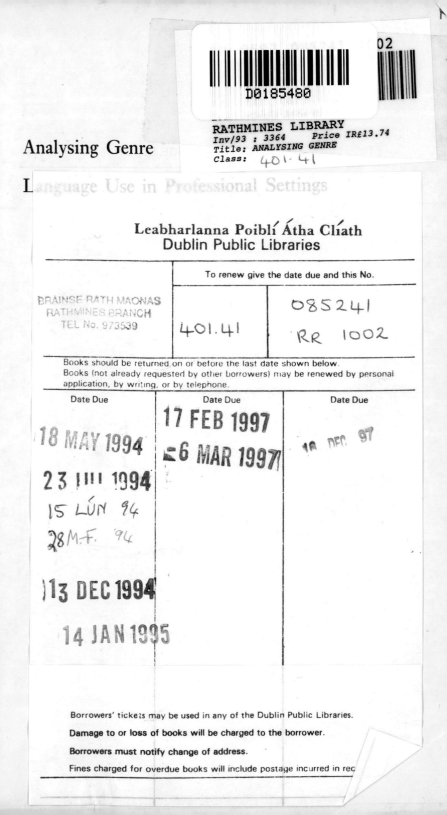

Analysing Genre

Language Use in Professional Settings

APPLIED LINGUISTICS AND LANGUAGE STUDY

General Editor
Professor Christopher N. Candlin, Macquarie University

For a complete list of books in this series see pages xvii and xviii

ANALYSING GENRE

Language Use in Professional Settings

VIJAY K. BHATIA

Longman
London and New York

Longman Group UK Limited,
Longman House, Burnt Mill,
Harlow, Essex CM20 2JE, England
and Associated Companies throughout the world.

*Published in the United States of America
by Longman Publishing, New York*

First published 1993

ISBN 0–582–08524–1 PPR

British Library Cataloguing-in-Publication Data
A catalogue record for this book is available from the British Library

Library of Congress Cataloging-in-Publication Data
Bhatia, V. K. (Vijay Kumar), 1942–
     Analysing Genre: Language use in Professional Settings / V. K. Bhatia.
         p.   cm. — (Applied linguistics and language study)
     ISBN 0–582–08524–1
     1. Discourse analysis.   2. Language and languages—Style.
3. Literary form.   4. English language—Study and teaching.
I. Title.   II. Series.
P302.B48   1993
401′.41—dc20
                                                                                    92–30733
                                                                                    CIP

Set by 8H in 10/12pt Ehrhardt
Printed in Malaysia by GPS

Contents

General Editor's Preface

One of the more diverting and harmless parlour-games one can play in any discipline is to calculate the current popularity and currency of particular terms – a kind of academic Trivial Pursuit. If one were to embark now on such an entertainment, a term like *discourse analysis* would have to be a sure-fire winner. The trouble would only come when the winners had to decide what it meant, and the reasons for its popularity. Common and encompassing terms have a sting in their tails. What is said about discourse analysis could equally be said of Vijay Bhatia's topic – *genre* – in this latest contribution to the *Applied Linguistics and Language Study Series*. What is it about the term and the area of study it represents that attracts such attention? What is it that will bring together under one terminological roof literary scholars, rhetoricians, sociologists, cognitive scientists, machine translators, computational linguists and discourse analysts, ESP specialists and language teachers? What is it that will bring together, to cite one local Sydney example, over 700 secondary school teachers of language and literacy to a weekend conference exploring *genre*? What it is, moreover, that will allow us to bring into the same fold, advertising copywriters, business communication experts and Plain English campaigners? Clearly, a concept that has found its time.

As Dr Bhatia carefully displays, text and its genres is a metaphor which invites attention by those whose role is linguistic analysis, those who seek evidence for the rhetorical preferences of contemporary media, those who seek to infer the processing strategies whereby texts are individually constructed and construed, those who wish through the analysis of individuals' textual preferences to connect language with social practices, and those literary and lexicographic scholars whose interests lie in stylistic choice and historical antecedent. It is this commonality of usage, however, which causes the problem and gives the reason for this book. Genre needs an explanation. The 'Theoretical Preliminaries' have this function and Part One sets out not only necessary definitions of genre in terms of events, structures, allowable practices and expert purposes, but does so with appropriate historical background and with an increasing commitment to practical exemplification. In doing so, this introductory section makes a case for genre analysis being seen as an extension of traditional discourse analysis into what the author calls a "thick description", one which precisely seeks to include those diverse traditions I refer to above. The issue of practical exemplification is important, given the focus on *analysis*. Indeed, in Chapter Two, the author's seven investigatory steps are as clear a practical guide as one might find anywhere, serving to display just how the various intellectual traditions and disciplines called up by the term may be brought into useful service.

If product, process and purpose are the three guiding principles of genre analysis, then in Part Two, Dr Bhatia demonstrates with his now customary display of data, how these principles can be drawn upon to explore the knotty question of the relationship between events, their associated genres and the texts these genres subsume. Thus, however well illustrated the Chapters are with detailed textual exemplification from specific corpora, there is always the reference to theory and to analytical traditions. Indeed, in reading Chapters 3, 4 and 5, one is inevitably reminded of the work of J. R. Firth, whose call for a 'sociological linguistics' might be seen as the precursor and begetter of the genre analysis of this book. Such a historical grounding is important since it emphasises that in calling afresh for an "explicit linguistic theory' to underpin pedagogy, those readers familiar for example with genre analysis in the context of literacy teaching, need to be aware that their concerns have a long tradition.

As John Swales notes with his customary generosity in his *Episodes in ESP*, Dr Bhatia has enjoyed a long and well-recognised involvement with the particular genre of legal texts, and a central place is accorded here to a display of their analysis. A close reading of the data shows how well justified the author's claims earlier are for the links to be made between generic analysis, the analysis of social institutions and the motives and purposes of their actors, even those as distinguished as Bhatia's parliamentary counsel. Furthermore, the legal data and their analysis offer important insights not only into the ways in which professional writers and draughtspersons position their readers to particular understandings (and guard against mischievous misunderstandings) but also into cross-cultural differences within the same genre, providing a cautionary warning about generic translatability. Like the law itself, legal texts are not universal in all particulars.

But perhaps as important as this generic analysis itself is the amplification in Part 3, an an introduction to the possibilities of application of genre analysis, of the author's concept of 'easification' by which means, rather than by simplifying the text itself, readers can be enabled to engage with the original. This concept and the author's apparatus of easifying techniques have proved to be of considerable pedagogic significance, especially in the context of special purpose language teaching. It is this special purpose language world which has, of course, been a major focus for the author's previous writing on the subject, and this final Part of the book is a rich source of worked example of the arguments laid out earlier. Of particular interest, given the overwhelming counter-pressures, is the author's proper orientation towards the *non*-native English speaker, as author, analyst and reader. It is easy to forget that it is the non-native speaker/writer (itself a somewhat unhelpful term for someone like myself working in Australia) who produces by far the largest quantity of English language generic material, and that it will be non-native English speaking and writing teachers who will find in this book very great support for their curriculum designs and classroom practice. More generally in the context of language education though, Dr Bhatia's unequivocal support for the making explicit to the learner of the lexicogrammatical resources for particular textualisations places **Analysing Genre** at one with current interests in consciousness-raising in the field of second language a cquisition and supports its interests in exploring the grammaticising processes of the developing learner. Most of all, however, it is the careful, explicit and questioning working out of explanatory principle upon exemplary texts which makes this book valuable to the applied linguistic researcher, the writer of instructional materials, the reflective teacher and the test designer.

Professor Christopher N Candlin
General Editor,
Macquarie University,
Sydney

Preface

This book attempts to provide a comprehensive introduction to a relatively new and unexplored area of discourse studies. Although genre analysis has a long-established tradition in literature, interest in the analysis of non-literary genres has been relatively recent.

In taking linguistic analysis from description to explanation, genre analysis brings significant enrichment to it, often providing an answer to the oft-repeated question in discourse studies: 'Why is a particular text-genre written the way it is?'. It takes as its key characteristic feature the communicative purpose that gives a particular text-genre its meaningful and yet typical cognitive structure. The analyst takes on the role of detective, in order to unravel the mysteries of the artifact under consideration and to emphasize the importance of motive as a clue to the nature of that artifact, thus introducing a kind of excitement rarely experienced in other approaches to linguistic analysis.

The book is divided into three parts. The first outlines the theory of genre analysis drawing on a variety of diverse disciplines that help the system define its key features, boundaries and methodology. The second part shows genre analysis in action, analysing texts from a wide variety of genres offering linguistic insights, and focusing on the conventional aspects of genre construction. The third part illustrates the use of genre analysis in language teaching, particularly English for Specific Purposes (ESP), and in language reform – especially in the writing of legislation and other public documents. Throughout, there are extensive discussions of cross-cultural variation in many of the academic and professional genres, taking examples from a wide range of non-native contexts.

The book is an attempt to contribute to the understanding of the use of language in a variety of academic and professional contexts. It will be of great value to those students, teachers of English (particularly of ESP), and applied linguists who are concerned with applied discourse analysis, and are interested in making use of the findings of linguistic analysis for a wide range of applied linguistic purposes, especially for planning and designing of ESP programmes. The book will also be of interest to members of the legal profession and to those involved in the simplification of public documents.

Acknowledgements

This book evolved from an attempt to develop a course on genre analysis entitled *Varieties of Written and Spoken English* and, subsequently, *Discourse Analysis*, at the National University of Singapore. So I am grateful to the students who have served as a trial audience for many parts of the book, during the teaching of this course over the years. My work for the UNDP-Government of Singapore Project on the *Teaching of English in Meeting the Needs of Business and Technology* has been a stimulus to organize my ideas on the applications of genre analysis to ESP. I am thankful to the project team for the opportunities for discussion, responses and challenges.

I am very much indebted to John Swales whose ideas and works have influenced me enormously ever since I came in contact with him about fifteen years ago. I have greatly benefited from numerous discussions with him at the University of Aston in Birmingham. I am sure he will find a proof of my gratitude to him in the book.

I am particularly grateful to Christopher Candlin, who not only helped me to acquire the confidence to undertake this project but has also been very supportive throughout the writing of the book. He has been extremely helpful in his very constructive criticism of the earlier drafts of the book, and has saved me from many an infelicity. Whatever weaknesses that still remain are entirely my own responsibility.

I am also grateful to a number of my colleagues and friends who have helped me during the writing of the book. My special thanks are to Paroo Nihalani for his comments on various aspects of the book and also for his general support. I am especially thankful to Nasir Kazmi for his close reading of the draft and for his useful comments. I have benefited from my discussions with Sujata Kathpalia on various aspects of genre analysis.

I am also grateful to the Department of English Language and Literature, National University of Singapore, for providing me with a helpful environment in which to write the book, especially to the Head of the Department, Professor Edwin Thumboo for his encouragement and support.

Last, but not, of course, least, I am indebted to my wife Archana and daughters Aditi and Astha, who have willingly sacrificed their numerous hours of leisure and pleasure and put up with my hectic schedule and often temperamental behaviour throughout the writing of the book.

Vijay Bhatia
Singapore

We are grateful to the following for permission to reproduce copyright material:

Adelaide Law Review Association for extracts from *Essays on Legislative Drafting: In Honour of J. Q. Evans* edited by D. Kelly; American Institute of Aeronautics for an extract by D. Almosnino from 'High Angle-of-Attack calculations of the Subsonic Vortex Flow on Slender Bodies' originally published in the *AIAA Journal*, vol. 23, No. 8. © 1983 AIAA; Butterworth Law Publishers Ltd for an extract from *Casebook on Torts* (1969) by D. M. M. Scott; Cambridge University Press Ltd & the author, John Swales for extracts from his *Genre Analysis*; The Department of Justice, Victoria for an extract from *Legislation, Legal Rights & Plain English – Discussion Paper 1* (1986) by the Law Reform Commission of Victoria; the Author, Tony Dudley-Evans for extracts from his article in *Talking About Text*, pubd. ELI, Birmingham University; Encyclopaedia Britannica International Ltd for the *Encyclopaedia Britannica* advertisement; The Motor Accidents Authority for text from *'Rego's Changed' Brochure*; National University of Singapore, the Department of English Language and Literature for an extract from *The Teaching of English in Meeting the Needs of Business and Technology*, UNDP Project Report by V. K. Bhatia and Mary Tay; The New York Times Syndication Sales for an extract from the article 'Why Mr. Reagan Blundered on SALT' by Al Gore in *The New York Times* 1/6/1986; Reuters Ltd for extracts from articles in *The Straits Times*; Singapore Press Holdings Group for an extract from the editorial 'Unwarrented and inequitable' in *The Straits Times*, Sept. 20, 1985; Sweet & Maxwell Ltd for an extract from *A Casebook on Tort* (1983) by Tony Weir; Times Newspapers Ltd for extracts from articles 'Moscow says. . .' by Chris Waller & 'Moscow says. . .' leading article both in *The Times* 29.5.86. © Times Newspapers Ltd 1986.

APPLIED LINGUISTICS AND LANGUAGE STUDY

General Editor
Professor Christopher N. Candlin, Macquarie University

PART 1: GENRE ANALYSIS – THEORETICAL PRELIMINARIES

The main purpose of this part is not to review literature in discourse analysis as such but to look at the developments in linguistics relevant to the analysis of professional and academic genres for applied linguistic purposes. It particularly focuses on discourse analysis as pure linguistic description, whether formal, functional or discoursal, and language description as explanation. Discourse analysis as description typically concentrates on the linguistic aspects of text construction and interpretation, whereas discourse analysis as explanation goes beyond such a description to rationalize conventional aspects of genre construction and interpretation, in an attempt to answer the question: Why do members of a specialist community write the way they do?

Part 1 also includes an extensive discussion of genre analysis as a multi-disciplinary activity, and outlines an approach to the analysis of professional and academic discourse. Its main strength is that it is primarily for applied linguistic purposes, which implies that the linguistic theory should be within the grasp of an average practitioner of English for Specific Purposes (ESP). In this respect, it is less of an extension of linguistic formalism, but more of a combination of essential grammatical insights and adequate socio-cognitive and cultural explanation. It focuses on the specific realizations of conventionalized communicative purposes rather than on the universals of discourse theory. Finally, it tends to offer a grounded description of language in use rather than a surface analysis of linguistic form.

1 From description to explanation in discourse analysis

Discourse analysis, as a study of language use beyond the sentence boundaries, has become an established discipline. It started attracting multidisciplinary attention in the early seventies and has developed into a variety of approaches motivated by a wide range of interests and orientations. In sociology, for example, analysis of language, under the name of ethnography of communication, provides insights into the structuring of communicative behaviour and its role in conduct of social life. Ethnomethodology, as developed by Garfinkel (1967, 1972), is concerned primarily with discovering the underlying processes which speakers of a language utilize in order to produce and interpret communicative experiences, including the unstated assumptions which are shared socio-cultural knowledge and understanding. In philosophy, speech act theory has motivated an interest in the formulation of rules of language use as against rules of grammar. In cognitive psychology, the study of discourse as schema theory, frame analysis, and conceptual analysis in terms of scripts, has been motivated by the interest in how knowledge of the world is acquired, organized, stored, represented and used by the human mind in the production and understanding of discourse. In literature, in the name of literary or linguistic stylistics, it provides an understanding of how literary writers achieve aesthetic value in their creative writing by describing, interpreting and analysing literary style. In linguistics, it has been given several names, such as: text-linguistics, text analysis, conversational analysis, rhetorical analysis, functional analysis, and clause-relational analysis. The main object of all these studies has been to understand the structure and function of language use to communicate meaning.

Within linguistics, discourse analysis has developed and can be distinguished along several parameters. The first one is that of **theoretical** orientation. On the theoretical orientation scale one could broadly identify at one end discourse studies as an extension of grammatical formalism, with a focus on formal, and sometimes functional, aspects of language use, including semantics and pragmatics; and, at the other end, discourse analyses of institutionalized use of language in socio-cultural settings with a heavy emphasis on communication as social action. The more theoretical studies are generally based on a particular theoretical framework in linguistics; text-linguistics pioneered by van Dijk and others, for instance, is based on transformational generative framework. Similarly, register and, to some extent, genre analysis within the systemic linguistic framework are other examples of this tradition. The studies at the other end of the scale are less concerned about the use of a particular linguistic framework but more with the actual communication in an institutionalized socio-cultural context. Examples of this second kind of discourse analysis are analyses of spoken interactions in the ethnomethodological tradition and analyses of professional and academic research genres by Swales (1981b) and Bhatia (1982).

The second parameter is that of **general-specific** scale. In the direction of generality we find discourse analyses of everyday conversation, analyses of written discourse in terms of descriptive, narrative, argumentative writing; whereas in the specific direction, we find analyses of research article introductions, legislative provisions, doctor-patient consultation and counsel-witness examination as genres. Somewhere in between, we can place register analyses of scientific and journalistic texts, etc.

The third parameter along which it is useful to distinguish discourse analysis is that of **application**. There are studies of discourse which have been motivated by an applied concern with language teaching, particularly for the teaching of ESP. Much of applied discourse analysis in linguistics, particularly on functional variation in written discourse, belongs to this strong tradition. Earlier work on discourse analysis by Widdowson, register analysis by Halliday, analysis of doctor-patient consultation by Candlin and others, rhetorical-grammatical analyses of scientific discourse by Selinker, Trimble and others, genre analysis of research writing by Swales, and analysis of legislative provisions by Bhatia all belong to this tradition. On the other hand, one finds analyses of spoken and written discourse which have not been directly motivated by any applied concern, although some of them have found useful applications in language teaching and elsewhere. Much of the work cited under an extension of grammatical formalism, i.e., text-linguistics, genre analysis under the systemic tradition, will come under this. It is true that some of these, particularly the work of the associates of Halliday on genre analysis, have found useful applications in the teaching of writing to children. However, at the same time, we find Sinclair and Coulthard's work on classroom discourse, which was initially motivated by applied concern but always had in mind an overriding concern for a general theory of discourse.

The fourth, and for our present purposes perhaps the most important, parameter along which much of discourse analysis can be distinguished, is that of **surface-deep** analysis, depending upon whether, or at what level, the analysis provides a thin or a thick (Geertz: 1973) description of language in use. This is particularly significant in the context of applied discourse analysis which has developed from a surface-level formal analysis to a deeper functional analysis, with a corresponding development in language teaching, which marks a movement from form to function, usage to use in Widdowson's terms, grammar to discourse and communication in recent years. This is particularly noticeable in the case of English courses for a variety of specific or, as Swales recently put it, specifiable purposes. Models of discourse analysis have steadily changed in the past three decades (see Barber, 1962; Gustafsson, 1975; Selinker, Lackstrom, Trimble and others, 1972, 1974; Trimble, 1985; Swales, 1981a; Candlin et al., 1976, 1980; Tadros, 1981; Widdowson, 1983; Bhatia, 1982 for the range and variety of linguistic descriptions of language use), moving from a surface-level description to a more functional and grounded description of language use, often bringing in useful explanation of why a particular type of conventional codification of meaning is considered appropriate to a particular institutionalized socio-cultural setting. Insights from such discourse analyses have been extensively utilized in language teaching and still provide the main source of strength for ESP theory and practice. If we look at the history and development of applied discourse analysis in the last thirty years, we notice that it has progressed through at least four levels of linguistic description.

1.1 Surface-level linguistic description: register analysis

One of the earliest approaches to the description of varieties of language use, characterized in terms of what Reid (1956) called 'register', became the focus of widespread attention in the Sixties and of fierce controversy in the Seventies. Developed by Halliday et al. (1964), within the 'institutional linguistics' framework of Hill (1958), register analysis focuses mainly on the identification of statistically significant lexico-grammatical features of a linguistic variety. Halliday, McIntosh and Strevens (1964:87) postulated that *language varies as its function varies; it differs in different situations. The name given to a variety of a language distinguished according to its use is register.* They further claimed that registers could be differentiated as sub-codes of a particular language on the basis of the frequency of lexico-grammatical features of a particular text-variety. They also proposed three situational and contextual dimensions in terms of **field**, **mode** and **style**, which later became **tenor** of discourse to identify various registeral characteristics. Although these situational and contextual categories have been variously refined and redefined in Gregory (1967), Crystal and Davy (1969), Ellis and Ure (1969), Hasan (1973) and Gregory and Carroll (1978) etc., registers have been defined essentially in terms of lexico-grammatical and, more recently, in semantic and semiotic terms.

Three of the most significant analyses of language use for applied linguistic purposes which belong to this tradition are those of Barber (1962), Crystal and Davy (1969) and Gustaffsson (1975). They draw interesting conclusions about the linguistic/stylistic variation in different varieties.

These studies on the frequency of syntactic properties of different varieties of English are interesting and useful in the sense that they provide necessary empirical evidence to confirm or disprove some of the intuitive and impressionistic statements we all tend to make about the high or low incidence of certain syntactic features of various varieties of languages. However, such studies tell us very little about the restricted values these elements of syntax realize in specific varieties. In fact, they tell us nothing whatsoever about the aspects of the variety these syntactic elements textualize or to what purpose such features are markedly present or absent in a particular variety. The findings remain severely constrained by their emphasis on surface features and do not provide adequate insights about the way information is structured in a particular variety. However perceptive these observations may be, they fall some way short of offering an explanation of why a particular variety takes the form that it does, and it is reasonable to suppose that specialized language courses will be more effective for being informed by insights into the rationale underlying selection and distribution of surface linguistic features.

1.2 Functional language description: grammatical-rhetorical analysis

Grammatical-rhetorical analysis, as indicated in Selinker, Lackstrom and Trimble (1973:1), aims *to investigate the relationship between grammatical choice and rhetorical function in written English for Science and Technology (EST)*. Selinker, Lackstrom, Trimble and others (1972, 1973, 1974), and Trimble (1985) begin by isolating two grammatical features, namely, tense and articles, which they thought were typical sources of difficulty for students of engineering – and also difficult to teach. Choices of tense and article were not solely dependent on syntactic and semantic considerations, but also involved rhetorical judgements, including the knowledge of the subject matter and its conventions. Substantiating their claim with real examples from scientific discourse, they conclude that whereas tense choices in general grammar of English are dependent on the notion of time, they are typically dependent on the notion of degree of generality in EST. Thus the present tense, they claim, is used to express generalization in EST and is used only where technical rhetoric requires the expression of this meaning. Investigating on similar lines the function of –en participles in chemistry texts, Swales (1974) discovered that *a given* in phrases like 'a given experiment' or 'a given temperature' has *two principle functions: one for clarifying the 'status' of the sentence, the other for specifying the 'determiner range' of the NP*. Which of these functions operates is itself determined by whether the author is exemplifying or generalizing.

The most interesting aspect of these two studies of scientific writing is not their attempt to discover which linguistic features are more frequent, but their attempt to discover how specific linguistic features take on restricted values in the structuring of scientific communication. Insights such as these are gained by reference to subject-specific conventions and rhetorical considerations rather than to syntactic or semantic specifications. However, in grammatical-rhetorical analysis, the analyst typically tends to investigate discourse from the vantage point of the writer to consider how a scientist-communicator makes certain grammatical choices as he writes and somehow limits the level of analysis to certain specific syntactic features of these texts. In spite of the significant specific explanations discovered for the use of these syntactic features, the analysis yields only limited information on discourse structuring in scientific discourse. Therefore, inadequate information on these aspects of text-structuring often leads to misleading generalizations. The most significant case of this kind of misleading generalization has been the case of definitions in scientific discourse, which was given a privileged status in the rhetorical structure of scientific writing (see Widdowson, 1973; Selinker, Trimble and Trimble, 1976). Swales (1981b), however, points out that definitions are frequently used only in science text-books and examination answers and are rare in other forms of scientific academic discourse and, therefore, it is rather misleading to look upon them as part of the scientific competence of the scientist. They are better regarded as part of his communicative and pedagogic competence as a text-book writer. In many of the later studies belonging to this tradition (see Tarone et al., 1981; Swales, 1981a; Pettinari, 1982; Oster et al., 1981; etc.) there have been clear attempts to pay more attention to specific scientific genres than to a general register of science.

1.3 Language description as discourse: interactional analysis

Discourse analysis as interaction represents the third level of language description. At the heart of interactional analysis – whether best described as **applied discourse analysis**, as in Widdowson (1973), or in terms of **speech functions**, as in Candlin et al. (1974, 1980), or **analysis of interactive discourse**, as in Sinclair and Coulthard (1975), or **analysis of predictive structures**, as in Tadros (1981), or analysis in terms of **clause relations**, as in Winter (1977) and Hoey (1979) – lies the notion of interpretation of discourse by the reader/listener. Discourse meaning, it is claimed, is not present in a piece of text ready to be consumed by the reader but is negotiated by the 'interactive' endeavour on the part of the participants engaged in the encounter, giving specifically appropriate values to utterances. In fact, Candlin and Loftipour-Saedi (1983) take this concept of negotiation of meaning by the reader through the mediation of the text, and propose a model of discourse analysis which depends on the balancing of what they define as the processes of discourse from two complementary perspectives – those of the writer and the reader. But, whether one characterizes discourse in terms of **rhetorical acts** (Widdowson, 1973), or in terms of **speech functions** (Candlin et al., 1974, 1980), or in terms of other communicative units like **initiation, response, elicitation** etc. (Sinclair and Coulthard, 1975), or in terms of **problem-solution** (Winter, 1977 or Hoey, 1979), or the writer's and the reader's discourse processes (Candlin and Loftipour-Saedi, 1983), the discourse in interactional analysis is viewed as essentially interactive in nature, being created as a result of the reader's interpretation of the text. If grammatical-rhetorical analysis can be referred to as the writer's discourse, discourse as interaction is the reader's discourse.

This view of discourse rests on the assumption that *the same interpretative procedures are brought into play whether one is involved in actual production of discourse or not* (Widdowson, 1979:147); it also takes for granted that in written discourse, the writer assumes a hypothetical reader for whom s/he is supposed to be writing, anticipating his/her reactions and adjusting his/her writing accordingly, to facilitate communication. In doing so, s/he follows what Grice (1975) calls 'the co-operative principle'. Although this approach works reasonably well in the case of many of the everyday occurring communicative contexts, it tends to simplify the relationship between the production and the interpretation of discourse in many of the conventionalized academic and professional contexts or what Levinson (1979) calls specific 'activity types' where one invariably needs to relax Grice's maxims. Fairclough (1985) points out that for a satisfactory application of Gricean maxims, the participants must relate as equals socially. In fact, a vast majority of institutionalized discourses that we are concerned with in this book happen to be instances of discourse where this kind of equality is exceptional rather than customary.

In the case of legislative genre, for instance, Bhatia (1982) points out that the parliamentary counsel often has to opt out of the maxim of quantity in order to incorporate in the legislative provisions every conceivable contingency that may arise during the application of the provision, thus making the writing 'over-informative' in Gricean terms. Similarly, the attempt to avoid obscurity and ambiguity often generates sufficient prolixity to transgress the maxim of manner at least as far as its 'brevity' aspect is concerned. Many of these so-called oddities of legislative variety could be attributable to a very different set of priorities and commitments on the part of the participants involved in discourse, which often require the specialist writer to adopt strategies which may be typical of the legislative genre. Similarly, in the case of many other academic or professional genres a successful achievement of the specific communicative purpose that the genre in question serves, depends on the use of specific conventionalized knowledge of linguistic and discoursal resources, depending upon the subject-specific, socio-cultural and psycholinguistic factors typically associated with the setting with which the genre is associated. In most of the language description models within this tradition, the specific requirements of a particular academic or professional culture are undermined, leaving the reader wondering why the members of a particular secondary culture write the way they do. Although much of interactional analysis in this tradition provides exhaustive description of language use in different social situations, and in some cases, as in Candlin and Loftipour-Saedi (1983), there is some indication of the role of socio-cultural factors in discourse processes, it does not pay adequate attention to the socio-cultural, institutional and organizational constraints and expectations that shape the written genre in a particular setting, particularly in the case of highly specific academic and professional genres. However, interactional analysis is valuable for the significant contribution that it has made to the theory and practice of discourse analysis by highlighting the interactive nature of discourse and also by focusing on the notion of structuring in language use.

1.4 Language description as explanation: genre analysis

Discourse analysis in all the three approaches discussed so far appears to have steadily moved from surface-level analysis to deep description of language use in three respects. First, in the values that features of language were assigned in specialist discourse, second, in the way the discourse was seen as underlying interaction between the writer and the reader, which Candlin and Loftipour-Saedi (1983) call equalization of the writer's and the reader's discourse processes; and, third, in the attention that was given to structuring in discourse. In the context of language teaching for specific purposes and applied linguistics in general – particularly after the work by Hymes and several others on ethnography of speaking and on the notion of communicative competence and subsequently its application by Munby (1978) to communicative syllabus design – applied discourse analysis appeared to represent a rather thin description of language in use and therefore, was inadequate at least in two major respects. First, it lacked adequate information about the rationale underlying various discourse-types, which, in other words, meant insufficient explanation of socio-cultural, institutional and organizational constraints and expectations that influence the nature of a particular discourse-genre. Second, it paid little attention to the conventionalized regularities in the organization of various communicative events. Although, as I pointed out in the previous section, there was some importance given to discourse organization in interactional analysis, there was no systematic handling of conventionalized aspects of discourse structure in many of the studies.

In order to move towards a thicker description, discourse analysis needs a model which is rich in socio-cultural, institutional and organizational explanation, relevant and useful to language teachers and applied linguists rather than to grammatical theorists, and discriminating enough to highlight variation rather than uniformity in functional language use; a model which is not seen as an extension of grammatical formalism but is truly applied in nature, in the sense that it requires minimum support and interference from grammatical theory, and exploits maximally the conventional aspects of language use. Also, such a model needs to be more towards the specific end of the continuum than the general end, because in language teaching for specific purposes, it is more realistic, and often desirable, to find pedagogically useful form-function correlations within, rather than across, specific genres.

In order to introduce a thick description of language in use, it is necessary to combine socio-cultural (including ethnographic) and psycholinguistic (including cognitive) aspects of text-construction and interpretation with linguistic insights, in order to answer the question, Why are specific discourse-genres written and used by the specialist communities the way they are? One such model has been proposed by Swales (1981b). The concept of genre, which had been so prevalent in literature, sociology and rhetoric for a long time, has started assuming importance in linguistics only recently. Genre analysis as an insightful and thick description of academic and professional texts has become a powerful and useful tool to arrive at significant form-function correlations which can be utilized for a number of applied linguistic purposes, including the teaching of English for specific purposes. That is one of the main reasons why it is often referred to as applied genre analysis.

The above historical development in the field of linguistic and discourse analysis indicates clearly that analysis has steadily progressed in the last thirty years or so from pure surface description to a thicker description of various aspects of texts or genres, whether these are specific features of lexico-grammar or discourse organization. It also underlines the fact that, in order to have an adequate depth of explanation for the analytical insights, one needs to utilize the nature of input from a variety of sources to the description and understanding of text-genres. In order to accomplish this, we shall consider the contribution to the development of a theory of genre analysis made by scholars of linguistics, theoretical and applied, sociology, including ethnography and ethnomethodology, psychology, cognitive as well as applied studies, and communication research. In this context, it is important to note that specialist informants also have an important role to play in the description, analysis and clarification of genres. And finally, one also needs to take into account cross-cultural factors, which sometimes influence the realization and understanding of specific genres. Our primary concern in the next chapter will be to look at how inputs from all these disciplines can be exploited to arrive at a viable framework for the analysis of various academic and professional genres.

2 Approach to genre analysis

Genre analysis requires inputs from a variety of disciplines to interpret, describe and explain the rationale underlying various professional and academic genres. But first, let me define what I mean by non-fictional genre for our immediate understanding and clarification.

2.1 Definition

Taking Genre, after Swales (1981b, 1985 and 1990), *it is a recognizable communicative event characterized by a set of communicative purpose(s) identified and mutually understood by the members of the professional or academic community in which it regularly occurs. Most often it is highly structured and conventionalized with constraints on allowable contributions in terms of their intent, positioning, form and functional value. These constraints, however, are often exploited by the expert members of the discourse community to achieve private intentions within the framework of socially recognized purpose(s).*

There are several aspects of this definition which need further elaboration.

First, genre *is a recognizable communicative event characterized by a set of communicative purpose(s) identified and mutually understood by members of the professional or academic community in which it regularly occurs.* Although there are a number of other factors, like content, form, intended audience, medium or channel, that influence the nature and construction of a genre, it is primarily characterized by the communicative purpose(s) that it is intended to fulfil. This shared set of communicative purpose(s) shapes the genre and gives it an internal structure. Any major change in the communicative purpose(s) is likely to give us a different genre; however, minor changes or modifications help us distinguish sub-genres. Although it may not always be possible to draw a fine distinction between genres and sub-genres, communicative purpose is a fairly reliable criterion to identify and distinguish sub-genres. We shall have more on this aspect of sub-genre identification in section 2.2.3.

Second, *it most often is a highly structured and conventionalized communicative event.* Specialist members of any professional or academic community are generally credited with the knowledge of not only the communicative goals of their community but also the structure of the genres in which they regularly participate as part of their daily work. It is the cumulative result of their long experience and/or training within the specialist community that shapes the genre and gives it a conventionalized internal structure.

Third, various genres display *constraints on allowable contributions in terms of their intent, positioning, form and functional value.* This means that although the writer has a lot of freedom to use linguistic resources in any way s/he likes, s/he must conform to certain standard practices within the boundaries of a particular genre. It is possible for a specialist to exploit the rules and conventions of a genre in order to achieve special effects or private intentions, as it were, but s/he cannot break away from such constraints completely without being noticeably odd. This is one of the main reasons why most of us are able to distinguish a personal letter from a business letter, an advertisement from a promotional letter or a newspaper editorial from a news report. Any mismatch in the use of generic resources is noticed as odd not only by the members of the specialist community, but also by the good users of the language in general. It may be the result of the use of some specific lexico-grammatical resources, certain kinds of meanings associated with specific genres, the positioning of certain rhetorical elements or even special meanings realized through certain expressions typically associated with only a restricted number of genres.

Swales (1990:204) cites an excellent example of this from the case study of Salwa, an Egyptian doctoral student in fish biology. In his draft of a research article introduction, Salwa begins like this:

[1] In aquaculture, the relations among nutrients, stocking rate, water quality and weather are complex . . .

The major problem with this opening, Swales comments, is that it has 'an explanatory textbook quality about it' and hence is 'unlikely to go down well with the expert readers of a specialized journal'. The remedy, he suggests, was to 'switch the proposition from new information to old information, from foreground to background', by inserting 'are known to be', so that we get the following perfectly acceptable opening:

[2] In aquaculture, the relations among nutrients, stocking rate, water quality and weather are known to be complex . . .

Although it is not always possible to find an exact correlation between the form of linguistic resources (be they lexico-grammatical or discoursal) and the functional values they assume in discourse, one is likely to find a much closer relationship between them within a genre than any other concept accounting for linguistic variation. Restrictions are also seen to operate on the intent, positioning and internal structure of the genre within a particular professional or academic context. This, perhaps, is another reason why most members of a particular professional or academic community are more likely than others to structure a particular genre more or less the same way.

Fourth, *these constraints are often exploited by the expert members of the discourse community to achieve private intentions within the framework of socially recognized purpose(s).* It is often found that the members of the professional or academic community have greater knowledge of the conventional purpose(s), construction and use of specific genres than those who are non-specialists. That is why expert genre writers often appear to be more creative in the use of genres they are most familiar with than those who are outside the specialist community. Obviously, one needs to be familiar with the conventions of the genre before one can exploit them for special effects. Experienced newspaper reporters often succeed in imposing desired perspectives on otherwise objective news reports. Similarly, in the case of counsel-witness examination in the court of law, the counsel's private intention to win the case often takes precedence over the real communicative purpose of cross-examination, i.e., bringing facts of the case to the attention of the court. For non-specialists, including a majority of discourse analysts, this lack of knowledge often presents serious difficulties, not only in the interpretation of the genre-content but also in the validation of analytical findings. It is for this reason that, in many of the studies of discourse analysis, including genre analysis, it has become almost a standard procedure to involve a specialist informant or to seek his or her reactions on various aspects of the investigation.

Although this definition of professional and academic genres owes its debt to Swales's work (1981, 1985, 1990), it differs from it in the way it brings in the psychological, particularly cognitive, level of genre construction. Swales offers a good fusion of linguistic and sociological factors in his definition of a genre; however, he underplays psychological factors, thus undermining the importance of tactical aspects of genre construction, which play a significant role in the concept of genre as a dynamic social process, as against a static one.

To sum up, each genre is an instance of a successful achievement of a specific communicative purpose using conventionalized knowledge of linguistic and discoursal resources. Since each genre, in certain important respects, structures the narrow world of experience or reality in a particular way, the implication is that the same experience or reality will require a different way of structuring, if one were to operate in a different genre. Although, as pointed out in the preceding paragraph, it is true that many professional writers do manage to exploit genre constraints to achieve effectiveness and originality in their writing, most of them still operate well within a broad range of generic rules and conventions. From the point of view of applied genre analysis, our primary concern is twofold: first, to characterize typical or conventional textual features of any genre-specific text in an attempt to identify pedagogically utilizable form-function correlations; and second, to explain such a characterization in the context of the socio-cultural as well as the cognitive constraints operating in the relevant area of specialization, whether professional or academic.

2.2 Function of orientation

Discourse analysis, of which applied genre analysis is a recent but very significant development, is a multidisciplinary activity to which a number of researchers from a variety of disciplines in the last quarter of a century have been drawn. Whereas interest in the analysis of linguistic variation is common to all of them, their training and background knowledge have encouraged them to formulate issues differently, adopt different methodologies and find answers that seem most interesting to them. While each one of them has a valid contribution to make, we need a fair amount of cross-fertilization in order to have a balanced approach to the construction and understanding of various genres. From the point of view of the analysis of functional variation in language, one envisages at least three different kinds of orientation, depending upon the nature of background knowledge and the motivating purpose the researcher brings to genre analysis.

2.2.1 *Linguistics and genre analysis*

As one more closely associated with linguistics, I would like to begin with a predominantly linguistic orientation. Much of what has come to be regarded as some form of register or stylistic analysis, and more recently certain types of discourse analysis, has been mainly concerned with a linguistic description of various texts. The analysts in most of these studies have generally been quite excited about an above-average incidence or even a lack of certain linguistic features, be they lexical, grammatical or even discoursal/rhetorical, in the texts under study. Earlier work on register analysis (see Barber, 1962; Halliday, McIntosh and Strevens, 1964; Huddleston, 1971; Gopnik, 1972, etc., on scientific English; Gustafsson, 1975, on legal English; and Crystal and Davy, 1969, on stylistic analysis of a number of varieties of English) belong to this category.

Later work in linguistic analysis on textualization and the use of rhetorical devices (Selinker, Lackstrom and Trimble, 1972, 1974; Swales, 1974; etc.) and rhetorical and discourse organization (Widdowson, 1973; Candlin et al., 1974, 1976 and 1980; Tadros, 1981; Hoey, 1983; Swales, 1981b; Bhatia, 1982 etc.) mark not only a movement from old to new but also from general to specific. This gradual progression in language description from one level to another appears to form a series of chinese boxes, each fitting into the other. Most of these studies are of great importance in linguistics because they tend to associate certain specific features of language with certain types of writing or styles. However, very few of them distinguished a variety (or register) from a genre. For many of them, a science research article, for example, is as legitimate an instance of scientific English as is an extract from a chemistry lab report. This creates two types of problem. Firstly, it potentially misrepresents not only the communicative purposes of the two genres, but also the relationship between the participants taking part in the linguistic activity, thus obscuring the very communicative nature as well as the distinct characteristics of the two genres. Secondly, by implication it gives a grossly misleading impression that a research article in science is likely to be very different from a research article in sociology, linguistics or psychology, for example. Swales (1981b), on the basis of his analysis of some forty-eight research article introductions from a variety of fourteen journals ranging from molecular physics through electronics, chemical engineering, neurology, radiology, educational research, educational psychology, management, language and linguistics, gives overwhelming evidence of the fact that a research article introduction in science is as good an example of this genre as is the one from psychology or sociology. Analyses of varieties or registers on their own reveal very little about the true nature of genres and about the way social purposes are accomplished in and through them in settings in which they are used. A number of significant questions like *Is this true of all the genres in a particular variety? How do these linguistic features realize social realities in a particular field of study or profession? Why do the users of the genre use these features and not others? Does the use of these features represent specific conventions in a particular genre, and if they do, what happens if some practitioners take liberties with these conventions?* remain largely unanswered.

2.2.2 *Sociology and genre analysis*

The second type of orientation is more of sociological concern, which makes it possible for the analyst to understand how a particular genre defines, organizes and finally communicates social reality. This aspect of genre analysis emphasizes that text by itself is not a complete object possessing meaning on its own; it is to be regarded as an ongoing process of negotiation in the context of issues like social roles, group purposes, professional and organizational preferences and prerequisites, and even cultural constraints. An exhaustive knowledge of sociological as well as cultural context provides one of the most important contributions to what Geertz (1973) refers to as a thick description of any social reality, including the linguistic behaviour of any speech community, academic or professional. Carolyn Miller (1984), taking primarily an ethnomethodological perspective, also underlines the importance of sociolinguistic input when she considers genre as social action. Kress (1985:19) too seems to separate linguistic factors from the sociolinguistic ones when he says:

> The social occasions of which texts are a part have fundamentally important effect on texts. The characteristic features and structures of those situations,

the purposes of the participants, the goals of the participants all have their effects on the form of texts which are constructed in those situations. The situations are always conventional. That is, the occasions in which we interact, the social relations which we contract, are conventionalised and structured, more or less thoroughly, depending on the kind of situation it is. They range from entirely formulaic and ritualised occasions, such as royal weddings, sporting encounters, committee meetings, to family rituals such as breakfast or barbecues or fights over who is to do the dishes. Other, probably fewer occasions are less ritualised, less formulaic; casual conversations may be an example. The structures and forms of the conventionalised occasions themselves signify the functions, the purposes of the participants, and the desired goals of that occasion.

At the time of writing, sociological studies of language use exist as a separate tradition of enquiry with hardly any overlap with the linguistic studies of similar genres. Research in scientific genres from these two traditions, for instance, has dealt with remarkably similar topics but rarely shows any awareness of studies done by various scholars in the two areas. Bazerman (1983) has an impressive list of over 140 references related to topics on scientific writing but very few of them familiar to (applied) linguists or ESP practitioners and I am sure the same is true the other way round. It is, therefore, necessary to point out that the two traditions have a lot to gain from each other. Sociological studies can become more alert to the use of linguistic resources for social ends whereas linguists can add the much needed sociological explanation to their interpretation of the use of language in professional and academic contexts.

The sociological aspect of genre analysis focuses on the conventional and often standardized features of genre construction and offers relevant, though non-linguistic, answers to the oft-repeated question *Why do members of what sociologists call 'secondary cultures' write the way they do?*

2.2.3 *Psychology and genre analysis*

The third type of orientation is basically psycholinguistic in nature, where the investigator tends to pay more attention to the tactical aspects of genre construction. The psycholinguistic aspect of genre analysis reveals the cognitive structuring, typical of particular areas of enquiry, whereas the tactical aspect of genre description highlights the individual strategic choices made by the writer in order to execute his or her intention. These tactical choices, appropriately called **strategies**, exploited by a particular writer are generally used in order to make the writing more effective, keeping in mind any special reader requirements, considerations arising from a different use of medium or prerequisites or constraints imposed by organizational and other factors of this kind. Such strategies are generally non-discriminative, in the sense that they do not change the essential communicative purpose of the genre. Non-discriminative strategies are concerned with the exploitation of the conventional rules of the genre concerned for the purpose of greater effectiveness in a very specific socio-cultural context, originality or very special reader considerations. Take, for example, the case of newspaper reports, which are generally recognized as a fairly well-established genre, with their own characteristic features, both linguistic and sociolinguistic. They serve a set of specific communicative purposes within newspapers. The reporters as well as the readers of newspapers have a common understanding of the function of this genre, in that a good reporter is generally well aware of what is expected of his news reporting, and the readers also have a fairly good understanding of the social function of the genre, i.e., to inform the readers about the day-to-day happenings in the world around them without bringing in any subjective interpretation or unnecessary bias. However, there are several types of non-discriminative linguistic strategies that reporters legitimately use to accomplish their intention in a particular news report. First, reporters use typical linguistic strategies in order to create various perspectives on news reports, thus bringing in some degree of subjective interpretation or even bias in their reporting. These may range from a convenient selection of facts to a subtle use of vocabulary. A news report in the *Guardian*, for example, is not written the same way as one in any of the tabloids, for example the *Sun*. Although both will be characterized as news reports, the one in the tabloid will be less detailed, and will generally have a more sensational headline, as well as a lot of visual input in order to ensure popular appeal. Many of these differences can be explained by reference to factors such as the purpose and nature of the newspaper and the nature of the readership. In addition to these strategies, newspaper reporters in various establishments are often required to follow guidelines imposed by the organization in which they work. These organizational constraints and pre-requisites are also generally of non-discriminative kind, in that they rarely change the nature of the genre within which a particular text is written.

Sometimes strategies used in the two texts representing the same genre differ because of the different nature of the medium involved. The case of print and TV advertisements is a good example of this phenomenon. Product description in the two advertisement-types is handled very differently because of the use of visuals on the TV.

Discriminative strategies, on the other hand, tend to vary the nature of the genre significantly, often introducing new or additional considerations in the communicative purpose of the text. This variation sometimes helps one to distinguish genres from sub-genres within them. A survey article, a review article, a state-of-the-art article, for example, can be distinguished as sub-genres of what is popularly known as the research article. Similarly, sports reporting is becoming increasingly different from general news reporting because of the greater use of popular explanation in reporting sporting events. The two text-types have a lot in common and yet they appear to use significantly different strategies to report objectively on two different types of events. In a case like this, it is best to regard them as two sub-genres of the same genre. However, it must be admitted that it seems almost impossible to draw up clearly defined criteria to make a satisfactory distinction between genres and sub-genres.

The communicative purpose is inevitably reflected in the interpretative cognitive structuring of the genre, which, in a way, represents the typical regularities of organization in it. These regularities must be seen as cognitive in nature because they reflect the strategies that members of a particular discourse or professional community typically use in the construction and understanding of that genre to achieve specific communicative purposes. This cognitive structuring reflects accumulated and conventionalized social knowledge available to a particular discourse or professional community. In this sense it is different from the organization of presupposed knowledge in an individual, which is primarily the case in schema theory, frames or scripts (Schank and Abelson, 1977). A good illustration of this inevitable connection between the communicative purpose of a particular genre and its typical cognitive structuring can be found in a comparison of the interpretative cognitive structures that one may discover in a typical news report and a feature article in a newspaper. In spite of all the other factors relating to the mode (including channel and nature of participation) and tenor of discourse (including the status and social distance between the participants) remaining the same, their communicative purposes change from an objective reporting in the news report to a balanced analysis of some interesting and controversial issue in the feature article. These differences in communicative goals require rather different strategies to be used in the two genres, and are reflected in the cognitive structuring of the two genres. In cases like these, where the communicative purposes of the genre-text are considerably different, requiring very different cognitive structuring, the two texts are viewed as different genres.

2.3 Analysing unfamiliar genres

In order to undertake a comprehensive investigation of any genre, one needs to consider some or all of the following seven steps, depending upon the purpose of the analysis, the aspect of the genre that one intends to focus on, and the background knowledge one already has of the nature of the genre in question.

1. Placing the given genre-text in a situational context

First, one needs to place the genre-text (i.e., a typical representative example of the genre) intuitively in a situational context by looking at one's prior experience, the internal clues in the text and the encyclopaedic knowledge of the world that one already has. This will include the writer's previous experience and background knowledge of the specialist discipline as well as that of the communicative conventions typically associated with it. The background knowledge of the discipline one gets from his/her association with, and training within, the professional community, whereas the knowledge of the communicative conventions one gets from his/her prior experience of similar texts. The user, therefore, gets the explanation of why the genre is conventionally written the way it is, from his or her understanding of the procedures used in the area of activity to which the genre belongs. This kind of knowledge is greater in those people who professionally belong to the speech community which habitually makes use of that genre.

For people who do not belong to the relevant speech community, this kind of knowledge is usually acquired by surveying available literature.

2. Surveying existing literature

This will include, among other things, literature on:

linguistic analyses of the genre/variety in question or other related or similar genres/varieties;

tools, methods or theories of linguistic/discourse/genre analysis which might be relevant to this situation;

practitioner advice, guide books, manuals etc. relevant to the speech community in question;

discussions of the social structure, interactions, history, beliefs, goals etc., of the professional or academic community which uses the genre in question.

3. Refining the situational/contextual analysis

Having intuitively placed the text roughly in a situational/contextual framework, one needs to refine such an analysis further by:

defining the speaker/writer of the text, the audience, their relationship and their goals;

defining the historical, socio-cultural, philosophic and/or occupational placement of the community in which the discourse takes place;

identifying the network of surrounding texts and linguistic traditions that form the background to this particular genre-text;

identifying the topic/subject/extra-textual reality which the text is trying to represent, change or use and the relationship of the text to that reality.

4. Selecting corpus

In order to select the right kind and size of corpus one needs to:

define the genre/sub-genre that one is working with well enough so that it may be distinguishable from other genres either similar or closely related in some ways. The definition may be based on the communicative purposes, the situational context(s) in which it is generally used, and some distinctive textual characteristics of the genre-text or some combination of these;

make sure that one's criteria for deciding whether a text belongs to a specific genre/variety are clearly stated;

decide on one's criteria for an adequate selection of the corpus for one's specific purpose(s) – a long single typical text for detailed analysis, a few randomly chosen texts for exploratory investigation, a large statistical sample to investigate a few specified features through easily identified indicators.

5. Studying the institutional context

A good genre analyst next attempts to study the institutional context, including the system and/or methodology, in which the genre is used and the rules and conventions (linguistic, social, cultural, academic, professional) that govern the use of language in such institutional settings. These rules and conventions are most often implicitly understood and unconsciously followed by the participants in that communicative situation in which the genre in question is used – or even explicitly enforced in some institutional settings (i.e., cross-examination in the law court). Quite a bit of information on these aspects of institutional contexts is available from guide books, manuals, practitioner advice and discussions of the social structure, interactions, history, beliefs, goals of the community in published or otherwise available literature. This step may also include the study of the organizational context, if that is seen to have influenced the genre construction in any way. This becomes particularly important if the data is collected from a particular organization, which often imposes its own organizational constraints and pre-requisites for genre construction.

6. Levels of linguistic analysis

The genre analyst then decides at which level(s) the most distinctive or significant features of language (for his/her motivating problem) occur, and carries out the appropriate analysis, which may concentrate on one or more of the following three levels of linguistic realization:

Level 1: Analysis of lexico-grammatical features

A text can be analysed quantitatively by studying the specific features of language that are predominantly used in the variety to which the text belongs. This is generally done by undertaking a large-scale corpus-based statistical analysis of a representative sample of the variety in question. Barber (1962), for example, undertook such a study of Some Measurable Characteristics of Modern Scientific Prose, and revealed the following figures of statistical significance in respect of the use of various tenses in the corpus.

Use of tenses in scientific English

	Active	Passive
Present simple	64%	25%
Present progressive	0.6%	0%
Present perfect	1.7%	1.4%
Past simple	1.2%	1.2%
Future simple	3.7%	0.7%
Imperative	1.3%	

Similar findings regarding the incidence of certain types of dependent clauses are reported in Gustafsson (1975) in the context of legislative genre which she calls English Law Language.

that-clauses   = 10%

adverbial clauses   = 31%

comparative clauses   = 11%

relative clauses   = 47%

Linguistic analyses of frequency of syntactic properties in different genres are interesting and useful in the sense that they provide necessary empirical evidence to confirm or disprove some of the intuitive and impressionistic statements that we all tend to make about the high or low incidence of certain lexico-grammatical features of various genres. However, this level of linguistic analysis tells us very little about what aspects of these genres are textualized (*pace* Widdowson, 1979) and to what purpose. The findings remain severely constrained by their emphasis on surface features and do not provide adequate information about the way communicative purpose is accomplished in a particular genre.

Focusing specifically on stylistic variation rather than on the frequency of certain lexico-grammatical features of a number of varieties of English, Crystal and Davy (1969) have added a useful dimension to text analysis under the name of stylistic analysis. They draw some interesting conclusions about stylistic variation in a number of varieties of language use, for example, on the legislative documents:

> It is a characteristic legal habit to conflate, by means of an array of subordinating devices, sections of language which would elsewhere be much more likely to appear as separate sentences.

> Legal English contains only complete major sentences. . . . Most of these complete sentences are in the form of statements, with no questions, and only an occasional command.

> One of the most striking characteristics of written Legal English is that it is highly nominal.

Although, as Bhatia (1982:20) points out, these are perceptive observations about the surface features of legislative genre, they fall short of offering an explanation of why legislative language takes the form it does, and it is reasonable to suppose that many of the applied linguistic purposes, particularly ESP, will be more effectively served if the findings are informed by insights into the rationale underlying selection and distribution of surface linguistic features.

Level 2: Analysis of text-patterning or textualization

This aspect of linguistic analysis highlights the tactical aspect of conventional language use, specifying the way members of a particular speech community assign restricted values to various aspects of language use (they may be features of lexis, syntax or even discourse) when operating in a particular genre. Widdowson (1979) calls this aspect of text analysis textualization.

An excellent example of this level of analysis comes from a very early analysis of data from chemistry textbooks by Swales (1974), where he was studying the function of past-participles in the pre- and post-modifying NP positions. Pre-modifying en-participles, he found, textualize two different aspects of chemistry text depending upon whether the author was exemplifying or generalizing. Since attribution, he claims, is an important convention in science, in a case where the author is exemplifying, the function of an -en participle is to signal unmistakably that the convention is being suspended, as in the following sentence.

[3] A *given* bottle contains a compound which upon analysis is shown to contain 0.600 gram-atom of phosphorous and 1.500 gram-atom of oxygen.

This, he claims, helps the author to prevent unnecessary and irrelevant enquiries regarding the details of the experiment. In the case of *generalizing*, Swales maintains, the function of *a given* is that of crypto-determiner which very precisely indicates the concept of definiteness without commitment to specificity, as in the following example.

[4] Figure 9.5 shows how the vapour pressure of *a given* substance varies with temperature.

If one were to substitute *a certain* instead of *a given* in the above example, he claims, the reading would become insufficiently generalized, as in the following case.

[5] Figure 9.5 shows how the vapour pressure of *a certain* substance varies with temperature.

On the other hand, if one were to substitute another ordinary English determiner like *any*, the reading would become overgeneralized, as in the following case.

[6] Figure 9.5 shows how the vapour pressure of *any* substance varies with temperature.

The above example indicates that statistical significance of a particular linguistic feature in a specific genre, by itself, is less interesting. However, it becomes more significant if it is possible to say what aspect of the genre it textualizes. This kind of insight into text-patterning in various genres tends to provide exciting answers to the question *Why do members of what sociologists call 'secondary cultures' write the way they do?* thus taking linguistic description a step further in the direction of explanation.

However, just as it is possible for a particular syntactic feature to perform several functions specific to a particular genre, similarly, it is also possible for a particular feature of language to perform different functions in different genres. A good example of that will be the use of NPs and nominalizations in advertising, legislation and scientific research articles.

In certain types of advertisements we find an overwhelming use of NPs. What purpose do they serve in the text? What aspect of the genre do they textualize? We all know that one of the most essential and typical strategies that advertisers use is the positive description of the product. The most useful linguistic feature for that purpose is the adjective. And, in order to be able to use as many adjectives as possible advertisers have no option but to use a number of NPs, because this syntactic category is likely to provide more slots for adjectival insertions than any other. So, in certain types of advertisements, NPs are used as facilitators, as it were, for positive product descriptions.

In scientific research writing, (compound) nominal phrases have an above-average incidence (Huckin and Olsen, 1983; Salager, 1984; Williams, 1984). Huckin and Olsen (1983) rightly point out that the use of these NPs promotes concise referencing and discourse cohesion and coherence. In fact, they serve as *ad hoc* names for concepts that will be referred to again, thus avoiding long descriptions. Dubois (1981), in a very interesting paper, goes a step further and suggests that various elements of NPs are generally rearranged to construct new NPs and that the choice between the two is not stylistic, but determined by the writer's assumptions concerning shared information on the part of his readers. She illustrates this by taking the following example:

[7] Studies of the oxidative NADP in enzymes in Drosophilla melanogaster have concentrated on the relationship of gene dosage to the in vitro tissue enzyme level and on allelozyme variation.

It is possible to rearrange the first NP in the above example in the form of a more complex nominal by changing post-modification phrases into a more concise pre-modification:

[8] Drosophilla melanogaster oxidative NADP-enzyme studies have concentrated on the gene dosage to in vitro tissue enzyme level relationship.

Dubois (1981) points out that although [8] is more concise, densely packed and hence space-saving than [7], it is less likely to occur in the beginning of an article, because, in that case, the author will be assuming a lot of information on the part of his readers right in the beginning of the article. It appears, therefore, that the scientific writer's use of complex NPs is not static but a dynamic one. He creates new nominals as he goes on building up new information for his readers.

In the case of legislative writing several studies have emphasized its nominal character (Crystal and Davy, 1969; Gustafsson, 1975; Bhatia, 1982; Swales and Bhatia, 1983). Let us take a simple but typical example from Bhatia and Swales (1983).

[9] The power to make regulations under this section shall be exercisable by statutory instrument which shall be subject to annulment in pursuance of either House of Parliament.

Now, compare this extract from Chapter 25/78: Nuclear Safeguards and Electricity [Finance Act] 1978, UK with its more verbal version given below.

[10] A statutory instrument can be used to make regulations under this section and such a statutory instrument can be annulled if either House of Parliament passes a resolution to that effect.

One can recognize [10] as similar to ordinary English writing, whereas [9] appears to be somewhat unnecessarily dense and self-contained.

Analysis of textual-patterning adds interesting explanation to the analysis of lexico-grammar of a genre. Such information on form-function correlations can be extremely useful for a number of applied linguistic purposes, particularly the teaching of ESP, which we shall take up in Part 3.

Level 3: *Structural interpretation of the text-genre*

As discussed in Section 2.2.3, structural interpretation of the text-genre highlights the cognitive aspects of language organization. Specialist writers seem to be fairly consistent in the way they organize their overall message in a particular genre, and analysis of structural organization of the genre reveals preferred ways of communicating intention in specific areas of inquiry. Swales (1981b) discovered that writers of academic research papers displayed remarkable similarities in the way they organized their article introductions. On the basis of some forty-eight article introductions from a variety of subject disciplines, ranging from physical and biological sciences to social sciences and linguistics, he posited a four-move structure for a typical article introduction, which he, in his later publication (1990), called Research Space Model for Article Introductions. Let us take a typical example of this kind of organization from his (1981) monograph.

[11] (1) The thermal properties of glassy materials at low temperatures are still not completely understood. (2) The thermal conductivity has a plateau which is usually in the range of 5 to 10K and below this temperature it has a temperature dependence which varies approximately at T2. (3) The specific heat below 4K is much larger than that which would be expected from the Dabye theory and it has an additional term which is proportional to T. (4) Some progress has been made towards understanding the thermal behaviour by assuming that there is a cut-off in the phonon spectrum at high frequencies (Zaitlin and Anderson 1975 a,b) and that there is an additional system of low-lying two level states (Anderson et al, 1972, Phillips, 1972). (5) Nevertheless more experimental data are required and in particular it would seem desirable to make experiments on glassy samples whose properties can be varied slightly from one to the other. (6) The present investigation reports attempts to do this by using various samples of the same epoxy resin which have been subjected to different curing cycles. (7) Measurements of the specific heat (or the diffusivity) and the thermal conductivity have been taken in the temperature range 0.1 to 80K for a set of specimens which covered up to nine different curing cycles.

[Kelham and Rosenberg, 1981:1737]

Swales (1981b) assigns a typical four-**move** cognitive structure to the above text as follows. (Sentences have been numbered for ease of reference.)

Move 1: **Establishing the research field** (1–3)
Move 2: **Summarizing previous research** (4)
Move 3: **Preparing for present research** (5)
Move 4: **Introducing the present research** (6–7)

The communicative purpose of the article introduction is accomplished through four rhetorical moves, which give this genre its typical cognitive structure. Just as each genre has a communicative purpose that it tends to serve, similarly, each move also serves a typical communicative intention which is always subservient to the overall communicative purpose of the genre. In order to realize a particular communicative intention at the level of a move, an individual writer may use different rhetorical strategies. In the case of article

introduction the writer may decide to **establish the research field**
either by

(a) asserting centrality of the topic, or
(b) stating current knowledge, or
(c) ascribing key characteristics

depending upon the constraints like the nature of the topic/field, the
background knowledge of the intended readership, reader-writer
relationship etc. In the above text, for example, the writer decides to
use option (b). These strategies, as pointed out in Section 2.2, are
essentially of non-discriminative type and in principle, one can add to
the list of strategies one wishes to use at this level by being innovative.

Similarly, move 2 can be realized by using any one or a combination
of the following three strategies:

(a) using a strong author-orientation and/or
(b) using a weak author orientation and/or
(c) using a subject orientation.

In [11] the author chooses to use a combination of (b) and (c). In the
case of move 3, Swales (1981b) points out the author has a choice of
three:

(a) by indicating a gap (in previous research) or
(b) by question-raising (about previous research) or
(c) by extending a finding.

In the example above the authors create research space for their own
work by indicating a gap in the previous research. Similarly, move 4
can be realized by either of the following options:

(a) by stating the purpose of present research
(b) by outlining the present research.

In [11], we find the use of the second strategy to introduce present
research. Although Swales in a number of his publications (1981,
1986, 1990) offers various versions of the interpretative **move-
structure** for this research genre, he has never clarified the use of

these non-discriminative strategies for an effective and successful accomplishment of the communicative purpose of the genre at various levels. I will say more on this aspect of genre analysis in later sections of the book when I take up other genres. For the time being, it is useful to think of moves as discriminative elements of generic structure and strategies as non-discriminative options within the *allowable contributions* available to an author for creative or innovative genre construction.

It is important to remember that although the notion of cognitive move-structure outlined here can be widely used for a variety of genres, it may not always be applicable to all of them. The idea is to interpret the regularities of organization in order to understand the rationale for the genre. Cognitive structuring, in a way, is very much like schematic structuring in schema theory, except that in the former, it is the conventionalized and standardized organization used by almost all the members of the professional community, whereas in the latter, it is often a reader's individual response to the text in question. Cognitive structuring in a genre is the property of the genre as such and not that of the individual reader. It depends upon the communicative purpose(s) that it serves in the genre and that is why it varies from one genre to another. In legislative genre, for example, the cognitive structuring displays a characteristic interplay of the main provisionary clause and the qualifications inserted at various syntactic openings within the structure of a sentence (Bhatia, 1982). In order to give some substance to this, let me take a very typical example of this from the British Housing Act 1980.

[12] Where the dwelling-house with respect to which the right to buy is exercised is a registered land, the Chief Land Registrar shall, if so requested by the Secretary of State, supply him (on payment of the appropriate fee) with an office copy of any document required by the Secretary of State for the purpose of executing a vesting order with respect to the dwelling-house and shall (nothwithstanding section 112 of the Land Registration Act 1925) allow any person authorised by the Secretary of State to inspect and make copies of and extracts from any register or document which is in the custody of the Chief Land Registrar and relates to the dwelling-house.

(Section 24, subsection 5)

The example above gives not only a clear indication of the complexity of individual qualification insertions in the legislative genre but also some indication of the variety of such qualifications. The following version of the same text displays more explicitly the structural organization of the genre.

Interactive move-structure in legislative writing

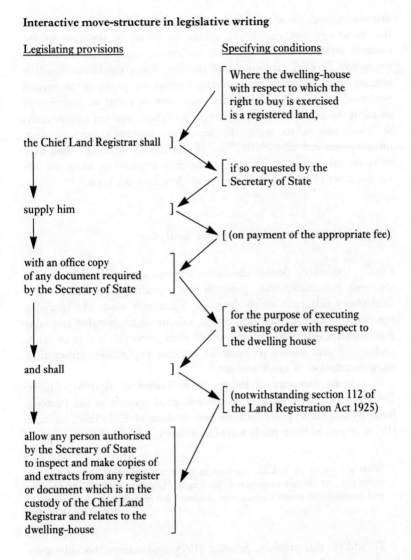

Legislating provisions   Specifying conditions

the Chief Land Registrar shall]

[Where the dwelling-house
with respect to which the
right to buy is exercised
is a registered land,

[if so requested by the
Secretary of State

supply him   ]

[(on payment of the appropriate fee)

with an office copy
of any document required
by the Secretary of State]

for the purpose of executing
a vesting order with respect to
the dwelling house

and shall   ]

(notwithstanding section 112 of
the Land Registration Act 1925)

allow any person authorised
by the Secretary of State
to inspect and make copies of
and extracts from any register
or document which is in the
custody of the Chief Land
Registrar and relates to the
dwelling-house

Both the density and the complexity of qualificational insertions serve a typically legal function in this genre in that each one is meant to answer legal questions and doubts, and offer clarifications about various aspects of the main provision. Any adequate structural description of the genre should explain this phenomenon. Therefore, it is more appropriate to think in terms of a two-part interactive cognitive structure consisting of the main provisionary clause, Legislating provisions, and the qualifications, Specifying conditions, rather than the linear organization of the moves as found in the case of the research article introductions. The analysis of cognitive structuring is interactive here in the sense that the Specifying conditions typically interact with several aspects of the Legislating provision at various positions, answering a number of questions that can be legitimately asked in the context. The main function of these inserted qualifications or conditions is to make the legislative provision precise, clear, unambiguous and all-inclusive (see Bhatia 1982, 1987a). We shall have more on this aspect of interactive cognitive structuring when we take up the cases of various legal genres in Part 2 of the book.

7. Specialist information in genre analysis

Finally, the analyst double checks his findings against reactions from a specialist informant, who, generally, is a practising member of the disciplinary culture in which the genre is routinely used. The specialist reaction confirms his findings, brings validity to his insights and adds psychological reality to his analysis. It is an important aspect of genre analysis, if one wishes to bring in relevant explanation rather than mere description in one's analysis.

In existing literature (Selinker, 1979; Tarone et al, 1981; Bhatia, 1982; Huckin and Olsen, 1984) there is good account of the problem faced by discourse/genre analysts and teachers of ESL/ESP. Selinker (1979) describes their predicament as follows:

> What are we to do as ESL teachers in the normal situation where we ourselves just do not understand the English language scientific textbooks and professional articles which our students are required to grapple with?
> (Selinker, 1979:190)

To address this problem, Selinker (1979) and some of his colleagues used a specialist genetics professor to help them interpret a journal article in genetics. They discovered that their meetings with the specialist informant were very useful and productive. They not only received quite a lot of help in understanding the nature of the text but were also able to establish somewhat tentative procedures to exploit specialist reactions in discourse interpretation. Huckin and Olsen (1984) did further work on the same problem using the author of the same genetics article which Selinker used with a genetics professor as a specialist informant. Both these studies, although they came up with slightly different interpretations of the target text, were very useful in clarifying some of the crucial issues often raised in the context of the use of specialist informants in discourse interpretation. Huckin and Olsen (1984) list their main conclusions as follows:

1. LSP researchers who use informants should have some familiarity with important conventions and ways of arguing in the field being studied – in this case, an understanding of scientific methodology and of the transitory nature of the results in a rapidly-progressing scientific field;
2. no specialist informant is likely to provide an optimally useful interpretation of a text for pedagogical purposes unless the LSP researcher can learn to see the information structure of the text more through the eyes of the specialist informant and less through the eyes of the linguist;
3. perhaps the most useful specialist informant one can find for an LSP text is the actual author of that text.

(Huckin and Olsen, 1984:129)

Tarone et al. (1981) went a step further and used the services of a subject-specialist as part of the investigating team for their analysis of astro-physics journal articles. The most extensive use of the specialist informant is reported in Bhatia (1982), where the investigator worked closely over a period of almost three years with a senior Parliamentary Counsel who was primarily responsible for the drafting of the British Housing Act 1980, which he used as corpus for his doctoral investigation. Consulting a specialist informant in genre analysis is a difficult job. In the first place, it is difficult to find a truly resourceful specialist informant. Secondly, even if one succeeds in finding a suitable person, it takes quite an effort, time and understanding to develop a common understanding of the purpose of enquiry. It is not always easy to ensure that the two parties, with their differing background knowledge, are able to speak the same language, as it were. In order to avoid any mishaps in the selection of an appropriate specialist informant for the analysis of a particular genre, Selinker (1979) mentions several characteristics that one should look for but it is possible to adapt the following three which appear to be crucial. The specialist informant, as far as possible, should

1. Be a competent and trained specialist member of the disciplinary culture in which the genre under study is routinely used.
2. Have a feel for the specialist language and also be prepared to

talk about it openly, when asked searching questions about various aspects of the genre under study.

3.   Be in a position to explain clearly what he believes expert members of the disciplinary culture do when they exploit language in order to accomplish their generic goals.

In order to ensure maximum co-operation from the specialist informant and to exploit his/her expertise adequately, the investigator needs to keep the following in mind:

1.   The investigator must have a good idea of what he is looking for, preferably in terms of possible hypotheses formulated on the basis of initial analyses of the data representing the genre in question.

2.   The investigator should formulate his/her questions in a manner which is least-biasing, although narrowly focused specific questions are sometimes very useful to prevent the discussion from going out of control.

3.   The investigator should be prepared to refine and reframe questions, keeping in mind the new information or interpretations offered by the specialist informant.

4.   The discussion sessions with the specialist informant should be recorded as far as possible, transcribed and sent back to the informant for confirmation. Sometimes, the informant can be surprised at his own contribution and might want to change or clarify his opinion or assertion.

5.   Sometimes it can be extremely useful to consult a second informant to validate some or all of the data from the first one.

These are just a few of the guidelines that can help the analyst to plan and organize discussion sessions with the specialist informant.

2.4 Cross-cultural factors in genre analysis

The relationship between linguistic communication and culture is widely recognized. Saville-Troike (1982:34) goes a step further to suggest that *the very concept of the evolution of culture is dependent on the capacity of humans to use language for purposes of organizing social cooperation.* Unfortunately, however, as Candlin (1978) points out, much of the available research in discourse interpretation *operates within a specific cultural and ethnographic frame; 'general principles of human cooperative behaviour' seem Western European, even Anglo-Saxon in their orientation.* In recent years researchers in ethnography and ethnomethodology have gone a long way towards producing a theory of conversation as a co-operative activity based on social rules of interaction. However, few of these studies consider norms other than pan-cultural from the West.

Cross-cultural variation in spoken interaction has become a well-established area of discourse study but very little has been published in the case of written genres, though recently there have been some indications of interest in cross-cultural variation in academic and professional discourse. It has been well known for some time that various cultures organize and develop ideas differently when writing expository texts and these differences persist when users of these languages and cultures learn to write in a new language. In a recent study, Hinds (1990:98), investigating expository writing in Japanese, Korean, Chinese, and Thai, discovered that in all these languages there is a common style which is characterized by 'delayed introduction of purpose'. This delayed introduction of purpose, he claims, has the undesirable effect of making the essay appear incoherent to the English-speaking reader, although the style does not have this effect on the native speaker. Others (Hinds, 1990; Clyne, 1981; Kaplan, 1983; Connor and McCagg, 1984; Cheng, 1985) have also come up with similar findings in the case of expository and argumentative prose. However, the situation is somewhat less than satisfactory in the area of professional and academic genres. There are two obvious reasons for the lack of research in this area. First, non-literary genre analysis has so far been more actively concerned with some of the well-established and more standardized genres, particularly those used in research settings. In research writing, the trend is still towards conformity because a majority of academics look for recognition through publications in the English-speaking world, where established conventions and standards are observed rather seriously by scientists and other academics in various disciplines. However, in the case of many other professional genres, particularly in some of the business letters (Teh Geok Suan, 1986; Bhatia and Tay, 1987), job applications (Bhatia, 1989) and some legal genres, the local socio-cultural constraints do seem to play a more significant role in their linguistic realizations. In a number of ESP situations where such genres are used, it therefore appears appropriate that genre analysts become aware of the local constraints which may seem to determine the nature and linguistic realizations of these genres in order to ensure pragmatic success in real life professional settings in local environments. At the moment, there is very little research in this area and a lot more input is needed to make sure that the findings of genre analysis, wherever necessary, are sensitive to local socio-cultural constraints.

In a majority of genres, particularly those with which we are concerned in this book, local cultural constraints are unlikely to effect substantially the essential move-structure of a specific genre; however it is very likely that they will have significantly interesting implications for the realization of certain moves and even in the way certain non-discriminative strategies are employed to accomplish specific intentions. These constraints are particularly important for genres employed in business transactions than anywhere else. Cultural taboos in the use of numbers, colours and shapes are well known. Aman (1982) has a number of interesting and useful suggestions for advertisers. One would do well in India to avoid zero and any number ending in zero. The number seven should be shunned in Ghana, Kenya and Singapore. About number 88, he reports:

> The number 88 recently has taken on offensive connotations in England. A British paramilitary terror group calls itself 'column 88'. The number 88 is derived from the eighth letter of the alphabet, 'H', and, in the minds of its users, is equivalent of HH, standing for the Nazi salute 'Heil Hitler'. It is unlikely that many English Jews who also know the meaning of 88 would be inclined to purchase a product containing the number 88, such as the Oldsmobile Delta 88.

Hawkins (1983) reports an interesting story about a US manufacturer of high-tech equipment, who was abruptly tossed out of the Middle East market, not because it had anything to do with the quality of his product, price or business expertise, but simply because he failed to understand the cultural baggage of his local partner. National culture, that elusive combination of customs, skills, art and ideas that distinguish each country, he points out, has always been a factor in international projects. As the business world is getting smaller and smaller every day, the trend towards increased cross-cultural understanding is likely to assume greater significance. The USA, he reports, is a 'low context' culture whereas Japan and China are 'high context' cultures. In 'low context' cultures, verbal messages are important, meaning and understanding come from what is said, relationships are often limited, and change is made easily and rapidly. In the 'high context' cultures, on the other hand, meaning and understanding come from looking at the position of the person in a company or the relationship between the business persons. No wonder, in Japan, unlike the USA, indirect and vague communication is preferred to direct and specific references.

The implications of cross-cultural input in business and management settings have also been recognized in organizational theories and practices. Hofstede (1983) rejects ethnocentric management theories based on the value system of a particular country as untenable. He undertook a massive project involving fifty countries between 1967 and 1978. His objective was to describe national cultures along four dimensions:

1. Individualism versus collectivism
2. Large and small power distance
3. Strong and weak uncertainty avoidance
4. Masculinity versus feminity

He claims that management practitioners and management theorists over the past eighty years have been blind to the extent to which activities like 'management' and 'organizing' are culturally dependent. His findings indicate that it was a *naive assumption that management is the same or is becoming the same around the world* and was *not tenable in view of the demonstrated differences in national cultures*. If Hofstede's claim is sustainable, and I think it is, then it has equally compelling implications for the analysis of business and perhaps a number of other professional genres. Genre, after all, is a socio-culturally dependent communicative event and is judged effective to the extent that it can ensure pragmatic success in the business or other professional context in which it is used.

2.5 Conclusions – strengths and limitations

The notion of genre analysis as presented here is a very powerful system of analysis in that it allows a far thicker description of functional varieties of written and spoken language than that offered by any other system of analysis in existing literature. As pointed out earlier, it expends linguistic analysis from linguistic description to explanation taking into account not only socio-cultural but psycho-linguistic factors too. Explanation of this kind is crucial to the understanding and construction of professional and academic genres because it not only clarifies the communicative goals of the discourse community in question, but also the individual strategies employed by the members to achieve these goals. This aspect of genre analysis is particularly relevant for any form of communicative language teaching, particularly ESP. Munby (1978) rightly emphasized the role of socio-cultural factors in communicative syllabus design. Unfortunately, however, his model turned out to be somewhat inadequate because of a neglect of psycholinguistic factors, which are equally important. An additional advantage of looking at linguistic description at the three levels proposed here is that it will allow for the findings to be used more creatively even when one wishes to focus on grammar, which is very much expected of an ESL/ESP teacher in a number of teaching situations, where learners do not feel happy unless the course includes some emphasis on grammar. In such cases, the findings at Level 1 (see section 2.3) can be used to focus on relevant areas of grammar, but the explanation for the use of grammatical features will come from findings at Levels 2 and 3, thus making it more specifically relevant to a particular genre.

One of the main limitations of such an approach appears to be that it might encourage prescription rather than creativity in application; however we must realize that one can be more effectively creative in communication when one is well aware of the rules and conventions of the genre. Exploiting rules and conventions for the sake of creativity and innovation is good but it is much better to do so after one has developed at least a good awareness of, if not a good mastery over such conventions. Moreover, analysis of generic conventions need not always be used prescriptively. As Hart (1986:280) points out, genre analysis is **pattern seeking** rather than **pattern imposing**.

The procedures for genre analysis outlined in the preceding sections appear to be atomistic; however, in actual practice they are part of an activity which is holistic and, in a way, indivisible. Every step described above is understood in the context of the whole. These steps have been artificially separated for the sake of convenient formalization and systematic discussion. Moreover, it is not the intention to suggest that in all such investigations, the analyst must go through all the stages listed above and certainly not in that order. The steps should be used selectively and in a flexible order depending upon the degree of prior knowledge (it may be the knowledge of the communicative setting, content or form) of the genre that the analyst brings to a particular analytical task. Under levels of linguistic analysis, for example, one does not go linearly from Level 1 to 3 in that order. Sometimes it is more convenient to begin with Level 3 looking at the regularities of organization, than with statistical analysis of surface features. In actual practice, analysis at any level helps the investigator to understand the structuring at other levels. For instance, analysis of text-patterning, on the one hand, will have to be based on some perception of the statistical significance of that feature in the genre (Level 1) and, on the other hand, it must be explained in terms of the communicative purpose of the genre, which is indicated in the cognitive structuring of the genre (Level 3). Similarly, Level 3 analysis of the cognitive structuring, to a large extent, has to be based on the study of the lexical signals that one reads in the genre (Level 1). Therefore, it is always advisable to think of linguistic analysis of genres as one major activity comprising these three components. An adequate description and a satisfactory understanding of any genre should provide answers to as many of the questions as can be legitimately raised within the framework outlined here. How this works and what sort of answers one can get and what conclusions one can draw from such analyses, will be taken up in Part 2.

PART 2: GENRE ANALYSIS IN ACTION

This section of the book can be seen as an illustration of the framework suggested in section 1. While offering analyses of professional and academic genres, it also tends to clarify the concept of *genre analysis*.

It begins with a set of two apparently *different* communicative events from the business world, and analyses them as instances of the same genre because both of them serve somewhat similar sets of communicative purposes. Then it considers two apparently *similar* communicative events from the academic world and analyses them as instances of two different genres because they serve different communicative purposes. This illustrates that of all the contextual factors associated with a conventionalized speech event, communicative purpose is the most privileged criterion for the identification of genres. This section then undertakes detailed genre analyses of two related genres from legal settings.

PART 2: GENRE ANALYSIS IN ACTION

3 Product and self promotion in business settings

In Chapter 2, I suggested that the communicative purpose which the genre is intended to serve is the most important factor in genre identification. In this chapter, I will take a closer look at the role communicative purpose plays in the identification and description of genres. In order to understand its function in genre identification, I will take up examples from two seemingly different and yet closely related areas of linguistic activity, namely, *product* and *self-advertising* through sales promotion letters and job applications, respectively. We begin with sales promotion letters as a genre in order to determine the role of communicative purpose in its identification and description.

3.1 Sales promotion letters

3.1.1 *Communicative purpose*

A sales promotion letter is an unsolicited letter addressed to a selected group of prospective customers (they may be individuals or companies) in order to persuade them to buy a product or service. Since most of these prospective customers may not be interested in the product or service that one is trying to promote, the writers of these sales promotion letters have a difficult task not only in capturing their attention but also in sustaining their interest, and eventually convincing them of the benefits of the product or service being promoted. A typical sales promotion letter thus tends to serve the following communicative purposes:

1.   The main function of a sales promotion letter is persuasive, in the sense that its writer aims to elicit a specific response from its reader(s). Eliciting a desired response in this setting is a complex communicative process and, in order to ensure its

pragmatic success, it needs to achieve the following additional communicative purposes:

2.   The letter should capture the attention of the potential customer, even if s/he has no immediate need for the product or service being offered.

3.   Sales promotion letters are generally addressed to those potential customers who are known to have some need (immediate or future) for the product or service being promoted. Therefore, the most important function of the letter is to offer an appraisal of the product or service in terms of the perceived interests, needs or inhibitions of the potential customer.

4.   Since most sales promotion letters are unsolicited, and busy businessmen are not likely to waste their precious time on such promotional efforts, the letter must be short and effective. However, this requirement contrasts sharply with another, i.e., there should be enough details about the product or service in the letter for those customers who already have some need for or intention to buy the product or service.

5.   Sales promotion letters should serve as the first link between a potential seller and a prospective customer. In this respect, they are generally seen as initiating business relations between the two parties. Therefore, all sales promotion letters need to encourage further communication between the two parties.

In the light of the above communicative purposes, let me now take up the following instance (p. 47) of a sales promotion letter (slightly adapted to preserve confidentiality) and consider in what way it satisfies these requirements.

3.1.2 *Structural description*

Using the framework discussed in Chapter 2, one may assign the following structural description (p.48) to the Standard Bank letter, in terms of the moves (see section 2.3) used by the writer to achieve his communicative purposes.

The structural interpretation assigned to the letter below indicates that the writer has used the following moves.

1.   **Establishing credentials**
2.   **Introducing the offer**

[1]

STANDARD BANK
268 Orchard Road, Yen Sun Building, Singapore 0923

4 December 1987

Mr Albert Chan
1 Sophia Road, 05–06
Peace Centre
Singapore 0922

Dear Sir

We are expertly aware that international financial managers need to be able to ask the right questions and work in the market place with confidence.

Corporate Treasury Services, Standard Bank, now provides a week-long Treasury Training programme designed to develop awareness and confidence in managers.

We explain the mechanics of foreign exchange and money markets. We discuss risk from an overall standpoint and practical hedging techniques to manage foreign exchange risks. We also discuss treasury management information systems, taxation and the latest treasury techniques.

We will be holding our next Treasury Training Programme from 24–28 February 1987, inclusive. The fee for the Training Programme will be US$1,500 per person to include all luncheons and a dinner as indicated in the schedule as well as all course materials.

The programme is both rigorous and flexible. It can be tailored to fit the needs of a whole corporation or just a few levels within the company.

We are pleased to inform you that if your company sponsors 6 or more staff for the course, we will offer you a discount of US$100 per person.

For your convenience, I enclose a reservation form which should be completed and returned directly to me. If you have any questions or would like to discuss the programme in more detail, please do not hesitate to contact me (Telephone No. 532 6488 / telex No. 29052).

As the number of participants at each training programme is limited, we would urge you to finalize as soon as possible your plans to participate.

Thank you very much for your kind consideration.

Yours faithfully

Mr. G. Huff

[2]

STANDARD BANK 268 Orchard Road, Yen Sun Building, Singapore 0923 4 December 1987 Mr Albert Chan 1 Sophia Road, 05–06 Peace Centre Singapore 0922 Dear Sir	
We are expertly aware that international financial managers need to be able to ask the right questions and work in the market place with confidence.	**Establishing credentials**
Corporate Treasury Services, Standard Bank, now provides a week-long Treasury Training programme designed to develop awareness and confidence in managers.	**Introducing the offer** *Offering product / service*
We explain the mechanics of foreign exchange and money markets. We discuss risk from an overall standpoint and practical hedging techniques to manage foreign exchange risks. We also discuss treasury management information systems, taxation and the latest treasury techniques.	*Essential detailing of the offer*
We will be holding our next Treasury Training Programme from 24–28 February 1987, inclusive. The fee for the Training Programme wil be US$1,500 per person to include all luncheons and a dinner as indicated in the schedule as well as all course materials.	
The programme is both rigorous and flexible. It can be tailored to fit the needs of a whole corporation or just a few levels within the company.	*Indicating value of the offer*
We are pleased to inform you that if your company sponsors 6 or more staff for the course, we will offer you a discount of US$100 per person.	**Offering incentives**
For your convenience, I enclose a reservation form which should be completed and returned directly to me.	**Enclosing documents**
If you have any questions or would like to discuss the programme in more detail, please do not hesitate to contact me (Telephone No. 532 6488 / telex No. 29052).	**Soliciting response**
As the number of participants at each training programme is limited, we would urge you to finalize as soon as possible your plans to participate.	**Using pressure tactics**
Thank you very much for your kind consideration.	**Ending politely**
Yours faithfully Mr. G. Huff	

    (i) Offering the product or service
    (ii) Essential detailing of the offer
    (iii) Indicating value of the offer

3.   **Offering incentives**
4.   **Enclosing documents**
5.   **Soliciting response**
6.   **Using pressure tactics**
7.   **Ending politely**

We shall now look at these moves in greater detail to see in what way they help the writer to fulfil his communicative purposes.

Establishing credentials

The writer of the letter begins by establishing his company's credentials, in the first paragraph, by referring to the needs of the potential customer. He gives a good indication of his own perception of the requirements of the international financial managers. (Obviously, such a letter will go only to those individuals or companies who are known to have some financial managers who could benefit from the training being offered.) By doing so, he obviously implies that they (his company) are the ones who can fulfil these needs. The most striking aspect of this move, therefore, is the indication to the addressee that it is to his advantage to participate in the decision-making process leading to product buying. There is another interesting phrase in the beginning of the letter, 'We are expertly aware ...' which implies that the reader of the letter can depend on the expertise of the company to meet the needs of his company. This is the first move that the writer makes and we shall call this **establishing credentials**.

As suggested earlier, a sales promotion letter is an unsolicited letter addressed to a group of individuals or companies in order to persuade them to buy a particular product or service. Since most of these prospective customers may not necessarily be interested in the product or service being promoted, the writers of these sales promotion letters have a difficult task not only of capturing the attention of the readers but also of convincing them of the benefits of the product or service. One way of capturing the attention of the prospective customers is to impress upon them that the writer of the letter represents a company which has a well-established reputation in the market by highlighting the achievements of the company, its speciality or the long experience that it can boast of in that particular line of products or services. To achieve this successfully, the writer will often use a 'we' orientation.

[3] We at Wright Services are well-established Management Consultants with experience in industries as diverse as mining, banking and manufacturing.

Alternatively, this can be achieved by indicating the writer's perception of the interests and needs of the potential customer, and implying that s/he or the company can fulfil them by offering the product or service being promoted. Jordan (1986:36) emphasizes this aspect of promotional writing.

A great deal of promotional writing, especially hard-sell advertising, relies on convincing readers that they have a problem or need, and the product or service being offered is not just a solution but is also the best solution.

This is frequently achieved by using a 'you' orientation.

[4] Have you ever wished that there was one computer course providing you with on-site consultancy to assist your staff in solving problems of implementing application?

or

[5] Does your company require a penthouse accommodation but may have perhaps put aside that consideration because of high cost?

Sometimes the writer may be tempted to use both orientations together as in [1]. But whatever orientation the writer may decide to use, he invariably will be trying to attract reader attention by establishing the credentials of the company he represents.

2. Introducing the offer

Having established his company's credentials in the eyes of the reader, the writer then goes on to introduce the service that he is promoting. In the next four paragraphs, he offers the service to his reader, informs him about the most essential details of the service, like what it consists of, when it can be offered, how much it costs, and in what way it can be valuable for the intended reader. In business terminology, this is known as product-detailing. Let us call this move **introducing the product or service**. Informing the customer about the product or service is always essential because if the product is not familiar to the consumer, it will not sell no matter how good it is. There are three important aspects of this move.

(a) Offering the product or service.
(b) Essential detailing of the product or service.
(c) Indicating value of the product or service.

This move is the most essential part of the sales effort. The first part of the move makes an offer, the second gives the essential description of the product or service, and the final part evaluates the product or service. Although it is true that in certain types of advertisements, especially the ones popularly known as image-building or picture-caption advertisements, the copy writer often undermines the value of product-detailing, in sales promotion letters it is rarely done. The most crucial aspect of this move is that the indication of the value of the product or service is essentially done in terms of the needs of the potential customer referred to in the first move. This seems to be a result of a strict observance of Grice's (1975) **maxim of relevance**, and any transgression of this maxim here tends to make the letter ineffective and even less credible. The moment the writer refers to the needs of the potential customer in the first move, he invariably promises the reader that he has a product or service to satisfy those needs and if the writer does not indicate how the product or service fulfils these needs, it is seen as non-fulfilment of the promise. Addressing your package to the interests, needs and inhibitions of your potential customer is the real secret of successful selling. In the Standard Bank letter, the writer indicates his perception of the needs of international financial managers in very general terms in move 1, and, after essential detailing of the training programme, indicates the value of the programme by emphasizing that the programme is rigorous as well as flexible and that it can be tailored to suit the requirements of inviduals as well as those of various groups – a strategy consistent with the first move in the letter.

In offering the product or service, writers tend to use typical formulaic expressions like the following:

[6] We are pleased to bring to your attention/to offer/announce/introduce . . .

In indicating value of the product or service, it is difficult to miss the predominant use of what Teh (1986) calls **lexical boost**:

[7] Domo toilet partition is *as solid as a brickwall!* Domo incorporates *the latest German Technology* and *superior quality standards* to make it *a perfect system* for the toilet, especially wet toilets in public places

or

[8] Apart from the *breathtaking* views and and the *delightful* environment of Ardmore Park's *renowned* "country club" facilities, the penthouse offers *exclusive* accommodation with a layout that provides *complete* flexibility and *excellent* opportunities for entertaining and conducting your business in *total* privacy.

The use of such modifiers is an essential part of product evaluation in the rhetoric of advertising and is fully exploited by the writers of sales promotion letters for product detailing.

3. Offering incentives

After the prospective customer has been informed about the product or service, the writer in the sixth paragraph attempts to make the offer more attractive by offering an incentive in the form of a discount of $100 per person if the reader decides to sponsor 6 or more staff. We shall name this move **offering incentives**.

This requirement may seem more cultural than universal. Bargaining is, for instance, an essential part of Singaporean business culture. Brochures distributed free to foreign tourists all over the country invariably advise them to negotiate the price of goods and services. This applies even more seriously to sales promotion letters. Consumers tend to expect attractive bargains in promotional activities and, if a sales promotion letter does not fulfil such an expectation, it is likely to be less successful in its persuasive effort. Even in the West, particularly in the promotion of credit cards, offering incentives in the form of introductory offers, special offers, discounts, special rebates etc. has become almost a norm. But it is more widely practised in countries like Singapore than in the West. In fact, the evidence I get from my interaction with the business community in Singapore indicates that a number of promotional efforts undertaken by some multinationals in Singapore are less successful than those undertaken by the local companies, simply because, in the local ones, the sales promotion letters are essentially seen and used as instruments of special discounted offers rather than simply as instruments of introducing new products or services. So the function of this move is to offer a discount to persuade the prospective customer to consider seriously the service being offered.

4. Enclosing documents

As mentioned previously, one of the important aims of the writer of the sales promotion letter is to keep its length within reasonable limits so that the busy businessman is not put off by its unnecessary details (at least for those readers who may not be terribly inclined to buy the product or service straight away). However, this requirement directly clashes with the requirement that a positively inclined customer should have readily available all the necessary details that s/he might need in order to make up his or her mind about the product or service. Clever business people find easy and effective solutions to such problems by enclosing detailed descriptions of products or services in the form of brochures, leaflets, pamphlets, reservation slips or request forms etc., so that a busy non-inclined reader can ignore the details, while a favourably inclined reader has the details readily available. This move on the part of the writer can be identified as **Enclosing documents**. The idea is that if, as a result of the promotional effort, a particular reader is even half-converted from a non-inclined to a somewhat positively-inclined customer, he should not be burdened with a situation where he will have to make additional effort to make the next move. All the effort at this stage must come from the seller rather than the buyer. However, the business community seems to be divided on this issue. There are people who feel that once the first move has been made by the seller, it is for the interested customer to make the second move, and they do not favour enclosing all the necessary details with the sales promotion letter. According to them, selling is a two-way process and once the first move has been made by the seller, the second move in the form of a letter of inquiry should come from the interested customer. This strategy, it is claimed, works better in the long run. So, the move **Enclosing documents** becomes optional, depending upon the strategy that the writer wishes to use.

5. Soliciting response

Whatever philosophy one may subscribe to in respect of the last move, there are no two opinions about the next one. All sales promotion letters are seen as efforts to initiate new business relations or strengthen the existing ones. Therefore one of the main communicative purposes of the sales effort is to encourage the reader, in this case the prospective customer, to continue further communication. That is the reason why in sales promotion letters the writers often make it a point to include a specific telephone number and/or the name of the person who will be all too willing to answer any queries that the reader may have about the product or service. **Soliciting response**, therefore, is yet another important move in the rhetoric of the sales promotion letter. Limaye (1984:28) confirms this in the following extract:

> All persuasive communication aims towards building a relationship between the sender and the receiver of the message since successful negotiations or transactions depend on relationships perceived as mutually gratifying to both parties.

This very interesting move is, therefore, characterized by a rather extravagant use of politeness markers and by its promise of a free, no-obligation and most often personalized service, as in the following two examples from Asia Commercial Bank Ltd and Hongkong Bank, respectively:

> [9] Please call on me if I can be of any service (my business card is attached). Alternatively, I shall be glad to visit you at your office at a date and time convenient to you.
>
> *or*
>
> [10] Please read through the enclosed leaflet. . . . Should you require further assistance, call our Prime Account Hotline – 5330088. There will be someone to answer your call 24 hours a day, including Sundays.

In the case of the Standard Bank letter [1], Mr Huff, the writer, personally offers his services for any further consultation or discussion.

6. Using pressure tactics

Sometimes it is considered rewarding, particularly in the context of Singapore, to use further pressure tactics to prompt the already half-inclined customer to take a quick decision about the product or service being promoted. This is generally realized in the form of an offer of some additional savings or gains if the customer decides to buy the product or use the service before a specified deadline. This move we shall call **using pressure tactics**. In some respects, this move may appear to be similar to the one we earlier called **offering incentives**. However, the two have a very distinct function and they appear at different positions in the rhetoric of sales promotion. The main function of **offering incentives** is to convince the potential customer about the attractiveness of the offer whereas the main focus of using pressure tactics is to push the already inclined or half-inclined customer to take an immediate decision, and that is one of the reasons why this move generally occurs towards the end of the letter. In the Standard Bank letter, the writer puts pressure on the reader in order to expedite his decision to participate by cautioning him about the limited number of participants required for the course. Here is another typical example of this move from American Express International, Inc:

[11] So join in our celebration now. . . . The American Express Card is a lot harder to get, but it means so much more when you get it. Once you carry the Card, you'll know why millions of successful people around the world never leave home without it!

PS: Joining Fee Waiver and Supplementary Card Gifts are valid only on the Special Form enclosed up to May 15, 1986.

7. Ending politely

Sales promotion letters invariably end on a polite, pleasant and courteous note, which we shall call **Ending politely**. One may think that all business letters should end politely. After all, business can flourish only by maintaining friendly, courteous and pleasant relations. It is generally true that most business letters observe the formality of ending communication on a pleasant note; however, there are cases, particularly in letters of complaint and adjustment, where the formality of polite ending is deliberately suspended to signal displeasure or to discourage further communication with regard to a particular matter (see Gan, 1989). Just as a formal close in business letters is significant in maintaining and strengthening business relations, its absence is also creatively used to signal subtleties of interpersonal relations without appearing to be either rude or discourteous. In fact, Gan (1989:21) distinguishes two types of discoursal functions of closings in business letters: **situational** and **relational**. The situational closings are directly derived from the function of the letter concerned whereas the relational ones indicate the attitude of the writer towards the following:

Future business relations (it can be used to initiate, maintain or terminate business relations)

Further communications (it can be used to encourage or discourage further communication with regard to a particular matter)

Reader (it can be used to build goodwill or threaten action).

A typical example of a **relational close** is from the following letter from City-Link International (S) Pte Ltd, where the writer makes a rather overwhelming attempt to initiate future business relations with the prospective customer.

[12] We sincerely hope that you will give us your kind support and we are looking forward to be of service to your esteemed organization.
We trust you will find our rates very competitive and we assure you of our best services and attention at all times.
Thank you and best regards.

And a typical example of **situational close** is the following one, from a collection letter from American International Assurance Company Ltd:

[13] Please give this matter your urgent attention. We look forward to an early settlement and to continue providing full coverage and our professional services to your company. However, if you have already sent the premium, please ignore this letter and we thank you sincerely for the action taken.

3.1.3 *Flexibility in move-structure*

The above structural interpretation clearly indicates that moves do not necessarily coincide with paragraphs; we may have two or more moves in one paragraph. For example, in example [1] paragraph seven beginning with *For your convenience . . .* we get two moves. On the other hand, the move **Introducing the offer** takes four paragraphs. Moreover, although this letter contains all the seven moves, it is not always obligatory for the writer to use all of them and in the same order. Just as there is a certain degree of flexibility in the number of moves used in a specific promotional effort by considering some moves more essential than others, there is a certain degree of freedom in the sequencing of these moves.

Move 1, **Establishing credentials**, appears to be more or less obligatory, particularly in the case of companies which consider themselves to be well established (see Bhatia and Tay, 1987), and certainly so in the case of multinationals (see Teh, 1986). So far as its positioning is concerned, **establishing credentials** is generally assigned the opening position, followed by the introduction of the offer. In fact, move 1 and move 2 are like the two potential opening batsmen in cricket. In most cases they are in that order but sometimes – particularly where a new product is being promoted – the letter opens with an announcement, and move 1 is either relegated to a later position as in the following instance:

[14] The Learn-a-Word-a-Day Calender 1986 is a new educational product for children between three and six years old. This product was launched into the market during the 17th Singapore Festival of Books and Book Fair '85 from 30 Aug to 8 Sept 1985 at the World Trade Centre. It received very good response from the parents and kindergarten teachers who visited the Fair.
We are the publisher and distributor for this product in Singapore.

or skipped altogether, as in the following example:

[15] We are pleased to bring to your attention an exclusive and fabulous condominium perched at the slope of Fraser's Hill called Fraser's Hill Condominium.
Fraser's Hill Condominium offers . . .

Move 2, **Introducing the offer**, is again obligatory in all sales promotion letters. Some form of product-detailing is necessary if the consumer is to be persuaded to buy the product. It may not always contain all the three aspects (see p. 51) and in that order. Indicating value of the offer, though often used to close the product-detailing section, does not always form a distinct unit by itself. In quite a few cases that I have seen, it is scattered throughout the essential detailing of the product or service. In terms of positioning, it is always one of the opening moves – generally after the writer has established his credentials.

Move 3, **Offering incentives**, is not obligatory in all promotional efforts, although in certain lines of products or business cultures it is likely to be more often used than in others. Although not an obligatory move, it is very commonly used in local sales promotion letters but less so in letters written by multinational concerns. However, it is worth noting that there is an increasing tendency these days, even in the West, to use it more often. The most prominent position (where it often occurs) is the one immediately after the product-detailing move. However, occasionally it is also seen as part of the opening move, particularly in those letters in which special offers are seen as the most attractive aspect of the offer, as in the following letter from a travel company.

[16] We are pleased to introduce to you our 5 DAY PHUKET/PHANG-NGA/PIPI ISLANDS TOUR for your incentive travel groups at a special price of £585.00 (normal £629.00 – exclusive for PIPI ISLANDS TOUR).

Move 4, **Enclosing documents**, is again widely used by some companies but is not really obligatory. As already mentioned earlier it really depends on the company's sales philosophy; if it is used, it generally occurs towards the end of the letter, but never finally.

Move 5, **Soliciting response**, is obligatory, in that it has been found to be present in most sales promotion letters, whether used by strictly local companies or multinationals (see again, Bhatia and Tay, 1987 and Teh, 1986). After move 2, this is perhaps the next most important move in sales promotion letters written both by local and multinational companies. It is also very versatile in its positioning. In fact, it not only paves the way for future business negotiations and successful relations but also, sometimes, serves a cordial and polite ending, as in the following case:

[17] Any one of us will be too glad to provide more product information and specification details.

or

[18] I hope that the above is of interest to you. If so, please contact us on Telephone Number 4695055 for a definite price and proposal.

Move 6, **Using pressure tactics**, once again is highly specific to certain lines of products or business cultures and thus is less likely to be an obligatory move, but whenever it occurs, it is more often than not positioned towards the end of the letter just before the close. Very occasionally, it can also be used as a closing move, instead of the more usual *polite ending*, as in the following example from the Standard Chartered Bank, promoting what they call their most comprehensive insurance coverage called the Ultra Plan. After move 5, it ends like this:

[19] Remember, you are completely covered by **UltraPlan** the moment your application is approved. So hurry, apply today. **LAST 10 DAYS TO APPLY**.

Move 7, **Ending politely,** marks the close and is found in most sales promotion letters. Gan (1989) found 100% incidence of this move in sales promotion letters, letters of enquiry and reply, whereas in letters of complaint, adjustment and collection, he found an absence of a proper close in as many as 40% of the letters. In most of these letters this deliberate omission of a close was used in a subtle manner to signal dissatisfaction, anger, unhappiness.

3.2 Job applications

On the face of it, job applications and sales promotion letters are considered two different types of texts, having little in common. However, when one looks at the communicative purpose of the two kinds of documents, one finds that both of them are meant to promote something. In the case of sales promotion letters, as we have just seen, it is the product or service that is promoted, whereas the job applicant attempts to promote himself. The emphasis in genre analysis on the shared communicative purpose on the part of the participants makes it possible for us to view sales promotion letters and job application letters as close cousins. In fact, job application is one specific realization of a rather large category of promotional literature, other typical realizations of which include sales promotion letters, advertisements in various forms, company brochures and leaflets of various kinds. A job application letter is closely related to a sales promotion letter not simply because both of them are persuasive in nature and both of them share the same communicative purpose (i.e., to promote a particular product or service) but also use the same medium, and exploit the same form. The only difference in the two is that the sales promotion letter generally is unsolicited whereas the job application letter is generally written in response to an advertisement, although it is not uncommon to find an unsolicited job application, where an applicant writes to a prospective employer to explore the possibility of a job opening.

If we consider the communicative purpose of the job application letter, we find that it is not very different from that of the sales promotion letter:

1.   As in a sales promotion letter, the main function of a job application letter is also persuasive, in the sense that its writer

aims to elicit a specific response from its reader(s), in this case a call for interview. Eliciting such a positive response is again a complex process and in order to ensure its pragmatic success it needs to achieve the following additional communicative purposes:

2. In the case of an unsolicited job application letter, the most important function of the opening is to establish the credentials of the candidate. It becomes even more difficult in cases where an applicant has to make an effort to persuade the reader to create a suitable job for him or her.

3. The most important function of a job letter, if written in response to an advertisement, is to offer a favourable, positive and *relevant* description of the abilities of the candidate in terms of the specifications or requirements of the job that has been advertised. This concern to indicate the value of the service being offered is taken as the main source of persuasion in this context.

4. Like a sales promotion letter, a job application letter does not give all the details of the services being offered. It is simply meant to highlight the most essential and the most important aspects of the candidature. The main purpose of the job application letter is thus seen as *clarificatory*.

5. Again like the sales promotion letter, the job application letter is the first attempt by the seller (the applicant or maybe a potential employee) to initiate a possible business relationship (a working relationship) with the potential customer (the employer). That is why the success or failure of a job application letter depends on the nature of the response it attracts from its reader.

Most of the Business Communication guides in some form or another point out these functions of a job application letter. Norman Sigband (1984:63), for example, advises his readers to do the following four things in their job application letters.

1. Gain the reader's attention
2. Describe qualifications and refer to more complete data in the résumé
3. Provide proof of your competence by referring to ... employment, degrees, etc.
4. Ask that an interview be scheduled as soon as possible.

In a similar manner, Love and Tinervia (1986:158) advise their readers to **stimulate interest, show confidence** (which means they should make their candidature relevant to the job specifications), **mention qualifications** (which requires them to enclose their detailed C.V.) and lastly **request an interview** in their job application letters, (which encourages the applicant to make an effort to invite further communication).

In the light of the above communicative purposes, let me now take up the following typical example of a slightly adapted version (to preserve confidentiality) of a job application letter and see how these are realized in practice.

[20]

> I wish to make application for a lectureship in the Department of English at this University.
>
> I have a Ph.D. in English from the University of Guelph in Ontario, Canada, where I studied under such distinguished scholars as Professors K.R. Sisson and P. Hogg. I also have an M.A. in English from Napoli University.
>
> I have taught English at a number of American and Canadian educational institutions, including Purdue and Oklahoma universities. I have also taught at Lohis College in Tehran, Iran, where I had experience teaching English as a second language. Currently I am on the staff of Riyadh University in Saudi Arabia.
>
> I have written about ten research articles in the last seven years, all of which have been published in scholarly journals. I have also written two books, one on Shakespeare and the other on the teaching of writing, which are being published by Guelph University and will be out in a few months.
>
> My speciality is Shakespeare and Renaissance drama in general, but I am also qualified to teach a wide variety of other courses, including the Novel, Poetry, Composition, writing and teaching of writing and ESL.
>
> I hope this letter of 'application' will clarify some of the information on the enclosed C.V., which outlines my qualifications, experience and research interests.
>
> I am required to give notice to Riyadh in early April and therefore look forward to hearing from you soon. Since I do not have a telephone, I will be happy to call you should a telephone discussion become appropriate.
>
> Sincerely yours
>
> XYZ

Like the sales promotion letter [1], this job application letter can also be assigned a seven-part structural description as in the following version:

[21]

I wish to make application for a lectureship in the Department of English at this University.	**Introducing candidature** *Offering candidature*
I have a Ph.D. in English from the University of Guelph in Ontario, Canada, where I studied under such distinguished scholars as Professors K.R. Sisson and P. Hogg. I also have an M.A. in English from Napoli University.	**Establishing Credentials**
I have taught English at a number of American and Canadian educational institutions, including Purdue and Oklahoma universities. I have also taught at Lohis College in Tehran, Iran, where I had experience teaching English as a second language. Currently I am on the staff of Riyadh University in Saudi Arabia.	*Essential detailing of candidature*
I have written about ten research articles in the last seven years, all of which have been published in scholarly journals. I have also written two books, one on Shakespeare and the other on the teaching of writing, which are being published by Guelph University and will be out in a few months.	*Indicating value of candidature*
My speciality is Shakespeare and Renaissance drama in general, but I am also qualified to teach a wide variety of other courses, including the Novel, Poetry, Composition, writing and teaching of writing and ESL.	**Offering incentives**
I hope this letter of 'application' will clarify some of the information on the enclosed C.V., which outlines my qualifications, experience and research interests.	**Enclosing documents**
I am required to give notice to Riyadh in early April and therefore look forward to hearing from you soon.	**Using pressure tactics**
Since I do not have a telephone, I will be happy to call you should a telephone discussion become appropriate.	**Soliciting response**
Thank you very much.	**Ending politely**
Sincerely yours	
XYZ	

Let us now look at the individual moves in order to see how they serve the various communicative purposes of a typical job application letter.

1. Establishing credentials

As in the sales promotion letter, this letter also opens with **establishing credentials**. The only difference is that, in the sales promotion letter, this move is more often realized by referring to the well-established nature of the company and less often by referring to the needs of the potential customer, although both of them are legitimate strategies to establish credentials. However, in the case of job application, it is not entirely impossible but very rare that we find a person well established in the profession and still looking for a job. So, generally one tends to find a predominant reference to the needs of the potential employer, always implying that the candidate can fulfil those needs.

In the above letter, the writer makes a reference to a lectureship in the department that he is applying for. In fact, it is so ambiguously worded that one almost takes it for granted that there is a position available. In most other cases, it is customary to refer to the job advertisement. By doing so, the applicant indirectly indicates his perception of the requirement of a specific job opening and then makes an offer in the form of his or her own candidature. In the process, it also becomes possible for the applicant to establish his or her credentials by bringing in his or her most important strengths. The following is a typical example from Comeau and Diehn (1987:214):

[22] This is in response to your recent advertisement in the *West Bend Tribune* for a part-time insurance secretary. I would like to apply for this position with your agency. I feel that my experience and education have prepared me for this position.

In the next one, from Lesikar (1984:287), we find a more daring and yet effective strategy to establish credentials, a seemingly perfect combination of what the employer needs and what the applicant thinks he can boast of.

[23] Sound background in advertising ... well-trained ... work well with others ... These key words in your July 7 advertisement in the *Times* describe the person you want, and I believe I am that person.

Occasionally, we come across a few instances of job application letters in which the first move, **establishing credentials**, is preceded by what Bhatia (1989) calls **adversary glorification** where the writer tends to glorify the credentials of the organization or institution of the prospective employer. Huseman and others (1986:450) give a good example of this kind of approach.

[24] The reputation and growth of your company in the textile industry have led me to make this application for a position in your management trainee program. In reading about Brockland, I have been impressed with your trainee program and the opportunities you offer to qualified university graduates.

2. Introducing candidature

Having established credentials, the writer goes to the next move, **introducing candidature**, which again, like the one in sales promotion letters, usually consists of three parts:

(a) Offering the candidature
(b) Essential detailing of the candidature
(c) Indicating value of the candidature

The first part of the second move sometimes presents a peculiar problem because of the availability of a typical syntactic possibility, which allows a writer to legitimately place this part of move 2 before move 1. Here is a typical opening for a job application letter:

[25] With reference to your advertisement in the *Straits Times* of 1 December, 1988 for the position of fashion copywriter I would like to offer myself as a candidate for your consideration.

The first part of the sentence, *With reference to your advertisement in the* Straits Times *of 1 December, 1988 for the position of fashion copywriter*, is an attempt to establish credentials by referring to the needs of the employer and the rest of the sentence, *I would like to offer myself as a candidate for your consideration* offers the candidature for the position referred to in the earlier part of the sentence. So far, there seems to be no problem with the order of the moves. However, because of the legitimate syntactic possibility of reversing the two parts of the sentence we end up with the following:

[26] I would like to apply for the position of fashion copywriter as advertised in the *Straits Times* of 1 December, 1988.

Here there seems to be a reversal in the ordering of the moves, in that, the first part of move 2 is realized by the first part of the sentence, and move 1 is realized by the second part of the sentence. Unfortunately this second version seems to be more commonly used than the first one. It can become even more complex in a case like this.

[27] With reference to your advertisement for the position of fashion copywriter as advertised in the *Straits Times* of 1 December, 1988, I would like to enclose my c.v. for your kind consideration.

Here the sentence realizes three moves. It establishes credentials by referring to job specification, offers candidature and also refers to the enclosed C.V. As in the sales promotion letter, the second part of move 2 is the most elaborate one, meant to give the most essential details of candidature, i.e., qualifications and experience, interests, abilities and achievements etc.

The third part is the most difficult and yet the most crucial one. A potentially successful application needs to stress that the writer is aware of the requirements of the job and that he has sufficient qualities and potential in the form of qualifications, relevant experience, personal attributes, strength of character, etc., to meet these requirements satisfactorily. Indeed, establishing the candidate's relevance to the job is the most complex form of self-representation in written discourse. Self-representation in job application is as complex as it is in literature. The applicant has a real self, on the basis of which he has to create his relevant self; this is similar to a literary author's fictional self, frequently referred to as *persona* in literary criticism. This relevant self of the applicant represents a relevant, positive and convincing selection of the applicant's real self based on Grice's principle of relevance, and it skilfully disguises or conceals the irrelevant, negative and less convincing aspects of the real self. Moreover, self-representation in job application letters needs to be persuasive and in order to be persuasive, in that it must arouse an appropriate emotional response in its readers, it must achieve credibility. It is a situation where even the best of *pathos*, *logos* and *ethos* in the true Aristotelian (see Aristotle, 1954) sense may not guarantee eventual pragmatic success.

One of the most frequently used strategies for self-representation in promotional literature, including job applications, is that of *self-appraisal*, which consists of an adequately relevant, positive and credible description of the product or service and a good indication of its potential value to its intended audience (Bhatia, 1989). The job application letter [20] illustrates this in the paragraph reproduced below.

[28] My speciality is Shakespeare and Renaissance drama in general, but I am also qualified to teach a wide variety of other courses, including the Novel, Poetry, Composition, writing and teaching of writing and ESL.

The paragraph tends to portray a relevant self in making claims about the general usefulness of his teaching abilities, which, he hopes will be perceived by the reader as useful and relevant to the job requirement. Self-appraisal of this kind is nothing but an account of one's fictional self made relevant to the specifications of the job for which the writer is an applicant. In sales promotion letters and advertisements this self-appraisal takes the form of product-detailing and indication of the value of the product in terms of the needs of the potential customer (Bhatia, 1988). Lesikar (1984:283) offers somewhat similar advice when he stresses the importance of making a job application letter reader-based rather than writer-based:

You can help your case . . . by presenting your information in reader viewpoint language whenever it is practical. More specifically, you should work to interpret the facts in terms of what they mean to your reader and to the work to be done.

Just as product-detailing and indication of the value of the product are the main strategies used in sales promotion letters to inform and persuade the prospective customer to buy the product, self-appraisal is used as the main strategy to persuade the prospective employer to accept the candidature of the applicant.

3. Offering incentives

In job application letters, it is rare to find applicants using this move, which seems to be the major difference between job applications and sales promotion letters. In letter [19], paragraph 5 can be interpreted as an attempt to make the offer more attractive. However, it can also be interpreted as **indicating the value of the candidature**. It is difficult to say which one is really intended by the applicant.

4. Enclosing documents

The following paragraph from letter [20] indicates two important aspects of this genre:

> [29] I hope this letter of 'application' will clarify some of the information on the enclosed C.V., which outlines my qualifications, experience and research interests.

Firstly it explains the function of the job application letter, i.e., it is clarificatory and not descriptive. That is the main reason why these cover letters are not exhaustive in details. Instead, the details are enclosed in the form of C.V., certificates, testimonials etc. Secondly, it refers to enclosed documents, which we listed as move 4, **enclosing documents**, in sales promotion letters.

5. Soliciting response

Like the sales promotion letter, the job application letter also has its primary indicator of success in its achievement of an interview. Lesikar (1984:283) refers to this aspect of job application letters as **action drive**.

> The presentation should lead logically to the action which comprises the close of the letter. . . It could be a request for an interview, if distance permits. It could be an invitation for further correspondence, perhaps to answer the reader's questions. Or it could be an invitation to write references. . . You are concerned mainly with opening the door to further negotiations.

In the closing part of the last paragraph of letter [20], the writer cleverly keeps initiative for further contact in his hands.

> [30] Since I do not have a telephone, I will be happy to call you should a telephone discussion become appropriate.

6. Using pressure tactics

Very occasionally we come across a case where a candidate would like to be so aggressive as to use pressure tactics to force the reader to take a quick decision, though it is fairly common in sales promotion letters. That makes the job application situation slightly more unequal than the one in sales promotion. In this competitive world of today, where jobs are not easy to get, an applicant can rarely claim parity with the employer. The stakes for the prospective employee are far higher than the ones for the employer. Nevertheless, it is not impossible to find a case where a candidate thinks that he or she can negotiate from a position of strength. In letter [20], the first sentence of the last paragraph seems to be performing that function:

[31] I am required to give notice to Riyadh in early April and therefore look forward to hearing from you soon.

7. Ending politely

Any promotional effort, whether it is for a product or service, largely depends on the goodwill that it creates. In this respect the function of closings in job application letters, like those in sales promotion letters, is crucial. On most occasions it may be a simple 'Thank you' or a more elaborate one like the following:

[32] I hope you will find my qualification and experience of use to you.

Although not very common these days, it is not impossible to find an odd job application letter with the following kind of antiquated closing.

[33] I assure you that if given a chance to serve your esteemed organization, I will give you full satisfaction with my work and conduct.

3.3 Cross-cultural variation

Many of the professional and academic genres, particularly in research and science, are of conformative type, in the sense that they are universally conventionalized to such an extent that even in their cross-cultural realizations, they rarely show any variation. The scientific research article is one such genre where one finds very little variation (Swales, 1981b; Hill et al., 1982; Zappen, 1983). However, the little research on business genres that has been reported indicates that in some contexts dominant socio-cultural factors do influence certain types of professional genres. In promotional literature, two important studies need some discussion: Teh's work (1986) on sales promotion letters and Bhatia's (1989) on job application letters.

3.3.1 *Sales promotion letters*

Teh (1986:94) reports results of her analysis of sales promotion letters from two sources, multinational companies (mostly from the West) and local Singaporean companies. She discovered that, although the two sets of data showed remarkable similarities in the use of lexico-grammatical resources and discourse regularities, they showed some very interesting variation in their discourse structure. Both sets of data displayed more or less obligatory use of move 2, **introducing the product or service**, and move 4, **soliciting response**. Letters from multinational companies invariably used move 1, **establishing credentials**, whereas in the letters from local companies this move was less common. Teh (1986:96) points out that

> The company's credibility can only be confidently established in the addressee's eyes if the company has a longstanding reputation in the market or a tradition of trust and reliability. Most local companies rarely enjoy the longstanding reputation that they can take advantage of.

One other possible explanation might lie in the fact that local companies rely more on the incentives they offer than their credentials, which as Teh points out are not very impressive anyway. And, perhaps for that reason, there is a much greater incidence of move 3, **offering incentives**, in her corpus from the local companies than from the multinational ones.

3.3.2 *Job application letters*

Bhatia (1989) reports on the nativization of job applications from South Asia. His corpus included some 200 applications for jobs and scholarships from India, Pakistan, Sri Lanka and Bangladesh. He reports that in South Asia the function of a job application letter appears to be different from what it is in the West. As the example quoted earlier [21] indicates the main function of the job application letter is to highlight and make relevant the qualifications and experience of the applicant to the specifications of the job. And that is one of the reasons why an overwhelmingly large number of promotional documents, whether sales promotion or job application letters, use product-detailing as the main strategy to persuade the reader to buy the product or service. In job application letters from South Asia, most applicants were found to be using the cover letter just to enclose the C.V., without taking advantage of the opportunity to offer self-appraisal to convince the reader of the strength of their candidature. The following is a typical example of this kind of use from his study:

[34] With reference to your advertisement for the post of *Personnel and PR Executive* published in *The Times of India* dated 12th March 1988, I hereby submit my personal resume for your kind consideration and disposal.
   Hope to be favoured.

A number of other cases, more particularly those of applications for scholarships, were even more interesting where, instead of using self-appraisal as the main strategy, many of the applicants used what Bhatia (1989) calls **Self-glorification**, **Adversary-glorification** or even **Self-degradation** as the main strategy to persuade the reader to accept their candidature.

Self-glorification is an unsupported claim of the writer's own superiority based simply on feelings or desires rather than on rational judgment. Such applicants frequently refer to their strong desire or personal ambition either to pursue higher education or to take up an attractive job. The following is a good example:

[35] I am a graduate in mining engineering having a shining academic record in my credit. I have been given admission in the graduate School, University of . . ., U.S.A. . . . But due to my financial un-ability I cannot afford to fulfill this long standing desire. . .

Self-glorification, Bhatia (1989) points out, lacks credibility and is likely to be viewed by the reader as purely subjective unless the applicant is a well-known authority in his area of expertise.

Job applicants in South Asia tend to become lyrical not only about their own achievements but they can, in the best traditions of Asian hospitality, bestow the same – even better in some cases – service on their adversaries (the reader, in this case) as well. The following is a rather extreme example of the use of this strategy from an application for scholarship from Bhatia (1989):

[36] First of all I would like to appreciate your activities/services which you are providing us. In our religion our prophet Mohammad (Son) encouraged/ appreciated those people who had provided educational facilities to the deserving people.
  So I personaly felt that you are really serving the nation in real sense. . .
  Sir, I would like to serve the human beings in real sense but I cannot do without the assistance of any organization such as yours. . .

In addition to adversary-glorification of this kind, where the organization is magnificently appreciated, sometimes even the country of final destination is given a similar treatment, particularly in the case of applications for scholarships to study abroad.

[37] I have secured first division marks (Grade B) in the said exam. and on the above basis I intend to complete my further studies in the field of Medicine in my loving great country, United States of America.

Besides such examples of target-glorification, Bhatia (1989) also cites instances from job applications where the applicant assigns glorified status to the organization of the prospective employer, indicating his or her eagerness to work with them.

[38] I am enclosing my brief 'Bio-data' for your kind consideration and confirmation. I request you kindly give me a chance to serve your esteemed organization. I assure you, Sir, I can prove worth of your selection by hard work and devotion to duties.

It is true that in job negotiation, both the prospective employer and the employee have their respective interests to serve. However, it is rare that they participate as equals. This inequality between the two parties tends to vary from situation to situation but also from one socio-cultural setting to another. It is maximum at the time of job application and tends to decrease as the employee becomes absorbed in the organization. It is likely to increase as one goes from affluent developed countries to less affluent developing or underdeveloped countries, where jobs are more difficult to get. In South Asia, this inequality between the two participants in the job situation becomes more pronounced and job applicants tend to magnify this inequality either by Adversary-glorification or Self-degradation. Self-degradation is more predominant in applications for scholarships (17.3%) than in those for jobs (2.3%) (Bhatia, 1989). It frequently takes the form of expression of lack of financial resources on the part of the candidate and/or his family.

[39] I may bring to your gracious knowledge that I belong to a very poor family and my parents are not financially sound enough to bear heavy expenses on my medical studies.

Presently I am being looked after by my brother (name of the brother) who is a driver by profession and his annual income is not more than 6000/ six thousand rupees. From this meagre amount, my brother has also to bear expenses on the maintenance of 2 sisters and 2 brothers besides himself. It is beyond his capacity to bear my expenses too, for the purposes of higher studies.

I would accordingly beseech your gracious, generous and benevolent honour to be kind enough to confer upon me a scholarship sufficient to cover my educational expenses in the United States of America.

For this noble act of kindness, I shall remain grateful deep down the depths of my heart.

In some cases Self-degradation does appear in the form of depreciation of financial and/or academic resources of a specific institution or even the country as a whole.

[40] I belong to a third world country whose most of the development depends upon the foreign aid majorly provided by your country. Due to this feeling of immense kindness and generosity of Americans both literally as well as practically, I a needy student of (name of the country) is able to pen-down this request for financial assistance in education.

The education system in (name of the country) is very unstable specially in the professional colleges and universities. In a calendar year the universities hardly work five months. This condition is even worse in my province... Here the universities are a year late than other universities of (name of the country). Because of this fact spirit and efficiency to study in students is fading. The students with real potential are trying to escape out from this monster of severe disorder, but the education abroad is very expensive and we cannot afford it. . . .

So, I request your honour to please support a poor student of (name of the country) financially. . ., so that he can become a bright mind (on the light provided by you) for humanity.

Although this strategy of Self-degradation is very common in applications for scholarship, it is not entirely absent in job applications.

[41] There are many openings for lecturers in colleges here, but the standard of the students has gone down very much and they insist on being lectured in the local language. I am not prepared to teach English Literature in (name

of the language), our regional language, and so have not applied for any posts here. Though my own college invited me to send in an application I did not do so.

Self-degradation in such application letters serves to highlight the disparity between the candidate's present situation and the one he is interested in. And since the addressee in all of them is the one who can bring about an adjustment, a move such as this can only invoke compassion and pity. There are some very explicit expressions of this kind in a number of applications.

> [42] My father is a rtd. primary teacher, he has 13 children and they are in different schools and different colleges. I am here at (name of the university) in third year.
> Sir, have pity on me. . . And search some scholarship for me.
> For the above act of kindness, I shall be thankful to you and pray for your long life and your prosperity.

Like product-detailing in advertising, self-appraisal is considered more or less a norm in self-advertising, yet it is surprising that in a number of Asian applications for jobs and scholarships we find some use of less effective strategies like Self- or Adversary-glorification, and Self-degradation. Is there any socio-cultural or cognitive predisposition on the part of Asians to prefer an emotional to a rational approach to persuasive self-advertisement? It is difficult to propose any definitive answer to this question. However, in the case of Self-glorification, it is true that in matters of higher education and careers Asians are commonly driven by their strong desires and ambitions of what they want to be rather than by a rational analysis of what they can or cannot successfully achieve. It is well known that the decisions of Asian parents to send their children for a career in medicine or engineering are taken long before they are even born. Unfortunately, however, the opportunities available for the fulfilment of their ambitions are desperately limited. Inadequate job specification and description in a majority of job advertisements and a lack of communicative skills in a foreign language make it even more difficult for an average applicant to identify and communicate his or her relevant self in job negotiation.

In the context of Self-degradation, it is interesting to note that economic dependence of any kind, whether at individual or national level, tends to promote a self-depreciatory approach to magnify economic and social distance between the participants involved in the negotiation process. It is true that economic inequality is likely to invoke compassion, which can be a useful persuasive strategy in applications for jobs and scholarships. Self-degradation and Adversary-glorification, jointly and severally (to use a legal expression), tend to serve the same end. This perhaps, is a natural consequence of too much of economic dependence on the developed countries. However, it will be interesting to compare similar data from a newly industrialized and affluent country, such as Singapore, to see to what extent people use self-degradation (if they do at all) as a persuasive strategy in applications for jobs and scholarships.

As we have seen, the primary function of a job application letter as an instrument for self-advertisement is to promote the candidature of the writer. The letter gives the applicant an opportunity to demonstrate possession of the relevant qualities for a particular job by clarifying the information on the enclosed C.V. The C.V., on its own, is not meant to and cannot do this job. It is simply taken as a documentary evidence for the claims the applicant makes in his letter. It is only through self-appraisal in the job application letter that one is legitimately allowed to relax the **maxim of quality** and observe the **maxim of relevance**. It is only because of this freedom that the applicant can manipulate Grice's maxims. It is this freedom that makes the job application letter, and quite a few other instances of promotional literature, a unique genre, and self-appraisal or product-detailing its most important characteristic feature.

3.4 Conclusions

In this chapter we discussed two closely related instances of promotional genre. We discovered in them a great deal of common ground, in spite of the fact that these two types of documents have rarely been treated as instances of the same text variety. However, if we adopt a genre perspective, we cannot but view them as instances of the same genre. Not only do both of them use the same medium, their participants have a similar role relationship. And above all, they share the same communicative purposes, which are adequately reflected in the structural interpretations that can be assigned to some typical instances of these two text-types. In this respect, the sales promotion letter and the job application letter should be regarded as instances of what we can call **promotional genres**. Although, it is not possible within the limited scope of this chapter to consider a number of other instances of similar texts in detail, it would be worthwhile to look at some more samples of promotional genres to see to what extent they can all be put together as one genre and to what extent they can be regarded as sub-genres of the same genre which we have called promotional genres. Some of the interesting ones worth considering are advertisements of various kinds (from newspapers or magazines, on radio or TV), publisher's blurbs promoting books (bestsellers or literary gems, academic textbooks or research reports), company brochures of various types, and even certain types of publicity brochures or leaflets very often used by social institutions to educate ordinary people about important social issues or problems or those used by tourist promotion organizations to inform holiday makers about places of tourist attraction. All these, I am sure, will have a number of shared characteristics, and many of them must be using somewhat overlapping linguistic resources in much the same way. It is a tremendous task for any one individual to take on; however, some of us might like to investigate further a few of the samples of texts which represent these text-types.

4   Research genres in academic settings

In the last chapter we analysed two of the genres from professional business settings, namely the sales promotion letter and the job application letter. At first, they appeared to be very different in terms of their contextual configuration, in that they are associated with two different professional settings. There are also some interesting differences in the participants and participant relationships. However, from the point of view of their communicative purposes, and hence from the point of view of generic structure, they turned out to be very similar. In fact, the two genres happen to be closely related and could be termed as sub-genres of the same genre, more generally known as promotional genre (see Kathpalia, 1992). In this chapter we shall look at two more instances – this time of research genres from academic settings. These are research article **abstracts** and **introductions**, which, unlike the previous case, appear to be very similar in terms of their contextual configuration: they are associated with the same research setting; they also use the same written mode or channel of communication, and share similar participant relationships as well as the level of formality. Indeed, even expert members of the academic community sometimes fail to make a proper distinction between the two. However, as we shall soon see, the two seemingly similar genres are very different in their communicative purposes, and, hence, are instances of different genres. Let me illustrate first the failure to distinguish the two genres, by taking an example each of a research abstract and an article introduction from the same research article.

[1] *Abstract*

It is commonly thought that children learning two languages simultaneously during infancy go through a stage when they cannot differentiate their two languages. Virtually all studies of infant bilingual development have found that bilingual children mix elements from their two languages. These results have been interpreted as evidence for a unitary undifferentiated language system (the unitary language system hypothesis). The empirical basis for these claims is re-examined and it is argued that, contrary to most extant interpretations, bilingual children develop differentiated language systems from the beginning and are able to use their developing languages in contextually sensitive ways. A call for more serious attention to the possible role of parental input in the form of mixed utterances is made.

[2] *Introduction*

It is commonly thought that children learning two languages simultaneously during infancy go through a stage when they cannot differentiate their two languages. In fact, virtually all studies of infant bilingual development have found that bilingual children mix elements from their two languages. Researchers have interpreted these results as evidence for an undifferentiated or unitary underlying language system. In this paper I will examine the empirical basis for these claims and I will argue that they are questionable because of serious methodological shortcomings in the research. I will then offer some tentative evidence based on speech perception studies and reanalyses of selected bilingual case studies that young bilingual children are psycholinguistically able to differentiate two languages from the earliest stages of bilingual development and that they can use their two languages in functionally differentiated ways, thereby providing evidence of differentiated underlying language systems.

(Genesee, 1989:161–179)

We do not find any difference whatsoever in the way these two genres are written, except that the introduction gives a slightly more elaborate account of the description of proposed research, and the abstract includes some indication of research conclusion. It is somewhat intriguing to note that the two are put together, one after the other, in the same article. Do they serve the same communicative purpose? If they do, then why this unnecessary repetition? Is there any justification for this kind of repeat performance on the part of the writer? Since it is assumed that both texts are written by the same person and are meant for the same readership, there must be some justification for the role that these two genres have in the rhetoric of the research article. As a matter of fact, the two genres have very different communicative purposes, and should, therefore, display different cognitive structuring, so that they remain distinct as genres. In order to understand what must be happening in such cases, let us first consider the two genres separately.

4.1 Research article abstracts

The research article abstract is a recognizable genre and has emerged as a result of a well-defined and mutually-understood communicative purpose that most abstracts fulfil, irrespective of the subject-discipline they serve. This is evident from the advice that various research institutions, organizations or publishing houses give to the writers of abstracts. The American National Standards Institute (ANSI) defines abstract as follows:

> An abstract is an abbreviated, accurate representation of the contents of a document, preferably prepared by its author(s) for publication with it.
>
> (ANSI, 1979:1)

An abstract, as commonly understood, is a description or factual summary of the much longer report, and is meant to give the reader an exact and concise knowledge of the full article. It contains information on the following aspects of the research that it describes:

1.   *What the author did*
2.   *How the author did it*
3.   *What the author found*
4.   *What the author concluded*

In order to find out how information on all these four aspects of research is put together in a concise manner, let us consider a typical example of an abstract.

[3] This paper sets out to examine two findings reported in the literature: one, that during the one-word stage a child's word productions are highly phonetically variable, and two, that the one-word stage is qualitatively distinct from subsequent phonological development. The complete set of word forms produced by a child at the one-word stage were collected and analysed both cross-sectionally (month by month) and longitudinally (looking for changes over time). It was found that the data showed very little variability, and that phonological development during the period studied was qualitatively continuous with subsequent development. It is suggested that the phonologically principled development of this child's first words is related to his late onset of speech.

(French, 1989:69–90)

This example seems to answer the four questions by using the following four moves:

1.   INTRODUCING PURPOSE: This move gives a precise indication of the author's intention, thesis or hypothesis which forms the basis of the research being reported. It may also

include the goals or objectives of research or the problem that the author wishes to tackle.

2.   DESCRIBING METHODOLOGY: In this move the author gives a good indication of the experimental design, including information on the data, procedures or method(s) used and, if necessary, the scope of the research being reported.

3.   SUMMARIZING RESULTS: This is an important aspect of abstracts where the author mentions his observations and findings and also suggests solutions to the problem, if any, posed in the first move.

4.   PRESENTING CONCLUSIONS: This move is meant to interpret results and draw inferences. It typically includes some indication of the implications and applications of the present findings.

We have all the four moves present, as shown below:

This paper sets out to examine two findings reported in the literature: one, that during the one-word stage a child's word productions are high- 1 ly phonetically variable, and two, that the one-word stage is qualitatively distinct from subsequent phonological development. The complete set of word forms produced by a child at the one-word stage were collected 2 and analysed both cross-sectionally (month by month) and longitudinally (looking for changes over time). It was found that the data showed very 3 little variability, and that phonological development during the period studied was qualitatively continuous with subsequent development. It is suggested that the phonologically principled development of this child's 4 first words is related to his late onset of speech.

The first sentence **introduces purpose** of the research being reported; the next sentence **describes methodology**, followed by sentence three, which **summarises results**; and then the final sentence **presents conclusions**. Let us see what we find in a typical example of a research article introduction.

4.2 Research article introductions

Introduction, as a genre, has conventionally been understood as a piece of discourse which introduces other forms of lengthy discourse, be it a research article, a project report, a laboratory report or even a student essay. Its communicative function is quite clear, but the way it is treated in a particular context depends largely on the requirements of the longer discourse it introduces; sometimes the subject discipline will also affect the way it is treated, as will, also, the organizational constraints imposed by the genre in question, particularly in the case of student lab reports and essays, which are generally written in direct response to the requirements made by the department or the teacher concerned. We shall take up the question of variation within introductions to research articles, lab reports, project reports etc. later. For the present, let us focus on the case of research article introduction, for which Swales (1981b, 1985, 1990) gives a very exhaustive account as a genre. We briefly referred to one of his examples in Part 1, where it was assigned a four-move structure (see p. 30).

Move 1: **Establishing field**
    (a) Showing centrality
    (b) Stating current knowledge
    (c) Ascribing key characteristics
Move 2: **Summarizing previous research**
    (a) Strong author-orientation
    (b) Weak author-orientation
    (c) Subject orientation
Move 3: **Preparing for present research**
    (a) Indicating a gap
    (b) Question-raising
    (c) Extending a finding
Move 4: **Introducing present research**
    (a) Giving the purpose
    (b) Describing present research

Let me take an example to illustrate this four-move structure:

[4] Amino-phosphonic acids such as glyphosate are known to chelate metal cations in aqueous media (Kabachink et al., 1974). Several studies have shown effects of metal ions on glyphosate efficacy in the field and the greenhouse. Hensley, Beverman & Carpenter (1978) reported that Fe^{2+}, Fe^{3+}, and Al^{3+} reduced glyphosate activity, but that Ca^{2+}, K^+, Na^+ had no effect. Stahlman & Philips (1979) found that monovalent metal cations had no effect on glyphosate toxicity, but that divalent metal cations reduced the herbicide's toxicity in the following order of effectiveness: $Fe^{2+} > Ca^{2+} = Zn^{2+} > Mg^{2+}$. Sprankle, Meggitt & Penner (1975), however,

found no interaction of Fe^{2+} with glyphosate efficacy and others have found Ca^{2+} to antagonize glyphosate activity (Philips, 1975; Sandberg, Meggitt & Penner, 1978; O'Sullivan, O'Donovan & Hamman, 1981; Schultz & Burnside, 1978). Turner & Loader (1978) observed that compounds with complex or chelate metal ions enhance the effects of glyphosate. They suggested that calcium and other metal cations might immobilize the herbicide.

Laboratory studies of the interaction of metal ions with glyphosate have also yielded mixed results. Hollander & Amrhein (1980) found no effect of Al^{3+}, Fe^{2+}, Co^{2+}, or Ca^{2+} on glyphosate-caused decreases in anthocyanin synthesis in excised buckwheat (*Fagopyrum esculentum* Moench) hypocotyls. Similarly, Gresshoff (1979) observed no effects of Zn^{2+}, Co^{2+}, or Fe^{2+} on glyphosate toxicity to unicellular organisms. Roisch & Lingens (1980), however, reversed the inhibitory effect of glyphosate on enzymes of aromatic amino acid synthesis of *Escherichia coli* by addition of Co^{2+}, and Mg^{2+} to the medium.

Using isolated bean (*Phaseolus vulgaris* L.) cells, Brecke & Duke (1980) demonstrated that glyphosate inhibited uptake of Rb^+ before effects on photosynthesis, respiration, or RNA and protein synthesis could be measured. The effect was apparently not due to loss of membrane integrity decrease in energy supply, or external ion chelation. No studies, however, have been made of the effects of glyphosate on uptake and translocation of metal cations in intact higher plants (Hoagland & Duke, 1982).

In this study, we examined the effects of glyphosate on uptake and translocation of Ca^+ in soyabean seedlings. A secondary objective was to determine the effects of Ca^{2+} on glyphosate phytotoxicity.

(Duke, Wauchope, Hoagland and Wills, 1983)

In this introduction, as in the abstract, we find a typical four-move cognitive structure. However, the nature and discourse value of the four moves are very different with very little overlap between the two. The authors of the introduction, in the first sentence, **establish field** by stating current knowledge in the field and also give a reference to support their claim. The second sentence beginning: *Several studies have shown* ... marks the beginning of the **summarization of previous research**, which goes right through to the middle of the third paragraph: ... *loss of membrane integrity decrease in energy supply, or external ion chelation.* **Preparation for present research** begins: *No studies, however, have been* ... and takes the reader to the end of the paragraph. The last paragraph beginning: *In this study, we examined* ... marks the **introduction of present research**.

In his recent work, Swales (1990) modifies his analysis of Research Article Introductions and assigns it a three-move structure, but we shall discuss this in section 4.3. For the present, let us consider the issue whether these two genres can be assigned separate status as two independent genres.

In terms of the communicative purpose(s), the abstract presents a faithful and accurate summary, which is representative of the whole article. Research article introduction, on the other hand, only introduces the article without giving out everything reported in the article. It only marks a link between what has gone before in the relevant field of research and the present work that is being reported. In other words, introduction serves a useful purpose of making 'the present story' relevant by placing it appropriately in the context of 'the first story', i.e., previous research in a particular field of study. That is one of the main reasons why we rarely, if ever, find any discussion of previous research in abstracts, whereas it is a very important part of the research article introductions. On the other hand, some indication of methodology, experimental procedures, data collection, etc. used for present research is considered crucial in research abstracts, whereas it is rarely mentioned in article introductions. Similarly, reporting of results or findings of research is an important part of abstracts but this is very rare in article introductions, except in some disciplines, where some preview is considered strategically desirable. In mathematics, for example, the introduction contains the end result of the report because, in this discipline, one invariably needs to work backwards to solve mathematical problems, but that is a very special case.

Therefore, if we look at the cognitive structuring in the two genres, we find that there is nothing that is common to these two, except the last move of the introduction, i.e., **introducing present research**, which in a number of cases reappears as move 1 of the abstract as **introducing purpose**. In other words, the article introduction ends where the abstract begins. The only point of overlap is in the indication of the purpose of research, which is necessary and quite logical, because the abstract not only always precedes the introduction but can also occur on its own, outside the research article. Now, if we consider the two genres, we find that in spite of the fact that they share all the contextual factors, including the intended readership that they are meant for, the background knowledge that the two genres assume on the part of their readership, and even the formal academic style that is commonly associated with them, the two genres differ significantly in terms of their communicative purposes and so they display different four-move generic structures. The research article abstract is meant to tell all the important aspects of the very much lengthier research report, whereas the research article introduction is meant to 'motivate' the present research and to 'justify' its publication (see Swales, 1990:138). It is from this perspective that Swales (1990) revised his earlier four-move model, and developed his three-move, **Create a Research Space (CARS)** model.

4.3 Form-function correlation and the CARS model for article introductions

In the preceding section, we mentioned that Swales (1990) revised his earlier four-move model in favour of a three-move CARS model, which he presents as follows:

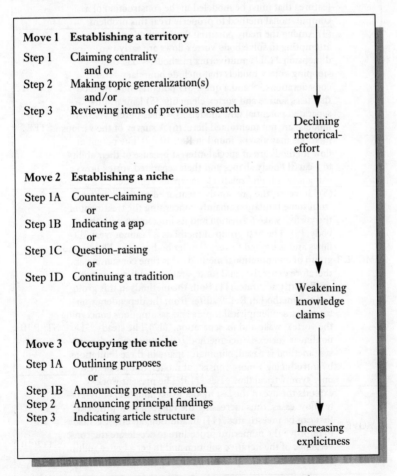

Move 1	**Establishing a territory**	
Step 1	Claiming centrality and or	
Step 2	Making topic generalization(s) and/or	Declining rhetorical-effort
Step 3	Reviewing items of previous research	
Move 2	**Establishing a niche**	
Step 1A	Counter-claiming or	
Step 1B	Indicating a gap or	
Step 1C	Question-raising or	
Step 1D	Continuing a tradition	Weakening knowledge claims
Move 3	**Occupying the niche**	
Step 1A	Outlining purposes or	
Step 1B	Announcing present research	
Step 2	Announcing principal findings	
Step 3	Indicating article structure	Increasing explicitness

As illustration of this he takes up the following example:

[5]

I Introduction

MOVE 1

(1) The increasing interest in high–angle–of–attack aero-dynamics has heightened the need for computational tools suitable to predict the flowfield and the aerodynamic co-efficients in this regime. (2) Of particular interest and complexity are the symmetric and the asymmetric separated vortex flows which develop about slender bodies as the angle of attack is increased.   STEP 1

(3) The viscous influence on the separation lines and the unknown three-dimensional (3D) shape of the vortex wake are some of the main flow features that must be modeled in the construction of a computational method to properly treat this problem.   STEP 2

(4) Among the many potential flow methods developed in attempting to solve body vortex flows are early two dimensional (2D) multivortex methods,[2-4] 2D time-stepping vortex models that include boundary-layer considerations,[5-8] and a quasi-3D potential flow method[9] that uses source and vortex elements. (5) Linear, un-separated potential flow models as well as purely viscous models, are not mentioned here. (6) A survey of the various methods may also be found in Ref. 10. (7) The potential flow methods are of special interest because of their ability to treat 3D body shapes and their separated vortex flows using a simple and relatively inexpensive model.   STEP 3

MOVE 2

(8) However, the previously mentioned methods suffer from some limitations mainly concerning the treatment of the vortex wake formation and its interaction with the body. (9) The first group of methods [2-4] cannot treat 3D flows and is limited to very slender bodies. (10) The second group of computational methods[5-8] is time consuming and therefore expensive, and its separation prediction is not sufficiently accurate. (11) Both the methods in this group and the method in Ref. 9 suffer from the dependency on too many semiempirical inputs and assumptions concerning the vortex wake and its separation. (12) The steady, 3D nonlinear vortex-lattice method,[11-12] upon which the pre-sent method is based, eliminates many of these limitations by introducing a more consistent model, but it can treat only symmetrical flow cases.   STEP 1B

MOVE 3

(13) The present work extends the use of the last model to asymmetric, body-vor-tex flow cases, thus increasing the range of flow problems that can be investigated. (14) In addition, an effort is made to improve the numerical procedure to accelerate the con-vergence of the iterative solution and to get a better rollup of the vortex lines representing the wake.   STEP 1B

(D. Almosino. 1985. High Angle-of-Attack Calculations of the Subsonic Vortex Flow in Slender Bodies *AIAA Journal* 23 (8): 1150–6)

In the revised model Swales (1990) combines moves 1 and 2 of the earlier model into a single move 1 and calls it **establishing a territory**. The most important reason for this is the difficulty of separating Move 1 and Move 2, as he points out:

> Several analysts (Lopez, 1982; Bley-Vroman and Selinker, 1984; Crooks, 1986a) have commented on the difficulty of separating Move 1 and Move 2. The fact that the original corpus was deliberately restricted to short introductions led to the creation of a separate citational category (Move 2 – Summarising Previous Research) clearly at odds with the increasing practice of spreading of references throughout the introduction (Jacoby, 1986).
>
> (Swales, 1990:140)

Clearly, Swales (1990) has been able to avoid the difficulty of distinguishing the first two moves in his earlier model. However, inadvertently perhaps, he has created a more serious problem by combining the two. Just as there can be arguments about the difficulty of separating move 2 from move 1, there are equally strong, and perhaps more valid, arguments in favour of assigning a separate status to move 2 **summarizing previous research**. Firstly, literature review in research reporting of various kinds has been well established for a long time. There is hardly ever a research project, dissertation or thesis that one can imagine being complete without an adequate section or even a chapter on the review of past literature. In the research article itself, it is very rare to find an example without an attempt of this kind. Even where there is no relevant literature of any consequence to discuss, conventionally a statement indicating that *there is hardly any work available in this area* is fairly common, which itself points out the traditional importance of the description of previous work in research reports.

The other evidence for the individual status of literature review comes from specialist reactions in various academic disciplines, particularly in the form of editorial reviews, comments, suggestions etc., which frequently indicate that the author must demonstrate his or her knowledge of the relevant literature, especially if the author happens to be less well established in the field. Comments like: 'Are you familiar with the work(s) of so and so?' or 'By the way, do you know that so and so has an interesting paper on this?' are fairly common on draft proposals for research publication, which emphasize the importance of literature review in research reporting. If it is true that literature review has conventionally acquired an independent status in research writing, and I strongly believe that it has, then the solution to the problem of distinguishing move 2 from move 1 does not lie in combining the two moves, but in finding adequate linguistic criteria to separate them.

In order to look for a principled criterion for identifying move-structure, let us first consider one of the fundamental principles of genre analysis, in fact of all kinds of discourse analysis – that the focus of analysis be on the functional rather than the formal characteristics of linguistic data. It is important for a genre analyst to know where the two moves, **establishing field** and **summarizing previous research**, become distinct. However, more important than that is to know which moves the authors conventionally make in order to realize their communicative purpose(s) effectively and the relative importance of these moves. How to distinguish them is an operational question. It has also been well known for quite some time that it is not always possible to find one-to-one correlation between formal and functional aspects of language use. Just as it is possible for a particular formal feature to serve one or more discourse values in different contexts, it is equally possible that a particular discoursal function may be served by two very different formal realizations. Let me illustrate this by going back to one of the points we noted in the previous chapter when we were discussing sales promotion letters. In that context we discovered that there were two major linguistic realizations of the move, **establishing credentials**. One of them is by referring to the good track record or the past achievements of the company, as in the example from data collected in Singapore and reproduced below.

[6] We are an established courier incorporated locally since 1971 when courier service was virtually unknown. We have come a long way and today we can boast that we have established ourselves as a specialist in the field of courier service, especially to destinations within Indonesia, i.e., Jakarta, Medan, Surabaya etc.

Here is a very straight-forward conventional way of **establishing credentials** of the company by referring to the reputation and long experience in a field of specialization. The same move is also quite frequently realized, differently, by referring to the needs of the prospective customers, as in the following example, once again collected from Singapore:

[7] Have you ever wished there were one computer course providing you

with on-site consultancy to assist your staff in solving problems or implementing application?

In surface realizations, the two examples are very different but in terms of discoursal value, the two serve exactly the same purpose. Whether one talks about one's own impressive track record in a business context, or about the potential customer's needs, one is essentially trying to establish credentials. When, in this sales promotion context, the needs of the prospective customer are mentioned, the writer is invariably implying that he or she is the one who can satisfy those needs. In other words, that he or she has the expertise, the necessary experience and, above all, the product to fulfil the needs in question. The whole point of the present discussion is that although surface signals are fairly reliable indicators of discoursal values in a majority of discourse contexts, the ultimate criteria for assigning discourse values to various moves is functional rather than formal. Let me take the reverse case now, where one linguistic realization (namely, citations or references in research writing) takes on different discoursal values and has thus been identified as a major problem in form-function correlation (see Swales, 1990).

In a number of research article introductions, there may be no problems in distinguishing the two moves, **establishing field** and **summarizing previous research**. However, what complicates the issue is the appearance of references and citations almost everywhere in the structure of the research article, rather than in the introduction alone. It is for this reason primarily that Swales (1990) decides against having a separate citational category in his revised generic structure of the article introduction. In other words, the misunderstanding is caused not by the status of the citational section in the introduction, but rather by its appearance in other parts of the article as well. Like any other feature of linguistic form, citations can also be assigned different discoursal values, depending upon where they occur and what communicative purpose they serve. Let me explain this by taking up a few examples.

[8] SELF-MONITORING, as conceptualized by Snyder (1972), was thought to encompass five underlying dimensions: (a) concern for appropriateness of social-behavior; (b) attention to social comparison information; (c) ability to control or modify self-presentation; (d) use of this ability in particular situations; and (e) cross-situational variability of social behavior. Factor analytic examination of Synder's self-monitoring scale by

Briggs, Cheek, and Buss (1980), however revealed an underlying factor structure consisting of three dimensions: (a) acting ability, (b) other-directedness, and (c) extroversion. This clarification of what is measured by the scale is germane to the research question examined here: Do self-monitoring and competence contribute differentially for males and females in the determination of social interaction?

Several recent studies have revealed differences between American males and females in the degree to which self-monitoring behaviour predicts emergent relationship and verbal participation in groups. Garland and Beard (1979) found that in same-sex trios working on an interactive task (brainstorming) high self-monitoring females emerged as leaders. For males, however, self-monitoring did not predict emergent leadership.

These results were affirmed and amplified by Oddous (1983) in a study of long-term discussion groups that revealed that higher levels of self-monitoring corresponded directly to increased likelihood of emergent leadership for females but not for males. The primary predictors of emergent leadership for males were commitment and competence.

Because the influence of competence might be expected to vary with the specific context, two studies were conducted: one used a task on which males would be expected to do better, the other a task on which females would be expected to excel.

(Stimpson, Robinson and Gregory, 1987:159–162)

There are four instances of citations or references, but all of them do not perform the same discoursal function. The first two citations of Snyder (1972) and those of Briggs, Cheek, and Buss (1980) help the writer to conceptualize self-monitoring in **establishing field**, which includes the introduction or identification of topic within the field of study. The two references essentially make it possible for the author to sharpen the area of research he is focusing on. This is further confirmed by the subject orientation in the first paragraph (see Swales, 1981b, for a discussion of subject-matter orientation in reporting previous research). On most occasions the author identifies, develops, if necessary, and establishes field at this stage. Once that has been done, the author begins **summarizing previous research** relevant to the field or topic thus established or identified. In the above case, this begins: *Several recent studies have revealed* ... and continues to the end of the third paragraph. The last two references, the first one to Garland and Beard (1979) and the other to Oddous (1983) are efforts to summarize previous research in order to create research space for the present work. In the illustration, therefore, we find two different discoursal values carried by the same citational form. In the same example we also find that identification of the topic of research is an important aspect of field establishment, which is necessary in some cases, particularly in longish introductions often found in project reports or theses, as reported in Dudley-Evans (1989). Whether or to what extent it can be assigned a separate move status is a different question and we shall come back to this in the next section. For the time being we shall consider it as part of the same move, **establishing field**.

Sometimes, we may find it difficult to distinguish two moves simply because syntactic possibilities allow them to be realized in the same sentence, often embedding one move within the other, as in the following article introduction:

[9] Although thermodynamic properties of binary liquid mixtures containing an associated component have been studied extensively, only a few have dealt with binary mixtures of sulfonamides. Dipole-dipole interactions appear between the molecules of these amides resulting in an ordered liquid structure[1]. N-Monosubstituted sulfonamides are able, in addition, to self-associate by hydrogen bonding.[2-5]
In earlier papers[6-8] we have reported the excess volumes and viscosities of different binary mixtures containing N-methylmethanesulfonamide as one component. In view of the importance of alcohols as solvents, it was of interest to continue this work with an investigation of the properties of the (methanesulfonamide + an aliphatic alcohol). In this study we report the excess volumes for NMMSA + methanol, + propan–1-ol, + propan–2-ol, + butan–1-ol, and + 2-methylpropan–2-ol.

(Pikkarainen, 1982: 503–507)

In this case, **establishing field** has been realized in the form of a subordinate adverbial clause embedded within the main clause which marks the beginning of the next move **summarizing previous research**. Although there seems to be rather unclear form-function correlation, in the sense that sentence and move boundaries do not coincide, it is still possible to distinguish the two moves. In some cases, the syntax may allow even the reversal of syntactic positioning of the two moves, which may make it even more difficult to distinguish them in a particular example. This is very common in abstracts, particularly of experimental studies where the first two moves, **introducing purpose** and **describing methodology** are often embedded one within the other, as in the following example:

[10] Children aged 2; 0 to 2; 6 participated in a longitudinal study examining their acquisition of the English auxiliary system following a six-week period in which they were exposed to additional auxiliary input in varying sentence contexts. Groups of children received enrichment utterances with the auxiliary *could* either in the first position in the sentence, in the middle position, or in both positions. Children in the front

position group were significantly advanced over the other experimental groups in acquiring modal auxiliaries but not non-modals. However, none of the experimental groups differed significantly from a baseline group which received no additional *could* input. The implications of these findings for understanding the mechanisms of auxiliary acquisition and the nature of children's grammatical categories are discussed.

(Shatz, Hoff-Ginsberg and Maciver, 1989: 121–140)

This example presents a typically interesting four-move structure for an abstract, which begins with move 2, **describing methodology**.

Children aged 2; 0 to 2; 6 participated in a longitudinal study examining their acquisition of the English auxiliary system following a six-week period in which they were exposed to additional auxiliary input in varying sentence contexts. Groups of children received enrichment utterances with the auxiliary *could* either in the first position in the sentence, in the middle position, or in both positions.

Move 1, **introducing purpose**, is embedded within move 2, **describing methodology** in the form of a reduced non-finite clause *examining their acquisition of the English auxiliary system.* Conventionally, as well as logically, move 1 should occur initially because one cannot talk about methodology before indicating the purpose for which a particular methodology has been used. However, English syntax allows not only the embedding of one move within the other, but also the reversal of syntactic positioning of the moves, thus making it difficult to distinguish the two moves in such discourse. This is not an isolated phenomenon in research abstracts of a particular kind, and it is very common in other professional genres. In fact, we find several instances of this kind in a variety of professional discourses, as in job application letters, which we discussed in the last chapter (see Section 3.2, examples 26–28), where three different moves are realized within the same sentence.

This difficulty of distinguishing one move from another is not associated only with the first two moves of article-introductions; it can occur in the context of any other set of moves in any genre, whether academic or professional. It can sometimes become problematic to distinguish move 2, **summarizing previous research**, from move 3, **preparing for present research**, because of the evaluative comments which can form part of both moves, as in the following case:

[11] The young child has at least two potentially competing conceptual

systems with which to organize his or her world. One system, the formation of complementary relationships, results from the child's direct observation of objects and events co-occurring in space and time. Thus, dogs are seen eating bones, and babies lie in cribs. Taxonomic relationships, for example, animals and fruit, form a second conceptual system that can be at odds with a categorization system based on complementary pairs.

Preschool children are capable of using both of these conceptual systems (Scott, Greenfield, & Urbano, in press; Scott, Scott & Serchuk, 1980; Scott, Serchuk, & Mundy, 1982) but find the complementary conceptual system easier (Scott et al., 1980; 1982), especially under demanding task situations (Scott et al, in press). On the other hand, older children are characterized as preferring a taxonomically based organizational system (Davis, 1976; Denney, 1975; Denney & Moulten, 1976; Smiley & Brown, 1979). This shift, which is hypothesized to occur somewhere between first and fifth grade, is characterized as representing "a change in preference rather than a shift to a fundamentally new way of organizing knowledge" (Smiley & Brown, 1979, p.249).

Although the literature strongly supports the notion that the use of taxonomic organization increases with age, there is some question whether a general shift in "preference" occurs. For example, Denney and Moulten (1976) found that although taxonomic choices increased from 3 to 9 years of age, complementary choices did not decrease over this age period. Davis (1976), who showed that complementary organization was not the dominant categorization mode in 11- to 17-years-olds, reported that 17% of his sample exhibited an "exclusive and pronounced preference" for complementary pairings, which increased with age. Research with adults (Rabinowitz & Mandler, 1983) has found superior recall in subjects using complementary versus taxonomic organization.

The generality of Smiley and Brown's (1979) findings, which provide the strongest evidence for a shift in conceptual preference, can also be questioned. Complementary picture pairs were based on verbal associations of first graders and taxonomic picture pairs based on verbal associations given by fifth graders. It is not clear whether verbal and pictorial associations are equivalent. Scott et al. (1980), for example, found little agreement between verbal association and picture pairs that served successfully for both complementary and taxonomic pairings. Nelson (1977) has argued that association to pictures is very different from association to words. Thus one may question whether associates derived from a verbal method have the same strength of relation when presented as visual pairs. Furthermore, the taxonomic pairs, derived from older children, may not have been as familiar to the younger children as the complementary pairs. Finally, the presence of the picture's "name" printed in large letters under the picture might have had differential impact across age.

In the present study, complementary and taxonomic preference was assessed with stimuli derived from picture pairs familiar to preschool children. . .

(Greenfield and Scott, 1986: 19–21)

This is an interesting introduction to a research article in *Psychology*, which examines the development of conceptual preference for complementary, as against taxonomic, relationships in children. Since the article questions the utility of conceptualizing the increased use of taxonomic organization as a shift in preference, it gives a rather negative review of literature which presents a shift from a complementary to a conceptual preference in the early school years, particularly in paragraphs 3 and 4. This review of literature is characterized by distinct evaluative expressions, as follows:

> Although the literature strongly supports the notion that the use of taxonomic organization increases with age, there is some question whether a general shift in "preference" occurs.

> . . . although taxonomic choices increased from 3 to 9 years of age, complementary choices did not decrease over this age period.

> The generality of Smiley and Brown's (1979) findings, which provide the strongest evidence for a shift in conceptual preference, can also be questioned.

> It is not clear whether verbal and pictorial associations are equivalent.

> . . . found little agreement between verbal association and picture pairs that served successfully for both complementary and taxonomic pairings.

> Nelson (1977) has argued that association to pictures is very different from association to words.

In fact, it is characteristic of **summarizing previous research** to evaluate rather negatively previous work, so as to create space for present research. But it is only the concluding section beginning with

> Thus one may question whether associates derived from a verbal method have the same strength of relation when presented as visual pairs

which focuses on the question that the authors want to raise in order to **prepare for present research**. All the other evaluative comments in the context of previous research indicate the involvement of the authors in the description of previous research, which is most often the case, particularly where research space is created by question-raising.

It would seem, therefore, that although it is not always easy to separate moves clearly because of a lack of form-function correlation, it is not always desirable either to look for solutions to that problem in terms of combining moves. In fact, the more reasonable solution lies in the sharpening of identification criteria for the move(s) concerned, so that at least one can justifiably account for a majority of clear cases of the move(s) in question. Moreover, there can still be cases which will pose problems and escape identification or clear discrimination, however fine a net one may use. After all, we are dealing with the rationale underlying linguistic behaviour rather than its surface form.

4.4 Introductions in student academic writings

In Section 4.2, it was pointed out that introductions tend to vary even within academic writing. Some of the closely-related introductions are the ones generally associated with student academic writings, particularly laboratory reports and project reports. Typical introductions to these reports are often found to be closely related to research article introductions in general terms but most of them display interestingly subtle variations in their cognitive structuring, which can be accounted for in terms of variations in their communicative purposes. Let us take the case of laboratory reports first.

4.4.1 *Student laboratory report introductions*

Although student laboratory reports and research articles are both accounts of scientific experimentation, they differ in one major respect. Research articles are reports on original and new experiments, which are meant to add to the existing knowledge of the discipline or field to which the research report belongs. Student laboratory reports, on the other hand, are mere repetitions of standard laboratory procedures, which are written in order to understand theory, to practise established procedures and to show awareness of relationship between theory and practice. The content of the laboratory reports, therefore, is not new knowledge, but established knowledge, and there is no attempt on the part of the writer to get it accepted as a contribution to the field or discipline. Whereas in the case of research articles, the content is new knowledge, which needs to be accepted by the academic community. The writer of the research article, therefore, needs to create what

Swales (1990) refers to as 'research space' to justify publication of his research report. In the case of student laboratory report introductions there is no need to create research space, and hence no need to evaluate previous research, but simply to show awareness and understanding of established research procedures or theory on which the experiment is based. Let us see how these changes are reflected in the structure of laboratory report introduction by looking at a typical example from a Civil Engineering and Building report (see Bhatia and Tay, 1987).

[12]

The Bulking Effect of Fine Aggregate

Aim: To determine the percentage bulking of fine aggregate due to the presence of moisture

Introduction

Bulking, an effect of the presence of water in aggregate, is an increase in the volume of a given weight of sand caused by the films of water pushing the sand particles apart. The volume is minimum when the sand is absolutely dry or when it is completely saturated. At immediate moisture content, fine aggregate shows an increase in volume. It is important to carry out an experiment of this kind as too much moisture is one of the reasons that can cause a building to collapse. The percentage of bulking for a given moisture content is calculated as follows:

$$S = \frac{hi - h}{hl} \times 100; \text{ when}$$

hi = immediate moisture content
hl = initial moisture content, and

hl is obtained by the following equation:

$$hl = \frac{hd \quad hs}{2}; \text{ when}$$

hd = the average of the dry volume
hs = the standard volume.

If we compare this introduction with the one from the research article [4], we find some very interesting differences. The lab report introduction contains three moves, as against the four we established in research article introductions. It begins with the statement of purpose or aim of the experiment, which is given some kind of a priority status at the top, immediately after the title of the experiment. The statement of purpose in research article introductions typically marks the end of the introduction. In the research article introduction, the writer needs to establish a case for the subject of the research report, whereas in the lab report it is treated as given. The writer does not, therefore, need to go through the lengthy and rather difficult process of establishing the research topic. Instead, it is enough for him to state the aim or purpose of the experiment as move 1 of the introduction, or even as a separate move outside the introduction.

Like the research article introduction, the lab report introduction also contains an attempt to **establish field** by

Indicating importance of the topic

or

Showing awareness of current knowledge

Since a lab report writer does not have to make an attempt to create a research space and then to occupy it, we do not see moves 2, 3 and 4 in such reports. Instead, very often, we find an attempt to show an awareness or understanding of the principle or theory which underlies the experiment. Let us call it **explaining theory**. The final move of research article introduction **introducing present research** appears in the form of a simple statement of the aim of the experiment and is invariably placed immediately after the title of the experiment. Lab report introductions are characterized by three moves in the following order:

Move 1: Stating aim of the experiment
Move 2: Establishing field
Move 3: Explaining theory

If we analyse example [12], we find the following discourse structuring underlying the introduction:

The Bulking Effect of Fine Aggregate

Aim: To determine the percentage bulking of fine aggregate due to the presence of moisture   1

Introduction

Bulking, an effect of the presence of water in aggregate, is an increase in the volume of a given weight of sand caused by the films of water pushing the sand particles apart. The volume is minimum when the sand is absolutely dry or when it is completely saturated. At immediate moisture   2
content, fine aggregate shows an increase in volume. It is important to carry out an experiment of this kind as too much moisture is one of the reasons that can cause a building to collapse. | The percentage of bulking for a given moisture content is calculated as follows:

$$S = \frac{hi - h}{hl} \times 100; \text{ when}$$

hi = immediate moisture content
hl = initial moisture content, and

hl is obtained by the following equation:

3

$$hl = \frac{hd \quad hs}{2}; \text{ when}$$

hd = the average of the dry volume
hs = the standard volume.

The foregoing discussion reveals that, although the two introductions are conventionally regarded as similar, they are in some way different from each other. The differences are the result of a slight variation in the two communicative situations they are associated with. Research articles are contributions to the field or discipline, whereas lab reports are indications of understanding as part of the process of learning. One is used in a professional context, the other is associated with an academic teaching/learning context. In the first, knowledge representation is new; in the second, it is old and established. In the first, the contribution is regarded as a knowledge claim, whereas in the second it is merely a claim to an understanding of whatever is known and established. In research article introductions the participants are equal in terms of expertise and shared professional knowledge, whereas in the case of lab reports, the participants operate in an unequal setting where teachers, for whom the lab reports are primarily written, have all the information being reported in the lab report. In research article introduction, therefore, it is necessary to evaluate (generally negatively) relevant past research, in order to create some kind of a niche for present research. Hence the importance of the move, **summarizing previous research**, to indicate a gap or raise a question, or to extend a finding. In the case of a lab report, on the other hand, the writer needs to show awareness and understanding of the principle or theory that is being used to perform an experiment. However, the communicative purposes, in very broad terms, overlap in that both kinds of introduction are attempts to place the reports in relevant context or to lead experimental or research efforts for a specific readership. In the light of this discussion there is a strong case for considering these two text-types as sub-genres of the genre which may be called **academic introductions**.

4.4.2 *Student dissertation introductions*

In the earlier part of the chapter we briefly mentioned a case of slight variation in academic introductions discussed by Dudley-Evans (1989) who looked at move-structure in introductions to M.Sc. dissertations. He discovered a six-move structure in his corpus, which I reproduce here:

Move 1: Introducing the field
Move 2: Introducing the general topic (within the field)
Move 3: Introducing the particular topic (within the general topic)
Move 4: Defining the scope of the particular topic by
    (i) introducing research parameters
    (ii) summarizing previous research
Move 5: Preparing for present research by
    (i) indicating a gap in previous research
    (ii) indicating a possible extension of previous research
Move 6: Introducing present research by
    (i) stating the aim of the research
    or
    (ii) describing briefly the work carried out
    (iii) justifying the research

The most significant difference between the above six-move structure and the four-move structure in Swales (1981b, 1985) is the more elaborate attempt in dissertations to establish field. The authors generally move rather slowly from field to general topic and then to particular or specific topic, which Dudley-Evans (1989) regards as three separate moves. The example he uses to illustrate this is on the opposite page.

One of the major differences between the move-structure presented by Dudley-Evans and the one presented by Swales may appear to be a proliferation of the introductory move, **establishing field**. In Swales (1981b) it is a single move whereas in Dudley-Evans (1989) it seems to be a much more elaborate one which is realized in terms of three separate moves. One of the simple reasons is that, in student dissertations and theses generally, the introduction is fairly elaborate, and long compared with introductions to research articles, because of a fairly well-established tradition to include literature review. Sometimes research article introductions are also fairly long, but fortunately such cases are not very common. Many such cases have elaborate descriptions of previous research. However, in the case of example [13], Dudley-Evans points out that dissertation writers need to go through three separate moves before they start handling previous research related to the topic. Although one may find objections, theoretical as well as practical, to the way Dudley-Evans identifies the first three moves, there is no doubt that there are three rather distinct stages indicated there. Whether these three stages should be regarded as sub-moves of the same move or as separate moves, is a difficult question to resolve. But it is clear that there is no attempt to **establish field** here; it is simply a matter of **introducing field**. In research articles, it is important to establish field because the authors invariably look for a larger readership than do students, and therefore have to 'sell' their research reports. Dissertations and theses, are mainly of an academic interest; there is very little professional competition from colleagues and other members of the academic community, and it is generally considered more appropriate to define the scope, or make claims for the research, which Dudley-Evans indicates in his move 4.

The main thrust of the argument that Dudley-Evans (1989) offers is that dissertation introductions are not very different in character but show some differences in their move-structure. In fact, these differences, as seen above, are accountable in terms of differences in the communicative contexts with which they are associated. Once again, there seems to be an excellent case for a sub-genre of the academic introduction.

[13]

Up to the middle of the nineteenth century, variability was a feature of every sexually reproducing crop. This variability, produced by mutation and natural hybridization, was maintained by natural selection – i.e., selection imposed by man (Frankel and Bennet 1970). The land races present had much potential for adaptive change, and the processes of gene exchange and introgression were allowed to occur freely. However, this situation changed with the introduction of individual selection during the nineteenth century, and since that time many biological, physical, cultural, economic and political factors have led to the evolution of the specialized crop forms found today. During this time, there has been much narrowing of the genetic base, by selection for both relative uniformity in the crops (for ease of harvesting, especially since the development of very intensive, mechanized agriculture) and for narrowly defined objectives, such as resistance to a particular disease.   **Situation**

The process of plant breeding, to produce new, improved crop varieties, is dependent on the variation in the existing crop races and their relatives. However, the amount of variation on which plant breeders can act is becoming very much reduced with the narrowing of the genetic base, and therefore, the need for the conservation of genetic resources – of related wild and weedy species, crop land races and primitive cultivars, as well as the more advanced cultivars, is becoming a widely recognized necessity.   **Problem**

Seed storage is probably the easiest and least expensive way of preserving plant genetic resources (Harrington, 1970). Under suitable conditions, the seed of many species is predicted to remain viable for up to hundreds of years. These conditions involve both the techniques used for seed preparation before storage, and the actual storage environment. The optimal storage environment differs for different species, but the two most important factors that require consideration are thought to be moisture content of the seeds, and storage temperature (Harrington, 1973; Roberts, 1975).   **Response evaluation**

The vast majority of species have seeds whose period of viability may be extended during storage by lowering the moisture content and temperature. Roberts (1973) used the term 'orthodox' for seeds with such viability behaviour. However, a second group of seeds cannot be reduced below a relatively high moisture content and temperature without decreasing the viability period. Roberts (1973) termed such seeds 'recalcitrant'. Included in this group are many large-seeded hardwoods, and many tropical tree crops – for example Citrus species (Barton, 1943), coffee (Huxley, 1964) and cocoa (Barton, 1965). This thesis examines the viability behaviour of the seeds of the latter of these crops.   **Negative evaluation**

4.5 Concluding remarks

In this chapter, we looked at two kinds of academic writings – professional research writing and student academic writing. We identified two professional research genres which are conventionally associated with the same communicative context but have different communicative purposes, and we established that they are, in fact, two different genres. This was the case of research abstracts v. research article introductions. Our analysis of the two genres indicated that they have practically nothing in common, except that the two occur one after the other in the same academic context. We then identified two more seemingly overlapping cases of academic genres, namely student laboratory report introductions and academic dissertation introductions. The analysis indicated that the two seemed to have quite different move-structures. However, on the analysis of the communicative contexts in which they are conventionally used we discovered that in spite of some differences in their cognitive structuring, they showed a great deal of overlap. The differences were accountable in terms of differences in their communicative contexts. Their communicative purposes did not show enough variation to regard them as two different genres, so they were considered sub-genres of the genre called **academic introductions**. The chapter, thus, makes a case for considering suitable criteria for sub-genres within the same genre.

5 Legal discourse in professional settings

In the last two chapters, we analysed examples of professional and academic genres; in this chapter, we look at one more area of professional writing, conventionally known as legal language.

5.1 Legal language

The term *legal language*, as Bhatia (1987b:227) indicates, *encompasses several usefully distinguishable genres depending upon the communicative purposes they tend to fulfil, the settings or contexts in which they are used, the communicative events or activities they are associated with, the social or professional relationship between the participants taking part in such activities or events, the background knowledge that such participants bring to the situation in which that particular event is embedded and a number of other factors.* He identifies several genres used in a variety of legal settings. Some of these are *cases* and *judgements* in written form used in *juridical settings*; *lawyer-client consultation, counsel-witness examination* in spoken form and *legislation, contracts, agreements* etc. in written form used in various *professional settings*. In this chapter, we shall take up two genres from the written medium, namely *legislation* and *cases* for an in-depth genre analysis.

5.2 Legislative provisions

Legislative writing has acquired a certain degree of notoriety rarely equalled by any other variety of English. It has long been criticized for its obscure expressions and circumlocutions, long-winded involved constructions and tortuous syntax, apparently meaningless repetitions and archaisms. To the specialist community these are indispensable linguistic devices which bring in precision, clarity and unambiguity and all-inclusiveness; however, to the non-specialist this is a mere ploy to promote solidarity between members of the specialist community, and to keep non-specialists at a respectable distance. It is, therefore, regarded by them as linguistic nonsense that is pompous, verbose, flabby, and circumlocutory. The truth, however, lies somewhere in between. In this chapter we shall examine a few instances of legislative provisions in an attempt to unravel the mysteries underlying this complex discourse form, and to answer the question *Why are legislative provisions written the way they are?* In order to appreciate the complexity of legislative statements, we need to have a better idea of the communicative purpose(s) these statements are meant to serve and the constraints that are imposed on the drafting of these provisions.

5.2.1 *Communicative purpose*

Legislative writing is highly impersonal and decontextualized, in the sense that its illocutionary force holds independently of whoever is the 'speaker' (originator) or the 'hearer' (reader) of the document. The general function of this writing is directive, to impose obligations and to confer rights. As legal draftsmen are well aware of the age-old human capacity to wriggle out of obligations and to stretch rights to unexpected limits, they attempt to guard against such eventualities, by defining their model world of obligations and rights, permissions and prohibitions as precisely, clearly and unambiguously as linguistic resources permit. A further complication is the fact that they deal with a universe of human behaviour which is unrestricted, in the sense that it is impossible to predict exactly what may happen within it. Nevertheless, they attempt to refer to every conceivable contingency within their model world and this gives their writing its second key characteristic of being all-inclusive.

Legislative writing differs significantly from most other varieties of English, not only in terms of the communicative purpose it is designed to fulfil, but also in the way it is created. In most other written varieties, the author is both the originator and the writer of what he creates, whereas in legislative provisions, the parliamentary draftsman is only the writer of the legislative act, which originates from the deliberations of a parliament in which he is never present. Similarly, in most varieties, the reader and the recipient for whom the document is meant are the same person, whereas in the case of legislative provisions, the document is meant for ordinary citizens but the real readers are lawyers and judges, who are responsible for interpreting these provisions for ordinary citizens. The result of this unique contextual factor is that the parliamentary draftsman finds his loyalties divided. On the one hand, he has to acknowledge his loyalty to the will of parliament and on the other hand he must use linguistic and discoursal strategies to help the intended readership towards what Candlin (1978) refers to as 'the equalising of interpretative opportunity'. In other words, he is required to use linguistic resources and discoursal strategies to do justice to the intent of Parliament and, at the same time, to facilitate comprehension of the unfolding text for ordinary readership. Reconciling the two is not always an easy task. His predicament is well summed up in the words of Caldwell, an experienced practitioner in the field.

> . . . there's always the problem that at the end of the day there's a system of courts and judges who interpret what the draftsman has done. It is very difficult to box the judge firmly into a corner from which he cannot escape . . . given enough time and given enough length and complexity you can end up with precision but in practice there comes a point when you can't go on cramming detail after detail into a bin . . . you've got to rely on the courts getting the message and deducing from what you have said or it may be often from what you haven't said, what implications they are to draw in such and such a case.
>
> (Reported in Bhatia 1982:25)

So, in spite of the seeming impossibility of the task, no effort is spared in legislative provisions to 'box' *the reader* 'firmly into a corner'. This is generally achieved by making the provision clear, precise and unambiguous. However, that does not seem to be the end of the story, because these provisions are meant to apply to real life situations and are invariably interpreted in the context of a particular dispute. Any specific interpretation will be dependent on and constrained by the facts of the case, which provide the context for its interpretation and it is possible that such an interpretation may not necessarily be the same as the one intended by parliament. In order to guard against such eventualities, the draftsman tries to make his provision not only clear, precise and unambiguous, but all-inclusive too. And it is this seemingly impossible task of achieving the dual characteristic of clarity, precision and unambiguity on the one hand, and all-inclusiveness on the other hand, that makes legislative provisions what they are.

5.2.2 *Types of legislative provisions*

Gunnarsson (1984:84) distinguishes three types of legislative rules:

Action rules

Action rules are applicable to only a set of specified descriptions of cases and are mainly meant to impose duties and obligations, to give rights, to prohibit actions, to assign power to certain members or bodies of the executive or other parties, or to state the law or just the penalties imposed on specific actions. A typical example will be the following:

> [1] When any person in the presence of a police officer commits or is accused of committing a non-seizable offence and refuses on the demand of a police officer to give his name or residence or gives a name or residence which the officer has reason to believe to be false, he may be arrested by that police officer in order that his name or residence may be ascertained.
> (Section 32(1) of Criminal Procedure Code, Republic of Singapore, 1980)

Stipulation rules

Stipulation rules define the domain of application of a particular act or any section of it, as in the following example:

> [2] Sections 35 to 46 of this Act do not apply to a tenancy at any time when the interest of the landlord belongs to a housing association which is a registered society.
> (Section 49(3) of the Housing Act 1980, UK)

Definition rules

Definition rules are applicable to the entire Act and are primarily meant to provide terminological explanation, as in [3] below.

[3] In this Chapter "landlord authority" means –
  (a) a local authority;
  (b)... a housing association which falls within section 15(3) of the 1977 Act;
  (c) a housing trust which is a charity within the meaning of the Charities Act 1960;
  (d) a development corporation...

(Section 42 (1) of the Housing Act 1980, UK)

However, a number of such definition rules, as Swales (1981a:109) points out, go well beyond such an objective and are treated as 'the Law itself *tout court*' and he cites the following example from the law of the Sudan (1955) defining 'kidnapping'.

[4] Whoever takes or entices any minor, under fourteen years of age if a male or under sixteen years of age if a female, or any person of unsound mind out of the keeping of the legal guardian of such minor or person of unsound mind without the consent of such guardian or conveys any such minor or person of unsound mind beyond the borders of the Sudan without the consent of some person legally authorized to consent to such removal, is said to kidnap such a minor or person of unsound mind.

He points out that the above definition is the law and provides eight different routes to kidnapping. Gunnarsson (1984:84) also claims a somewhat similar position when she says that definition rules have implications for action. Whatever the relative merits of the claims, both of them agree that the bulk of legislation consists of action rules rather than the other two types. So our discussion will primarily focus on these, which I have elsewhere (Bhatia, 1982, 1983b) called 'legislative provisions'.

5.2.3 *Syntactic properties of legislative provisions*

It has been claimed (Swales and Bhatia, 1983) that syntactic and discoursal features of legislative writing are, in various ways, interconnected, in the sense that the apparent legal requirement of expressing something by means of nominal expressions with a variety of qualifications would bring in syntactic discontinuities, thus making the discoursal structure of the sentence not only complex but compound as well. Therefore, it is necessary to look at some of the predominant syntactic features of the legislative provisions before we go to the discoursal features of this genre. Let us begin with a typical instance of this genre.

[5] For the purpose of ascertaining the income for any period of any person who has incurred expenditure on lawfully searching for, or for discovering and testing, or winning access to any mineral deposits in Singapore, there shall, if the person has within that period permanently abandoned such activities without having carried on any trade which consists of or includes the working of deposits in respect of which the expenditure was incurred, be deducted the amount of the expenditure wholly or exclusively incurred by that person in connection with such activities as if the expenditure were incurred at the time when such activities were so abandoned:
    Provided that no deduction shall be made –
(a) in respect of the value at the date of the permanent abandonment of such activities of any machinery or plant used in such activities or, if the machinery or plant is subsequently sold or transferred, any sum of money or other consideration received by that person in respect of it;
(b) to the extent that any sum of money or other consideration is received by such person from the sale of any rights or other benefits derived from such activities, or from the use of any such machinery or plant by any other person;
(c) in respect of any sum which is, apart from this section, allowed to be deducted in computing for the purposes of income tax, the gains or profits of any such person;
(d) in respect of any expenditure met directly or indirectly by the Government or by any government, public or local authority, whether within Singapore or elsewhere, or by any person other than the person claiming relief.
(Section 14A (1) of The Income Tax Act, 1984, The Republic of Singapore)

This legislative provision from the Singapore Income Tax Act is about the deductions allowed in relation to certain expenditure on abortive mining operations. Like any other instance of legislation, this also displays a number of syntactic and discoursal characteristics typical of the genre. Let us consider some of the most important syntactic properties, particularly those which will help us understand regularities of organization in this genre.

Sentence length

To begin with, the whole section consists of a single sentence of an above-average length – 271 words compared with 27.6 words in a typical sentence in written scientific English (Barber, 1962).

Nominal character

Legislative sentences are more nominal in character than the ones generally encountered in ordinary everyday usage. Swales and Bhatia (1983) claim that example [6] is likely to be preferred in this writing to its more typically verbal version [7].

[6] The power to make regulations under this section shall be exercisable by statutory instrument which shall be subject to annulment in pursuance of a resolution of either House of Parliament.
     (Ch.25/78: Nuclear Safeguards and Electricity (Finance Act) 1978)

[7] A statutory instrument can be used to make regulations under this section and such a statutory instrument can be annulled if either House of Parliament passes a resolution to that effect.

Although [5] gives some indication of nominalization, as in the use of 'permanent abandonment of such activities', it is not highly nominal in character. A more typical example of the nominal character of this genre will be the following section from The Wills Act, 1970 of the Republic of Singapore.

[8] No will shall be revoked by any presumption of an intention on the ground of an alteration in circumstances.
     (Section 14 of the Wills Act, Republic of Singapore)

Complex prepositional phrases

The next striking syntactic feature of the legislative genre is the use of what Quirk et al. (1982:302) refer to as complex-prepositional phrases. They give its structure as P-N-P (Preposition + Noun + Preposition). Some of the typical examples from legislative writing include *for the purpose of, in respect of, in accordance with, in pursuance of, by virtue of*, etc. The first two have been used a few times in [5]. The use of complex prepositions rather than the simple ones, for example, 'by virtue of' instead of 'by', 'for the purpose of' in place of 'for', and 'in accordance with' or 'in pursuance of' instead of a simple preposition 'under' is rather preferred in legislative writing simply because the specialist community claims, with some justification, of course (see Swales and Bhatia, 1983), that the simple ones tend to promote ambiguity and lack of clarity.

Binominal and multinomial expressions

Binomial and multinomial expressions have also been typically associated with legislative texts (see Gustafsson, 1975, 1984). What I mean by binomial or multinomial expression is a sequence of two or more words or phrases belonging to the same grammatical category having some semantic relationship and joined by some syntactic device such as 'and' or 'or' (see Bhatia, 1984:90). Typical examples include 'signed and delivered', 'in whole or in part', 'to affirm or set aside', 'act or omission', 'advice and consent', 'by or on behalf of', 'under or in accordance with', 'unless and until', and 'consists of or includes', 'wholly and exclusively', 'the freehold conveyed or long lease granted' and many many others. The provision in [5] offers a few more, some very much more complex and interesting ones, including 'machinery or plant', 'sold or transferred', 'any sum of money or other consideration', 'from such activities or from the use of any such machinery or plant', 'directly or indirectly', 'by the Government or by any government, public or local authority . . . or by any person other than the person claiming relief', 'within Singapore or elsewhere' and many more. It is not very difficult to see why legal draftsmen have a special fascination for expressions like these. This is an extremely effective linguistic device to make the legal document precise as well as all-inclusive. Here is an excellent example from the Prevention of Corruption Act 1947 from India.

[9] Where in any trial of offence punishable under section 161 or section 165 of the Indian Penal Code or of an offence referred to in clause (b) of subsection (1) of section 5 of this Act punishable under subsection (2) thereof it is proved that an accused person has accepted or obtained, or has agreed to accept or attempted to obtain, for himself or for any other person, any gratification (other than legal remuneration) or any valuable thing for any person, it shall be presumed unless the contrary is proved that he accepted or obtained, or agreed to accept or attempted to obtain that gratification or that valuable thing, as the case may be, as a motive or reward such as is mentioned in the said section 161, or, as the case may be, without consideration or for a consideration which he knows to be inadequate.

(Section 4(1) of the Prevention of Corruption Act 1947)

In order to appreciate better the use of binomials and multinomials to achieve all-inclusiveness in legislative provisions, let us take a look at example [10] broken down in the following way:

Where in any trial of offence
punishable under section 161

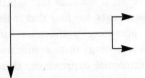

[or section 165 of the Indian Penal Code

[or of an offence referred to in clause (b)
of subsection (1) of section 5 of this Act
punishable under subsection (2) thereof

it is proved that an accused
person has accepted

[or obtained,

[or has agreed to accept

[or attempted to obtain,

for himself

[or for any other person,

any gratification (other
than legal remuneration

[or any valuable thing for any person,

it shall be presumed
unless the contrary is
proved that he accepted

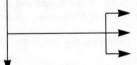

[or obtained

[or agreed to accept

[or attempted to obtain

that gratification

[or that valuable thing, as the case may be,

as a motive

[or reward such as is mentioned in the said
section 161, as the case may be,

without consideration

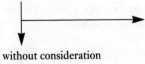

[or for a consideration which he knows
to be inadequate

The left-hand column of the provision gives one way each of accepting any gratification and of determining whether such a gratification has been accepted without consideration. However, if we read through the entire provision from left to right and downwards, we find that it lists at least forty-eight different ways of accepting gratification and nothing less than thirty-two ways of accepting that gratification without consideration. Binomial and multinomial expressions, therefore, serve as a useful tool for making legislative statements all-inclusive.

Initial case descriptions

Legislative statements typically begin with fairly long initial case descriptions. The legal subject is conventionally delayed by the introduction of a long case description in the form of an adverbial clause beginning with 'where', 'if' or sometimes 'when'. Here is a rather extreme example from the Housing Act 1980, UK.

> [10] Where a conveyance or grant executed in pursuance of this chapter is of a dwelling-house situated in a National park, or an area designated under section 87 of the National Parks and Access to the Countryside Act 1949 as an area of outstanding natural beauty, or an area designated by order of the Secretary of State as a rural area, and it is executed by a local authority (as defined in section 50 of this Act), a county council, the Development Board for Rural Wales or a housing association ("the landlord") the conveyance or grant may contain a covenant limiting the freedom of the tenant and his successors in title to dispose of the dwelling-house in the manner specified below.
>
> (Section 19 (1) of the Housing Act 1980, UK)

The main motivation for the pre-positioning of the case description comes from the requirement that very few legislative statements are of universal application and it is absolutely crucial for the writer to specify the kind of case description(s) to which the rule applies. In [5], there is no initial case description of the kind exemplified in [10], however we do find a fairly long qualification beginning with *For the purpose of. . .* delaying the introduction of the legal subject.

Qualifications in legislative provisions

The most important characteristic of the legislative statement is the use of qualifications without which the provision will lose its essential nature. Most legislative provisions are extremely rich in qualificational insertions within their syntactic boundaries. Let us see how this is done by taking this time a made-up provision based on a section from the Housing Act 1980 for illustrative purposes.

[11] Where a secure tenant serves on the landlord a notice in writing claiming to exercise his right to buy the dwelling-house, and if the landlord refuses to admit the tenant's right to buy the dwelling-house, then, subject to the following provisions of this Section, the Secretary of State, if he thinks proper, may by means of a written notification make special regulations in pursuance of his powers under Section 15 of this Act for the purpose of enabling the tenant to exercise his right to buy the dwelling-house (notwithstanding anything contained in Section 51 of the land Registration Act 1925) within a period of six months from the date of such a refusal, provided that the dwelling-house, or any part of it, is not being used for charitable purposes within the meaning of the 'Charitable Purposes Act 1954'.

In very simple words, this provision is meant to give powers to the legal subject, in this case, the Secretary of State, to make special regulations. But he is not given the authority to make special regulations as and when he likes. The attached qualifications make the provision extremely restricted. In fact, without these qualifications the legislative provision will be taken to be of universal application and it is very very rare that a rule of law is of universal application. The qualifications seem to provide the essential flesh to the main proposition without which the provision will be nothing more than a mere skeleton, of very little legal significance. In the words of Caldwell, a very senior practising parliamentary counsel:

. . . if you extract the bare bones . . . what you end up with is a proposition which is so untrue because the qualifications actually negative it all . . . it's so far from the truth . . . it's like saying that all red-headed people are to be executed on Monday, but when you actually read all the qualifications, you find that only one per cent of them are.

(Reported in Bhatia, 1982:51)

Syntactic discontinuities

It is not simply the presence of qualifications that makes legislative provisions an interesting genre but more interestingly the way these qualifications are inserted within the syntax of the legislative sentence. It is understandable that, if one needs to incorporate a variety of qualifications within a single sentence, one would like to have as many syntactic points at which to insert them as are possible. But one consideration that makes this task even more difficult is the fact that if qualifications on the one hand make the main provisional clause more precise and clear, they can also promote ambiguity if they are not placed judiciously. That is the main reason why legal draftsmen try to insert qualifications right next to the word they are meant to qualify, even at the cost of making their legislative sentence inelegant, awkward or tortuous but never ambiguous, if they can help it. The result of all this effort is that these qualifications are inserted at various points where they create syntactic discontinuities rarely encountered in any other genre. In example [5] we have a rather longish qualification,

> if the person has within that period permanently abandoned such activities without having carried on any trade which consists of or includes the working of deposits in respect of which the expenditure was incurred

inserted immediately after the modal *shall*, thus creating discontinuity within the main verb phrase *shall be deducted*. So far as qualificational insertions are concerned, legal draftsmen do not consider any phrase boundaries sacrosanct, be it a verb phrase (as in [5]), a noun phrase, binomial phrase or even a complex prepositional phrase. Let us look at some of the examples from the British Housing Act, 1980.

Discontinuous noun phrase

[12] A secure tenant has *the right* –
    (a) if the dwelling-house is a house, *to acquire the freehold of the dwelling-house*;
    (b) if the dwelling-house is a flat, *to be granted a long lease of the dwelling-house*
                                    (Section 1 (1) of the Housing Act, 1980, UK)

Discontinuous binomial phrase

[13] Where a secure tenant serves on the landlord a written notice claiming to exercise the right to buy, the landlord shall (unless the notice is

withdrawn) serve on the tenant, *within four weeks, or,* in a case falling within subsection (2) below, *eight weeks,* either

    (a) a written notice admitting the tenant's right; or

    (b) a written notice denying the tenant's right and stating the reasons why, in the opinion of the landlord, the tenant does not have the right to buy.

                       (Section 1 (5) of the Housing Act, 1980, UK)

Discontinuous complex prepositional phrase

[14] Any power of the Secretary of State to make an order or regulation under this Act shall be exercisable by statutory instrument *subject*, except in the case of regulations under section 22(1), 33(2), 52(3), 56(7) or paragraph 11 of Schedule 3 or an order under section 52(4), 60 or 153, *to annulment* in pursuance of a resolution of either House of Parliament.

                       (Section 151(1) of the Housing Act, 1980, UK)

Discontinuous constituents with fairly long qualificational insertions like these, and many others embedded within them, add considerably to an already complex syntactic character of the legislative sentence and cause serious psycholinguistic problems in the processing of such provisions, especially in the case of non-specialist readership (see Bhatia, 1984, for a detailed discussion of this aspect of legal writing).

5.2.4 *Cognitive structuring in legislative provisions*

Having discussed some of the important lexico-grammatical features of this genre, let me now consider how these features, particularly the complexity of intervening qualifications, are reflected in the cognitive structuring that is typically associated with the legislative provision. Looking more closely at the law-making process, one may find two important aspects. The first, of course, is the main provisionary clause, by which we mean essentially two things. One, the legal subject, i.e., the person or the party which is the subject of the provision. In other words, the person who is either given a right or some power to do something or is being prohibited from doing something. And, the second is the legal action, i.e., the nature of power or right he is given to do or prohibited from doing, that flows from the provision. But, the main provisionary clause, by itself, can only provide the bare bones. The essential flesh is provided by what we earlier referred to as *case description*, by which we mean the nature and specification of circumstances to which the main provisionary clause applies. Crystal and Davy (1969) give a good indication of this when they claim that most legal sentences have one of the following forms.

If X, then Y shall do Z,

or

If X, then Y shall be Z,

where 'If X' stands for the description of case(s) to which the rule of law applies, although they do not say so explicitly, 'Y' is meant to be the legal subject and 'Z' indicates the legal action.

George Coode, as early as in 1848, made a significant contribution to this aspect of law-making when he identified four essential elements in legal statements and placed them in the following order.

Where any Quaker refuses to pay any church rates, (CASE)

if any church warden complains thereof, (CONDITION)

one of the next Justices of the Peace (SUBJECT)

may summon such Quaker. (ACTION)

Although Coode's analysis of the legislative sentence is insufficiently developed for application to all legislative sentences, particularly those with multiple and complex modifications, it certainly is of considerable value, because of the attention it pays to the sentence structure and the arrangement of qualifying clauses in the 'best' position.

Both Coode (1848) and Crystal and Davy (1969) point out the essential nature of the legislative sentence however, they oversimplify the picture. Although it is true that the four essential elements in the syntax of the legislative provision are: *the case description*, *the legal subject* and *the legal action*, *condition*, as pointed out by Coode, is also very important, if not obligatory. However, as Bhatia (1982, 1983) points out, legislative statements can, and most of them do, have a number of qualifications other than the case description, without which they will become universally applicable. Basically, there are three types of qualifications and they tend to provide three different types of information about the rule of law. The first type are

preparatory qualifications, which outline the description of case(s) to which the rule of law applies. The second type are **operational** qualifications, which give additional information about the execution or operation of the rule of law. And finally there are **referential** qualifications, which specify the essential inter-textual nature of the legislative provision. In the words of Caldwell, a practising parliamentary counsel:

> ... very rarely is a new legislative provision entirely freestanding ... it is part of a jigsaw puzzle ... in passing a new provision you are merely bringing one more piece and so you have to acknowledge that what you are about to do may affect some other bit of the massive statute book.
>
> (Reported in Bhatia, 1982:172)

Qualifications, therefore, form an important part of the structuring of the legislative statements. In fact, most legislative provisions can be written and understood in terms of a two-part interactive move-structure consisting of the main **provisionary clause** and the attendant **qualifications** of various kinds, which are inserted at available syntactic positions within the structure of the main clause. To illustrate the two-part move structure, let us take a very simple example from the British Housing Act 1980.

> [15] Where the dwelling-house with respect to which the right to buy is exercised is a registered land, the Chief Land Registrar shall, if so requested by the Secretary of State, supply him (on payment of the appropriate fee) with an office copy of any document required by the Secretary of State for the purpose of executing a vesting order with respect to the dwelling-house and shall (notwithstanding section 112 of the Land Registration Act 1925) allow any person authorised by the Secretary of State to inspect and make copies of and extracts from any register or document which is in the custody of the Chief Land Registrar and relates to the dwelling-house.
>
> (Section 24(5) of the Housing Act, 1980, UK)

Cognitive structuring as used here is an excellent tool to interpret the regularities of organization in order to understand the rationale for the genre. In legislative provisions cognitive structuring displays a characteristic interplay of the main provisionary clause and the qualifications inserted at various syntactic openings within the structure of a sentence (Bhatia, 1982). The example above gives not only a clear indication of the complexity of individual qualificational insertions in the legislative genre but also some indication of the variety of such qualifications. In order to have a more explicit display of the structural organization of the genre and to understand the rationale for such an organization, let us look at the text broken down:

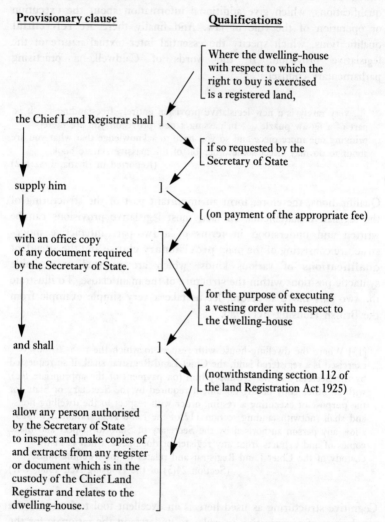

Provisionary clause

Qualifications

Where the dwelling-house with respect to which the right to buy is exercised is a registered land,

the Chief Land Registrar shall]

if so requested by the Secretary of State

supply him   ]

[(on payment of the appropriate fee)

with an office copy of any document required by the Secretary of State.

for the purpose of executing a vesting order with respect to the dwelling-house

and shall   ]

(notwithstanding section 112 of the land Registration Act 1925)

allow any person authorised by the Secretary of State to inspect and make copies of and extracts from any register or document which is in the custody of the Chief Land Registrar and relates to the dwelling-house.

Both the density and the complexity of qualificational insertions serve a typically legal function in this genre in that each one of them is meant to answer legal questions and doubts, and offer clarifications about various aspects of the main provision. Any adequate structural description of the genre should explain this phenomenon. Therefore, it is more appropriate to think in terms of a two-part **interactive** cognitive structure consisting of the main provisionary clause and the qualifications rather than the linear organization of the moves as found in the case of a number of other genres (see Swales, 1981a; Bhatia, 1982, 1991). The analysis of cognitive structuring is interactive here in the sense that the move **qualifications** typically interacts with several aspects of the move **provisionary clause** at various positions, answering a number of questions that can be legitimately asked in the context. The main function of these inserted qualifications or conditions is to make the legislative provision precise, clear, unambiguous and all-inclusive (see Bhatia 1982, 1987a).

Legislative statements, thus, have a conventionalized communicative purpose which is shared by the practising members of the specialist community. This shared communicative purpose is largely reflected in the way legislative statements are conventionally written and read by members of the community, particularly in the way some of the syntactic and discoursal resources are used in this genre. The typical use of complex-prepositions, binomial and multinomial expressions, nominalizations, the initial case descriptions, and a large number and variety of qualificational insertions make syntactic discontinuities somewhat unavoidable in the legislative statements and, to a large extent, account for the discourse patterning that is typically displayed in such provisions.

It has also been suggested that legislative statements have good reasons to be what they are, and one should try to understand this genre in its own terms rather than by imposing standards of ordinary expression from the outside, as it were, on a genre which has its own specialized concerns and specific constraints under which they are written and read. Many of the attempts to reform legislative writing in the western world have largely been ineffective because of their failure to recognize the value of an ethnomethodological position that the legislative provision reflects a sphere of practical reasoning which needs to be understood in its own terms. However, one often gets a feeling, quite justifiably in many cases, that this concern on the part of the specialist community for clarity, precision, and unambiguity on the one hand, and all-inclusiveness on the other, has been taken rather too seriously and, perhaps, too far. It is true that legislative writing has a long and well-established tradition and the style of legal documents has become firmly standardized, with the inevitable result that legal draftsmen tend to become comfortable with tried, tested and time-honoured linguistic expressions and style of writing over a period of time. This becomes particularly significant where each subsequent generation of parliamentary draftsmen is trained by the preceding one while on the job.

It is true that there have been some improvements in style that have taken place in the past few decades, especially in the way textual-mapping devices are used to reduce information load at a particular point in the provision (see Bhatia, 1987a) but such reforms have been few and far between and as a consequence have gone unnoticed by ordinary readers. On the part of the specialist community, therefore, there is a need to show two kinds of concern: firstly, a need to show greater awareness of their loyalty to the real readers of legislative documents; secondly, a need to use linguistic resources more consistently, particularly in the cases where certain linguistic forms are traditionally associated with some very specific meanings (see Swales and Bhatia, 1983). This is especially desirable in the use of what specialists call *proviso-clauses*; it would create fewer problems of interpretation for both specialist and non-specialist readers. Syntactic discontinuities should be used more sparingly – ideally as the exception rather than the rule.

5.3 Legal cases

Legal cases form the most significant part of a law specialist's reading list whether he is a law student or a practising lawyer. Cases assume importance because law courts follow their previous judgments within more or less well-defined limits. This means that cases are generally decided the same way if the material facts are the same. But this does not mean that all the facts of the case must recur in order for an earlier judgment to become relevant to the subsequent ones. In fact, legally material facts might recur, and it is these facts that legal specialists are generally concerned with. Legal cases are abridged versions of court judgments, which are very elaborate and detailed. These cases are summarized by various case writers for the benefit of specialists. There may be a large variety of versions written by various authors for different purposes; some can be very detailed and others very brief, but most are written to serve a definite purpose.

5.3.1 *Communicative purpose*

Legal cases are used in the law classroom, the lawyer's office and in the courtroom as well. They are essential tools used in the law classroom to train students in the skills of legal reasoning, argumentation and decision-making. Cases represent the complexity of relationship between the facts of the world outside, on the one hand, and the model world of rights and obligations, permissions and prohibitions, on the other. The process of legal argumentation in cases is, as Wisdom (1964:157) puts it,

> ... not a 'chain' of demonstrative reasoning. It is a presenting and representing of those features of the case which 'severally co-operate' in favour of the conclusion, in favour of saying what the reasoner wishes said, in favour of calling the situation by the name by which he wishes to call it. The reasons are like the legs of a chair, not the links of a chain.

The cases, therefore, represent the most potent instrument to train the learner of law in legal reasoning, argumentation and decision-making. In the lawyer's study, these cases act as guides as to what line of reasoning a lawyer should take and also as appropriate authorities either in favour of or against that line of reasoning. In the courtroom, cases function as legal authorities along with legislative provisions. They can be used both ways, to argue for a particular conclusion or against it. However, one thing that is common to all the three situations is the important role of cases in the negotiation of justice as well as in legal education. Cases in legal contexts serve four major **communicative purposes**:

1. In their full form (also referred to as legal judgments), as in Law Reports, cases serve as authentic records of past judgments. In this form they are taken as faithful records of all the facts of the case, the arguments of the judge, his reasoning, the judgment he arrives at and the way he does it, the kind of authority and evidence he uses and the way he distinguishes the present case from others cited as evidence either by him or by the opposing lawyers.

2. Legal judgments (including legal cases) also serve another important function. The judgments and the rule of law (*ratio decidendi*, in legal terminology) derived are meant to serve as precedents for subsequent cases, and are generally used as evidence in favour of or against a particular line of argument or decision.

3. Cases, as reported in some casebooks are meant to serve as reminders to legal experts, who use them in their arguments in the classroom or in the court of law. These versions are

generally very brief and contain nothing more than the essential material facts and the decision of the judge.

4.   Cases also serve as illustrations of certain points of law. Such cases are carefully selected and appropriately abridged. They form an important part of a law student's bibliography. They are generally abridged in casebooks and are also used prominently in law textbooks in support of or against a particular point of view. Law students learn the law from such cases.

The first of these purposes is difficult to illustrate within the scope of this book. The original judgments, as reported in the Law Reports, are very detailed and run to several pages. On most occasions they consist of several judgments delivered by the several judges constituting the bench. The other two purposes are realized in terms of cases reported in various casebooks. To illustrate these last two purposes, we shall take up three different versions of the case of Roles v. Nathan. First, we shall take up an example of type three.

[16]

Roles v. *Nathan*
[1963] 1 W.L.R. 1117

Two chimney-sweeps were killed by carbon monoxide emitting from the ventilation system of the boiler on which they were working. They had chosen to ignore a prior warning of this danger. The Court of Appeal held that the defendants were not liable, for, in the words of Lord Denning M.R., "When a householder calls in a specialist to deal with a defective installation on his premises, he can reasonably expect the specialist to appreciate and guard against the dangers arising from the defect."

(*Cases and Statutes On Tort*, Bradbury, 1984:107)

As we can see, this version of the case is very brief, highlighting the main points of the individual case. The purpose of the casebook is made clear by the author in the preface to the book:

> The purpose of this latest addition remains that of being a useful case source . . . it is hoped that the materials collected will serve as a straightforward revision aid for all law students. . .

The selection of the most important aspects of law cases seems to serve a good starting point for the analysis of legal cases. Most cases in this volume cover three important aspects of legal judgments, as illustrated in example [16]. The first two sentences,

> Two chimney-sweeps were killed by carbon monoxide emitting from the ventilation system of the boiler on which they were working. They had chosen to ignore a prior warning of this danger.

inform the reader about the description of the case by mentioning the most important, or what in legal terminology is known as the *material*, facts of the case. The second aspect of this case is the verdict given by the court.

> The Court of Appeal held that the defendants were not liable. . .

And, finally the case mentions the principle of law, or what specialists call *ratio decidendi*, which is derived by the judge, Lord Denning in this case, and is likely to be used as precedent in all subsequent cases of similar description.

> When a householder calls in a specialist to deal with a defective installation on his premises, he can reasonably expect the specialist to appreciate and guard against the dangers arising from the defect.

Let us now look at another version of the same case, from another casebook, which serves the third communicative purpose, outlined above.

> [17] An occupier may be regarded as having complied with his duty under the Act in respect of a visitor who comes to exercise his calling, either (i) if he gives an adequate warning of danger (s.2(4)(a)); or (ii) by relying on s.2(3)(b), which entitles him to expect that the visitor will guard against special risks.

Roles v. Nathan
Court of Appeal. [1963] 2 ALL E.R. 908

A building was centrally heated by a boiler in which coke was used as fuel, there being an old system to carry away the smoke and fumes, which included a horizontal flue running from the boiler under the floor to a

---

Continued overleaf

Roles v. *Nathan continued*

vertical flue which went up a chimney. In the vertical flue there was a sweep-hole, about twelve inches in diameter and nine feet above the ground. It was sometimes difficult to get the boiler lighted up, the difficulty being to get a draught going along the flues. In December, 1958, the fire was lit and there was a lot of smoke. A boiler engineer was consulted; he said that the flues needed cleaning. Two chimney sweeps were called in, and, ignoring the engineer's warning of the danger from fumes, one of them crawled into the horizontal flue. The fire was let out and the chimney sweeps cleaned out the flues, but when the fire was re-lit there was further trouble with fumes and smoke. Another expert was called in; he advised that the fire should be withdrawn and told everyone present to get out into the fresh air. The chimney sweeps said that they did not need any advice, but eventually were more or less dragged out by the expert. Later, the expert made his inspection and gave his advice, and, in the presence of the chimney sweeps and of C, the occupier's son-in-law (who was looking after the building, the occupier being ill), advised that, *inter alia* the sweep-hole was to be sealed up before the boiler was lit again, and that the chimney sweeps, while doing the sealing, ought not to stay too long in the alcove. The following day, the fire was re-lit by the caretaker. By the evening, the chimney sweeps had not finished sealing up the sweep-hole, and C arranged with them to finish the work the next morning. The next morning, both the chimney sweeps were found dead by the sweep-hole. Apparently, they had returned the previous night to complete their work and had been overcome by carbon monoxide fumes.

Held, the warnings given to the chimney sweeps by the expert on behalf of the occupier of the danger which in fact killed them were enough to enable them to be reasonably safe, and therefore the occupier had discharged under s.2(4)(a) of the Occupiers' Liability Act 1957 the common duty of care that he owed to the chimney sweeps.

Lord Denning, M.R.: A warning does not absolve the occupier unless it is enough to enable the visitor to be reasonably safe. Apply s.(2)(4) to this case. I am quite clear that the warnings which were given to the chimney sweeps were enough to enable them to be reasonably safe. The sweeps would have been quite safe if they had heeded these warnings. They should not have come back that evening and attempted to seal up the sweep-hole while the fire was still alight. They ought to have waited till next morning and then they should have seen that the fire was out before they attempted to seal up the sweep-hole. In any case they should not have stayed too long in the sweep-hole. In short, it was entirely their own fault. The judge held that it was contributory negligence. I would go further and say that, under the Act, the occupier has, by the warnings, discharged his duty.

I would, therefore, be in favour of allowing this appeal and enter judgment for the defendants.

(*Casebook on Torts*, by D.M.M. Scott, London, Butterworths, 1969, pp:246–48)

The author of the case (Scott, 1969, vii) writes in his preface to the book:

> The law student . . . if he is to get at the reality of law, the raw material behind the opinions of the textbook writers, must study the words of the judges and of the statutes.

How does the author, then, make it possible for his readers to learn from the words of the judges? Although version [17] is more detailed than version [16], it is not very different in terms of the type of information it incorporates. Initially, we have a number of facts mentioned about the situation, many of which may not even be of any legal significance. For example, it is legally immaterial that the whole incident took place in December, 1958; the building was centrally heated; the sweep-hole was about twelve inches in diameter and nine feet above the ground; and that C was the son-in-law of the occupier. But these interesting details highlight the fact that we are dealing with an everyday universe of human behaviour and help the reader to identify legally material facts and to distinguish them from those that may be legally immaterial.

Next, the case reports the judgment in a more elaborate form giving supporting evidence by referring to legal authority; in this case, to a statutory provision from the Occupiers' Liability Act 1957. Details of legal reasoning and the evidence considered were ignored in the first version of the case. So, like the initial case description, the judgment part of the text is also more elaborate and not very different in character from the second section of [16], although one may notice that the judgment is pronounced in very specific terms: there is a mention of *chimney sweeps, the expert* and *the occupier*.

The third part of the case, once again, differs from its corresponding section in [16] not so much in character as in details. It does not simply reproduce the rule of law that the judge wants to lay down as precedent for subsequent cases of similar description but it also takes the reader through a very brief process of legal reasoning on which the verdict is based. It also refers to the legal authority in the form of a statutory provision which helps the judge to arrive at the rule of law. The rule of law (*ratio decidendi*), however is not mentioned in the text. Instead, it is prominently displayed at the very beginning of the text, as the most important aspect of the case.

Let us now look at the third version of the case.

[18]

Roles v. Nathan

Court of Appeal [1963] 1 W.L.R. 1117; 107 S.J. 680;
[1963] 2 All E.R. 908

The Manchester Assembly Rooms, owned and occupied by the defendant, were heated by an old coke-burning boiler which smoked badly. Two chimney sweeps were called in to clean it, but it was no better after they had done so. An expert, Collingwood, was called, saw that the boiler-room was dangerous through fumes and succeeded, though only by force, in removing the sweeps from it. He said that the sweep-hole and inspection chamber should be sealed before the boiler was lit and the sweeps undertook to do that. On Friday evening the defendant's son-in-law, Mr Corney, went to the boiler-room and found the sweeps working there with the fire on. They had not finished sealing off the apertures, and were to return the next day with more cement. On Saturday morning they were found there dead, the fire still burning brightly.

Elwes J. gave judgment for the widows of the sweeps, but the Court of Appeal allowed the defendant's appeal, Pearson L.J. dissenting.

LORD DENNING M.R.: . . . The judge found Mr Corney guilty of negligence because "he failed to take such care as should have ensured that there was no fire lit until the sweep-hole had been sealed up." He said, "Unfortunately Mr Corney did not tell the caretaker to draw the fire, or at any rate not to stoke it up." On this account he held that Mr. Corney was at fault, and the occupier liable. But he found the two sweeps guilty of contributory negligence, and halved the damages. The judge said, "That negligence" – that is to say of the chimney sweeps – "consisted in the knowledge that there was gas about, or probably would be, the way they ignored the warnings and showed complete indifference to the danger which was pointed out to them in plain language, and this strange indifference to the fact that the fire was alight, when Mr. Collingwood had said it ought not to be, until the sweep-hole had been sealed."

The occupier now appeals and says that it is not a case of negligence and contributory negligence, but that, on the true application of the Occupiers' Liability Act 1957, the occupier was not liable at all. This is the first time we have had to consider that Act. It has been very beneficial. It has rid us of those two unpleasant characters, the invitee and the licensee, who haunted the courts for years, and it has replaced them by the attractive figure of a visitor, who has so far given no trouble at all. The Act has now been in force for six years, and hardly any case has come before the courts in which its interpretation has had to be considered. The draftsman expressed the hope that "the Act would replace a principle of the common law with a new principle *of the common law*; instead of having the judgement of Willes J. construed as if it were a statute, one is to have a statute which can be construed as if it were a judgement of Willes J." [in

Roles v. *Nathan continued*

Indermaur v. Dames (1966) L.R. 1 C.P. 274]. It seems that his hopes are being fulfilled. All the fine distinctions about traps have been thrown aside and replaced by the common duty of care.

"The common duty of care," the Act says, "is a duty to take such care as in all the circumstances of the case is reasonable to see that the visitor" – note the visitor, not the premises – "will be reasonably safe in using the premises for the purposes for which he is invited or permitted by the occupier to be there." That is comprehensive. All the circumstances have been considered. But the Act goes on to give examples of the circumstances that are relevant. The particular one in question here is in subsection (3) of section 2: "The circumstances relevant for the present purpose include the degree of care, and of want of care, which would ordinarily be looked for in such a visitor, so that (for example) in proper cases. . . (b) an occupier may expect that a person, in exercise of his calling, will appreciate and guard against any special risks ordinarily incident to it, so far as the occupier leaves him free to do so."

That subsection shows that *General Cleaning Contractors* v. *Christmas* ([1925] 1 K.B. 141) is still good law under this new Act. There a window cleaner (who was employed by independent contractors) was sent to clean the windows of a club. One of the windows was defective; it had not been inspected and repaired as it should have been. In consequence, when the window cleaner was cleaning it, it ran down quickly and trapped his hand, thus causing him to fall. It was held that he had no cause of action against the club. If it had been a guest who had his fingers trapped by the defective window, the guest could have recovered damages from the club. But the window cleaner could not do so. The reason is this: the householder is concerned to see that the windows are safe for his guests to open and close, but he is not concerned to see that they are safe for a window cleaner to hold on to. The risk of a defective window is a special risk, but it is ordinarily incident to the calling of a window cleaner, and so he must take care for himself, and not expect the householder to do so. Likewise in the case of chimney sweep who comes to sweep the chimneys or to seal up a sweep-hole. The householder can reasonably expect the sweep to take care of himself so far as any dangers from the flues are concerned. These chimney sweeps ought to have known that there might be dangerous fumes about and ought to have taken steps to guard against them. They ought to have known that they should not attempt to seal up a sweep-hole whilst the fire was still alight. They ought to have had the fire withdrawn before they attempted to seal it up, or at any rate they ought not to have stayed in the alcove too long when there might be dangerous fumes about. All this was known to these two sweeps; they were repeatedly warned about it, and it was for them to guard against the danger. It was not for the occupier to do it, even though he was present and heard the warnings. When a householder calls in a specialist to deal with a defective installation on his premises, he can reasonably expect the specialist to appreciate and guard against the dangers arising from the defect. The householder is not bound to watch over him to see that he comes to no harm. I would hold, therefore, that the occupier here was under no duty of care to these sweeps, at any

Continued overleaf

Roles v. Nathan *continued*

rate in regard to the dangers which caused their death. If it had been a different danger, as for instance if the stairs leading to the cellar gave away, the occupier might no doubt be responsible, but not for these dangers which were special risks ordinarily incidental to their calling.

Even if I am wrong about this point, and the occupier was under a duty of care to these chimney sweeps, the question arises whether the duty was discharged by the warning that was given to them. This brings us to subsection (4) which states: "In determining whether the occupier of premises has discharged the common duty of care to a visitor, regard is to be had to all the circumstances, so that (for example) – (a) where damage is caused to a visitor by a danger of which he had been warned by the occupier, the warning is not to be treated as absolving the occupier from liability, unless in all the circumstances it was enough to enable the visitor to be reasonably safe."

We all know the reason for this subsection. It was inserted so as to clear up the unsatisfactory state of the law as it had been left by the decision of the House of Lords in *London Graving Dock Co. v. Horton* ([1951] A.C. 737). That case was commonly supposed to have decided that, when a person comes on to premises as an invitee, and is injured by the defective or dangerous condition of the premises (due to the default of the occupier), it is nevertheless a complete defence for the occupier to prove that the invitee knew of the danger, or had been warned of it. Suppose, for instance, that there was only one way of getting into and out of the premises, and it was by a footbridge over a stream which was rotten and dangerous. According to Horton's case, the occupier could escape all liability to any visitor by putting up a notice: "The bridge is dangerous," even though there was no other way by which the visitor could get in or out, and he had no option but to go over the bridge. In such a case, section 2(4) makes it clear that the occupier would nowadays be liable. But if there were two footbridges, one of which was rotten, and the other safe a hundred yards away, the occupier could still escape liability, even today, by putting up a notice: "Do not use this footbridge. It is dangerous. There is a safe one further upstream." Such a warning is sufficient because it does enable the visitor to be reasonably safe.

I think the law would probably have developed on these lines in any case; see *Greene v. Chelsea Borough Council* ([1954] 2 Q.B. 127), where I ventured to say "knowledge or notice of the danger is only a defence when the plaintiff is free to act upon that knowledge or notice so as to avoid danger." But the subsection has now made it clear. A warning does not absolve the occupier, unless it is enough to enable the visitor to be reasonably safe.

Apply s.(2)(4) to this case. I am quite clear that the warnings which were given to the chimney sweeps were enough to enable them to be reasonably safe. The sweeps would have been quite safe if they had heeded these warnings. They should not have come back that evening and attempted to seal up the sweep-hole while the fire was still alight. They ought to have waited till next morning and then they should have seen that the fire was out before they attempted to seal up the sweep-hole. In any case they should not have stayed too long in the sweep-hole. In short, it was entirely

> **Roles v. Nathan** *continued*
>
> their own fault. The judge held that it was contributory negligence. I would
> go further and say that, under the Act, the occupier has, by the warnings,
> discharged his duty.
> I would, therefore, be in favour of allowing this appeal and enter judgment
> for the defendants.

(*A Casebook on Tort*, by Tony Weir, London, Sweet and Maxwell,
1983, pp. 131–134)

The third version of the case, once again, does not differ so much in
terms of its essential character and information structuring but is
markedly different in terms of essential detailing, particularly in the
area of legal argumentation offered by the judge. Initial description of
the facts of the case is more elaborate than in [17] but less elaborate
than in [18], but the essential legally-material facts are included in all
the three versions. The interesting thing about this last version is that
the judgment is not reported before the argument of the judge, but is
derived, as it were, through a process of legal reasoning offered by the
judge in a very elaborate manner so that the reader does not miss out
any important piece of evidence, aspect of argument, or other related
issues. It includes several aspects of the development of the law in this
area of occupiers' liability. This makes good sense in the context of
what the author of the book claims in the preface to the first edition of
the casebook:

A casebook has several uses. It may be taught with . . .; it may be learnt
from (which is a very different thing); or it may be used as a *bibliotheque
de chevet*. Any casebook should answer all these purposes, but its structure
will be affected by the purpose which the compiler had principally in mind.

This one is designed primarily to be learnt from. . .

The three versions of the case of *Roles* v. *Nathan* differ not so much
in the type of information incorporated or the way they are structured,
as in the detailing of the information. We shall have a look at the
structure of the genre in the next section.

5.3.2 *Structural interpretation of legal cases*

Like any other genre, the legal case also displays a typical cognitive
structuring which accounts for the structural interpretation of the case.

Let us look at [18] more closely for a detailed structural description of the genre. It has a typical four-move structure.

1. Identifying the case

Since cases are quoted and used as evidence in law classes, textbooks, casebooks, in the courtrooms and in a number of other legal contexts, whether academic or occupational, they need to be identified and referred to in a consistent manner by the professional community. It is for this reason that an overwhelming majority of cases, whether reported in Law Reports or listed in casebooks, always begin with the move 1, **identifying the case**. This move, like many others in a number of professional genres, has a typical formulaic realization as follows:

Roles* v. *Nathan
Court of Appeal [1963] 2 ALL E.R. 908

Here the title, *Roles* v. *Nathan*, is traditionally written like this (the two parties to the dispute written on either side of a small v. for versus) and is followed by the type of case, the court it was tried in and the year it was decided or reported. We have this move in all the three versions of the case. Even the way dates are mentioned has fairly standardized conventions (see Williams, 1982: 43, for more information on the conventions governing the citation practices).

2. Establishing facts of the case

English courts follow the doctrine of precedent, which, in the words of Williams (1982:67) means that *Cases must be decided the same way when their material facts are the same*, though *obviously it does not require that* all *the facts should be the same. We know that in the flux of life all the facts of a case will never recur; but the legally material facts may recur and it is with these that the doctrine is concerned.* Therefore, in order to decide the relevance of a particular case for a subsequent one, it is absolutely crucial that the reader must have a good idea of the facts of the case, at least the facts of the case that are considered legally material for a particular decision. So, in cases which are listed for revision purposes as in the case of version [16], we tend to find a bare minimum description of the case in terms of a few very important legally-material facts. However, if the casebook is viewed as a means of cultivating techniques of legal reasoning and argumentation, then the facts of the case need to be established by bringing in greater detailed account of what actually happened that led to the dispute. This detailed account of facts may include a number of those not legally significant for the judgment in the case, but they are considered important in at least two ways.

First, this detailed and realistic account of the happenings provides answers to some of the questions that a reader might ask. Take, for example, the facts of the case as in [17], where it is said that *They* [chimney-sweeps] *had chosen to ignore a prior warning of this danger*. It is true that readers familiar with the case will probably know the kind of warning they had ignored but those who are learning the law from such cases should know more about the warning the sweeps had chosen to ignore. Who gave the warning? Was it from the occupier's agent or was it from an expert? What constitutes a warning in a situation like that? In order to be able to discuss questions like these it is appropriate for the reader to be familiar with a more detailed account of the facts of the case, as in the extract below from example [17]:

> Another expert was called in; he advised that the fire should be withdrawn and told everyone present to get out into the fresh air. The chimney sweeps said that they did not need any advice, but eventually were more or less dragged out by the expert. Later, the expert made his inspection and gave his advice, and, in the presence of the chimney sweeps and of C, the occupier's son-in-law (who was looking after the building, the occupier being ill), advised that, *inter alia* the sweep-hole was to be sealed up before the boiler was lit again, and that the chimney sweeps, while doing the sealing, ought not to stay too long in the alcove.

Second, such a detailed account of facts will help the learner/reader to distinguish legally significant facts from those that are less significant and hence legally immaterial so far as the judgment is concerned. This elaborate description of facts will help the reader to appreciate better the argument of the judge, which is the subject of the next move.

3. Arguing the case

This is the most complex and perhaps the most important (for the learners of law) section of the legal case and will generally have several sub-moves depending upon the nature of the case and the length. It invariably begins with the name of the judge delivering judgment and may cover the history of the case in the courts including the judgment(s) delivered by earlier judges (particularly found in appeal cases), the arguments of the present judge, the evidence he or she uses in the negotiation of justice, leading to the derivation of the principle of law that the judge wants to record for use in subsequent cases (*ratio decedendi*), etc.

Let us propose three major sub-moves in this case.

(a) **Giving a history of the case**
(b) **Presenting arguments**
(c) **Deriving** *ratio decidendi*

In version [16] of the case, we have move 3 realized simply in terms of a clear statement of the *ratio decidendi* of the case, which leads to and justifies the pronouncement of the judgment.

> Lord Denning M.R., "When a householder calls in a specialist to deal with a defective installation on his premises, he can reasonably expect the specialist to appreciate and guard against the dangers arising from the defect."

In version [17], there is no indication of the history of the case, so sub-move (a) **giving a history of the case** is missing. Then we have a rather brief presentation of the argument beginning with a general statement of the principle based on section 2 (4) of the Occupiers' Liability Act 1957, which the judge thinks will provide the basis for his judgment.

> A warning does not absolve the occupier unless it is enough to enable the visitor to be reasonably safe.

The argument is taken farther by applying section 2 (4) to the facts of the case, move 2, **establishing facts of the case**, which eventually leads to the conclusion that *it was entirely their* [the chimney sweeps'] *own fault*. This constitutes sub-move (b) **presenting arguments**. The third sub-move, **deriving** *ratio decidendi*, consists of a principle of law derived by the judge for application to subsequent cases, and the case does contain a statement to that effect. However, this does not figure in the main body of the case but is prominently displayed in the beginning of the case, as its most important aspect.

Let us now see a very much more elaborate version of sub-move (1), in version [18] of the case.

The move begins with a good historical description of the case because this is an appeal case and, without the history of the case, it is less likely to be fully understood by the law student. It begins with the statement about the earlier judgment by J. Elwes and the subsequent permission for the defendant to appeal to the Court of Appeal.

> Elwes J. gave judgment for the widows of the sweeps, but the Court of Appeal allowed the defendant's appeal, Pearson L.J. dissenting.

It then includes sections from the judgment by the same judge, thus explaining the judgment given by the judge.

> LORD DENNING M.R.::...The judge found Mr Corney guilty of negligence because "he failed to take such care as should have ensured that there was no fire lit until the sweep-hole had been sealed up." He said, "Unfortunately Mr Corney did not tell the caretaker to draw the fire, or at any rate not to stoke it up." On this account he held that Mr. Corney was at fault, and the occupier liable. But he found the two sweeps guilty of contributory negligence, and halved the damages. The judge said, "That negligence" – that is to say of the chimney sweeps – "consisted in the knowledge that there was gas about, or probably would be, the way they ignored the warnings and showed complete indifference to the danger which was pointed out to them in plain language, and this strange indifference to the fact that the fire was alight, when Mr. Collingwood had said it ought not to be, until the sweep-hole had been sealed."

It then goes on to make a statement about the basis on which the defendant has appealed.

> The occupier now appeals and says that it is not a case of negligence and contributory negligence, but that, on the true application of the Occupiers' Liability Act 1957, the occupier was not liable at all.

Lord Denning then goes on to present his own argument, which marks the beginning of sub-move (b), **presenting arguments**. This sub-move is much more complex than a similar one in version [17] of the case. It begins with an attempt to establish the usefulness of the Occupiers' Liability Act 1957b because that is the basis on which the defendant has challenged the earlier decision of the court. The writer also uses the judgment in the case of *Indermaur* v. *Dames* [1966] L.R. 1 C.P. 274 as evidence to confirm his own point of view:

> This is the first time we have had to consider that Act. It has been very beneficial. It has rid us of those two unpleasant characters, the invitee and the licensee, who haunted the courts for years, and it has replaced them by the attractive figure of a visitor, who has so far given no trouble at all. The Act has now been in force for six years, and hardly any case has come

before the courts in which its interpretation has had to be considered. The draftsman expressed the hope that "the Act would replace a principle of the common law with a new principle *of the common law*; instead of having the judgement of Willes J. construed as if it were a statute, one is to have a statute which can be construed as if it were a judgment of Willes J." [in Indermaur v. Dames [1966] L.R. 1 C.P. 274]. It seems that his hopes are being fulfilled. All the fine distinctions about traps have been thrown aside and replaced by the common duty of care.

The next strategy the judge uses is to identify a relevant principle of law based on the Act, which he intends to apply to the present case.

"The common duty of care," the Act says, "is a duty to take such care as in all the circumstances of the case is reasonable to see that the visitor" – note the visitor, not the premises – "will be reasonably safe in using the premises for the purposes for which he is invited or permitted by the occupier to be there." That is comprehensive. All the circumstances have been considered. But the Act goes on to give examples of the circumstances that are relevant. The particular one in question here is in subsection (3) of section 2: "The circumstances relevant for the present purpose include the degree of care, and of want of care, which would ordinarily be looked for in such a visitor, so that (for example) in proper cases . . . (b) an occupier may expect that a person, in exercise of his calling, will appreciate and guard against any special risks ordinarily incident to it, so far as the occupier leaves him free to do so."

This statement of legal position is further confirmed by a marked reference (Swales, 1982:142) to the case of General Cleaning Contractors v. Christmas ([1925] 1 K.B. 141) with a fairly elaborate account of the facts of the case and the decision thereon, making a useful distinction between an ordinary risk and a special risk ordinarily incident to the calling of a window cleaner or any other professional group.

That subsection shows that *General Cleaning Contractors v. Christmas* ([1925] 1 K.B. 141) is still good law under this new Act. There a window cleaner (who was employed by independent contractors) was sent to clean the windows of a club. One of the windows was defective; it had not been inspected and repaired as it should have been. In consequence, when the window cleaner was cleaning it, it ran down quickly and trapped his hand, thus causing him to fall. It was held that he had no cause of action against the club. If it had been a guest who had his fingers trapped by the defective window, the guest could have recovered damages from the club. But the window cleaner could not do so. The reason is this: the householder is concerned to see that the windows are safe for his guests to open and close, but he is not concerned to see that they are safe for a window cleaner to hold on to. The risk of a defective window is a special risk, but it is ordinarily incident to the calling of a window cleaner, and so he must take care for himself, and not expect the householder to do so.

The statement of legal position thus established is then applied to the case of the chimney sweeps for a decision in favour of the defendant.

Likewise in the case of chimney sweep who comes to sweep the chimneys or to seal up a sweep-hole. The householder can reasonably expect the sweep to take care of himself so far as any dangers from the flues are concerned. These chimney sweeps ought to have known that there might be dangerous fumes about and ought to have taken steps to guard against them. They ought to have known that they should not attempt to seal up a sweep-hole whilst the fire was still alight. They ought to have had the fire withdrawn before they attempted to seal it up, or at any rate they ought not to have stayed in the alcove too long when there might be dangerous fumes about. All this was known to these two sweeps; they were repeatedly warned about it, and it was for them to guard against the danger. It was not for the occupier to do it, even though he was present and heard the warnings.

Once the presentation of the argument is complete, the judge goes on to derive the principle of law, *ratio decidendi*, that he would like to lay down for application to subsequent cases of similar description.

When a householder calls in a specialist to deal with a defective installation on his premises, he can reasonably expect the specialist to appreciate and guard against the dangers arising from the defect. The householder is not bound to watch over him to see that he comes to no harm. I would hold, therefore, that the occupier here was under no duty of care to these sweeps, at any rate in regard to the dangers which caused their death. If it had been a different danger, as for instance if the stairs leading to the cellar gave away, the occupier might no doubt be responsible, but not for these dangers which were special risks ordinarily incidental to their calling.

However, the final verdict is not based just on this principle of law. The judge takes up the other aspect of the law as well. Once again, sub-moves (b) and (c) are taken up, starting once again with the statement of a legal position based on the Act.

Even if I am wrong about this point, and the occupier was under a duty of care to these chimney sweeps, the question arises whether the duty was discharged by the warning that was given to them. This brings us to subsection (4) which states: "In determining whether the occupier of premises has discharged the common duty of care to a visitor, regard is to be had to all the circumstances, so that (for example) – (a) where damage is caused to a visitor by a danger of which he had been warned by the occupier, the warning is not to be treated without more as absolving the occupier from liability, unless in all the circumstances it was enough to enable the visitor to be reasonably safe."

Once again the judge discusses the main rationale for the Act and makes another marked reference to the case, this time, of *London Graving Dock Co.* v. *Horton* ([1951] A.C. 737) to establish the importance of the principle of law, pointing out that it is not enough to give a warning of impending danger to a visitor unless it is considered sufficient for the visitor to be reasonably safe.

We all know the reason for this subsection. It was inserted so as to clear up the unsatisfactory state of the law as it had been left by the decision of the House of Lords in *London Graving Dock Co.* v. *Horton* ([1951] A.C. 737). That case was commonly supposed to have decided that, when a person comes on to premises as an invitee, and is injured by the defective or dangerous condition of the premises (due to the default of the occupier), it is nevertheless a complete defence for the occupier to prove that the invitee knew of the danger, or had been warned of it. Suppose, for instance, that there was only one way of getting into and out of the premises, and it was by a footbridge over a stream which was rotten and dangerous. According to Horton's case, the occupier could escape all liability to any visitor by putting up a notice: "The bridge is dangerous," even though there was no other way by which the visitor could get in or out, and he had no option but to go over the bridge. In such a case, section 2(4) makes it clear that the occupier would nowadays be liable. But if there were two footbridges, one of which was rotten, and the other safe a hundred yards away, the occupier could still escape liability, even today, by putting up a notice: "Do not use this footbridge. It is dangerous. There is a safe one further upstream." Such a warning is sufficient because it does enable the visitor to be reasonably safe.

To confirm the legal position taken up by him, the judge refers to the case of *Greene* v. *Chelsea Borough Council* ([1954] 2 Q.B. 127) and then reproduces the principle of law laid down there.

I think the law would probably have developed on these lines in any case; see *Greene* v. *Chelsea Borough Council* ([1954] 2 Q.B. 127), where I ventured to say "knowledge or notice of the danger is only a defence when the plaintiff is free to act upon that knowledge or notice so as to avoid danger." But the subsection has now made it clear. A warning does not absolve the occupier, unless it is enough to enable the visitor to be reasonably safe.

The principle of law arrived at is then applied to the case of the chimney sweeps and the judgment favoured earlier on is further confirmed.

Apply s.(2)(4) to this case. I am quite clear that the warnings which were given to the chimney sweeps were enough to enable them to be reasonably safe. The sweeps would have been quite safe if they had heeded these warnings. They should not have come back that evening and attempted to seal up the sweep-hole while the fire was still alight. They ought to have waited till next morning and then they should have seen that the fire was out before they attempted to seal up the sweep-hole. In any case they should not have stayed too long in the sweep-hole. In short, it was entirely their own fault. The judge held that it was contributory negligence. I would go further and say that, under the Act, the occupier has, by the warnings, discharged his duty.

4. Pronouncing judgment

Although move 4 is generally very brief, the law case can never be complete without the pronouncement of judgment. Generally signalled by the term, 'Held', it is very brief, formulaic, highly standardized in character and inextricably part of the case. In version [16] it is realized by *The Court of Appeal held that the defendants were not liable*, whereas in version [17] it is rather more elaborate,

> Held, the warnings given to the chimney sweeps by the expert on behalf of the occupier of the danger which in fact killed them were enough to enable them to be reasonably safe, and therefore the occupier had discharged under s.2(4)(a) of the Occupiers' Liability Act 1957 the common duty of care that he owed to the chimney sweeps.

The judgment is repeated in its more formulaic form at the end of the case when the judge adds,

> I would, therefore, be in favour of allowing this appeal and enter judgment for the defendants.

In version [18], this move again appears in its formulaic form at the end of the case.

> I would, therefore, be in favour of allowing this appeal and enter judgment for the defendants.

The legal case, therefore, displays a typical four-move structure consisting of the following moves.

1.   **Identifying the case**
2.   **Establishing facts of the case**

3.   **Arguing the case**
       (a) Stating history of the case
       (b) Presenting arguments
       (c) Deriving *ratio decidendi*
4.   **Pronouncing judgment**

In the structure of the legal case, all the four moves are more or less obligatory. However, depending upon the purpose that a particular case is meant to serve, cases may vary in the amount of detailed information included, and also in choice of sub-moves, which are not obligatory. Some cases may have a very brief realization of one or more moves, while others very detailed ones. Similarly, in a number of cases, move 3 may not have all the three sub-moves present. In fact, non-appeal cases will invariably be without sub-move (a). Sometimes, one may find only a brief account of sub-move (b) realizing move 3, while in others the judge may not choose to lay down any *ratio decidendi*. There is also some degree of variability in the positioning of these moves. Move 1 is always realized in the title of the case. Move 2 is also fixed and is invariably placed after the identification of the case. Moves 3 and 4 often change positions, depending upon the purpose of the casebook in which they occur. If the purpose of the casebook is to remind the legal expert of the case references, then move 4 is more likely to appear before move 3, and is generally signalled by the heading Held. Occasionally, one may find sub-move (c) making an independent appearance somewhere outside the case, generally before move 1, as in version [17] of the case of *Roles* v. *Nathan*.

5.4 (Cross-cultural) variation in legal discourse

It is obvious that law is less universal than science. One may distinguish two major kinds of variation in legal genres. First, there are different kinds of legal systems and we may distinguish three leading ones. The common law, which is the basis for much of the law written and practised in the countries of the Commonwealth; the civil law, which provides the basis for many of the European countries, except the UK; and the Shariat law, which has its roots in most of the Muslim world. This variety of legal systems throughout the world provides for the first kind of variation in the way legal discourse is written and used. The second kind of variation, which is very significant in a number of ways, is found in the way legal discourse is realized in different countries within the same legal systems. Let me take up first the case of variation as a result of the different legal systems.

It is generally agreed that common law, which forms the basis for all legislation in the UK, and the civil code, which is the basis for most of the Continental legislation, including the French, are different in two main respects. First, the civil code prefers **generality** whereas the common law goes for **particularity**. And, second, the civil code draftsman is *eager to be widely understood by the ordinary readership*, whereas the common law draftsman seems to be more *worried about not being misunderstood by the specialist community*. A good comparison of the two styles of legislative drafting is cited by Millett (1986) when he compares the British and French Nationality Laws.

'The British Nationality Act 1981' is much longer than 'The French Code de la Nationalité' (approximately 22,500 words, whereas the Code runs to approximately 6,000 words). The Act consists of 53 sections and nine schedules, whereas the Code consists of 161 articles and no schedules. The sections of the Act are generally much longer than the articles of the Code: an average of 40 lines each, as against an average of 4 to 5 lines for an article of the Code. The schedules to the Act are even longer, several of them being subdivided into paragraphs themselves as long as the sections of the Act.

(Millett, 1986:137)

Let me cite comparable sections providing for nationality by descent from the two Nationality Acts. First, translation of Articles 17 and 19 of the Code de la Nationalité:

[19] Art.17 – A legitimate or illegitimate child is French if at least one of his parents is French.

Art.19 – However, if only one of the parents is French, a child who is not born in France shall have the right to renounce French nationality within the six months before attaining the age of majority.

That right is lost if the alien or stateless parent acquires French nationality while the child is a minor.

Now, compare this with its counterpart from the British Nationality Act, 1981:

[20] S.2. – (1) A person born outside the United Kingdom after

commencement shall be a British citizen if at the time of the birth his father or mother –

(a) is a British citizen otherwise than by descent; or
(b) is a British citizen and is serving outside the United Kingdom in service to which this paragraph applies, his or her recruitment for that service having taken place in the United Kingdom; or
(c) is a British citizen and is serving outside the United Kingdom in service under a Community institution, his or her recruitment for that service having taken place in a country which at the time of the recruitment was a member of the Communities.

(2) Paragraph (b) of subsection (1) applies to –

(a) Crown service under the Government of the United Kingdom; and
(b) service of any description for the time being designated under subsection (3).

(3) For the purposes of this section the Secretary of State may by order made by statutory instrument designate any description of service which he considers to be closely associated with the activities outside the United Kingdom of Her Majesty's government in the United Kingdom.

(4) Any order made under subsection (3) shall be subject to annulment in pursuance of a resolution of either House of Parliament.

S.14. – (1) For the purposes of this Act a British citizen is a British citizen "by descent" if and only if –

(a) he is a person born outside the United Kingdom after commencement who is a British citizen by virtue of section 2(1)(a) only or by virtue of registration under section 3(2) or 9; or
(b) subject to subsection (2), he is a person born outside the United Kingdom before commencement who became a British citizen at commencement and immediately before commencement –
(i) was a citizen of the United Kingdom and Colonies by virtue of section 5 of the 1948 Act (citizenship by descent); or
(ii) was a person who, under any provision of the British Nationality Acts 1948 to 1965, was deemed for the purposes of the proviso to section 5(1) of the 1948 Act to be a citizen of the United Kingdom and Colonies by descent only, or would have been so deemed if male; or
(iii) had the right of abode in the United Kingdom by virtue only of paragraph (b) of subsection (1) of section 2 of the Immigration Act 1971 as then in force (connection with United Kingdom through parent or grandparent), or by virtue only of that paragraph and paragraph (c) of that subsection (settlement in United kingdom with five years' ordinary residence there), or by virtue of being or having been the wife of a person who immediately before commencement had that right by virtue only of the said paragraph (b) or the said paragraphs (b) and (c); or
(iv) being a woman, was a citizen of the United Kingdom and Colonies as a result of her registration as such a citizen under section 6(2) of the 1948 Act by virtue of having been married to a man who at commencement became a British citizen by descent or would have done so but for his having died or

ceased to be citizen of the United Kingdom and Colonies as a result of a declaration or renunciation; or

(c) he is a British citizen by virtue of registration under section 3(1) and either –
(i) his father or mother was a British citizen at the time of the birth; or
(ii) his father or mother was a citizen of the United Kingdom and Colonies at the time and became a British citizen at commencement, or would have done so but for his or her death; or. . .

(The British Nationality Act, 1981, UK)

And it goes on to include paragraphs (d), (e), (f), (g) and (h) under subsection (1) and then has subsections (2) and (3) as well. There are many significant differences in the way the two laws have been written. The first, of course, is the length of the two sections. The section from the Act is very detailed whereas the one from the Code is only a statement of the general principle. Second, the Act contains numerous instances of the use of specialist lexis which may require terminological explanation, whereas the Code exploits ordinary words and their familiar meanings. Third, the Act is full of what we earlier on referred to as textual-mapping devices providing numerous instances of cross-referencing, thus making the task of unpacking very difficult, whereas the Code relies mostly on the good offices of the reader to interpret and construe the right meaning for application (see Millett, 1986 for a detailed comparison of the two Nationality Laws). The important thing, however, is that the two styles of writing are the result of two very different legal systems. As mentioned earlier, the Code is based on the French legal system, which relies heavily on the judiciary to construe, interpret and apply general principles of the Code to specific situations. It is often said that the Code attains simplicity of expression at the cost of certainty. But the Code draftsman is never bothered by any judicial hostility and the system allows members of the judiciary to make their own decisions. The British system is firmly based on the principle of precedence, where the decisions taken by one member of the judiciary may become binding on all subsequent cases of a similar description. The system, therefore, allows comparatively little scope for vagueness in judicial interpretation, and, hence, regards certainty of expression as the most valued quality in common law drafting.

Having looked at variation in different legal systems, let us now turn to variation within a single legal system, namely, variation in drafting styles within the Commonwealth countries. It is well known that legislation, unlike fictional literature and many other varieties of English, where creativity and innovation in the processes of coding as well as interpretation are considered positive virtues, belongs to what has traditionally been called a frozen variety of English, where the emphasis is definitely on conformity rather than creativity or innovation. The legal draftsmen rarely, if ever, seem to go for innovative or personal expressions. Instead, they prefer to use terms which have stood the test of time. They feel, quite justifiably in most cases, that if in a particular act a term has been used to express a particular kind of meaning, then in the later versions of or additions to the same body of acts, that same meaning must be expressed by the same term. The emphasis in all legislation, they say, is on avoiding litigation rather than giving elegant expression to the will of Parliament. If there is any tension between the two, obviously certainty will be preferred to elegance and conformity will thus be considered more valuable than innovation. This, perhaps, is one of the main reasons that legislative expression has not been able to keep pace with creativity in other genres. Instead, we notice a degree of orthodoxy in the use of linguistic resources in legislative writing that is rarely encountered in other areas of discourse. This is particularly significant in countries where, though English is used as a second language, it is also used as a vehicle of communication in legislative settings. A very good example of this comes from the use of what is commonly known in legal terminology as the *proviso-clause*, invariably introduced by *provided that*. If we look at the history of this expression in legislative writing, we find that in the earliest statutes it was used as enacting formula as *It is provided that*, where it was clearly a term of enactment (see Dreidger, 1957). In those days, it was customary for each enactment in a statute to have its own enacting clause because most statutes were written in one piece without distinctions by paragraphs or sections. In 1850, with the introduction of dividing statutory enactments into sections, the practice of having an enacting clause for every enactment was dropped. However, its use continued as an all-purpose conjunction, sometimes to introduce an exception to the rule, sometimes to mark a consecutive stage in the operation of the rule and very often, to add a new rule unconnected to the present one, thereby creating problems of interpretation for the users of these acts. The use of so-called *proviso-clauses* has undergone considerable change in Britain, where it is still used, though not very often, to introduce exceptions or additional conditions to the rule in question. However, in many of the Commonwealth countries *proviso-clauses* are still used overwhelmingly to indicate a variety of legal meanings. Ramachandra (1988:33) discovers twenty-four different uses of the *proviso-clause* in the Singapore Income Tax 1984. These different uses took on a variety of meanings commonly conveyed in everyday English usage by 'if', 'and', 'or' and 'but'. They are used to introduce exceptions to the rule, to specify preparatory conditions to the rule, to introduce a separate enactment, or as a cover term to introduce a variety of qualifications to limit or extend rights and obligations, powers and scope of application etc. *Sometimes*, she claims, *the phrase took on no meaning whatsoever – it was 'mere surplusage' and could be dropped.* In a number of cases, therefore, the phrase was being used as a formula 'to heap together matter wholly unconnected', to borrow an expression from Dreidger (1957). Many of these uses have become obsolete in present-day British legislation. However, they have survived and will thrive, perhaps, for a long time to come, in many of the Commonwealth countries, indicating orthodoxy in the bilingual's use of English in legislative settings.

Legislative writing has also changed considerably in the past few decades in its use of what Bhatia (1987a) calls **textual-mapping devices** to express complex contingencies. These are discoursal strategies which serve primarily a text-cohering function relating one aspect of the text to another, either in the same act or in some other, thus helping the draftsman to reduce information load at a particular point in the expression of legislative content. Let us take a typical example of the use of this device from the British Housing Act 1980.

[21] (1) The price payable for a dwelling-house on a conveyance or grant in pursuance of this Chapter is –

(a) the amount which, under this section, is to be taken as its value at the relevant time; less

(b) the discount to which the purchaser is entitled under this Chapter.

(2) The value of the dwelling-house at the relevant time shall be taken to be the price which, at the relevant time, it would realise if sold on the open market by a willing vendor on the assumptions stated, for a conveyance, in subsection (3) below, and for a grant, in subsection (4) below, and disregarding any improvements made by any of the persons specified in subsection (5) below and any failure by any of those persons to keep the dwelling-house in good internal repair.

(3) For a conveyance the assumptions are that –
(a) the vendor was selling for an estate in fee simple with vacant possession;
(b) neither the tenant nor a member of his family residing with him wanted to buy; and
(c) the dwelling-house was to be conveyed with the same rights and subject to the same burdens as it would be in pursuance of this Chapter.

(4) For the grant of a lease the assumptions are that –
(a) the vendor was granting a lease for 125 years with vacant possession (subject to paragraph 11(2) of Schedule to this Act);
(b) neither the tenant nor a member of his family residing with him wanted to take the lease; and
(c) the ground rent would not exceed $10 per annum; and
(d) the grant was to be made with the same rights and subject to the same burdens as it would be in pursuance of this Chapter.

(5) The persons mentioned in subsection (2) above are –
(a) the secure tenant
(b) any person who under the same tenancy was a secure tenant before him; and
(c) any member of his family who, immediately before the secure tenancy was granted, was a secure tenant of the same dwelling-house under another tenancy.
(Section 6 of the Housing Act, 1980, UK)

The above provision is about the purchase price of a dwelling-house, which is given as the value of the dwelling-house less the discount which the purchaser is entitled to. The term 'value' is further defined in subsection (2) as the price that it would attract if sold in the open market on certain assumptions and keeping in mind certain other conditions. The assumptions and the conditions, however, are not incorporated in the same sentence. Instead, the draftsman has postponed the discussion of these to subsections (3), (4), and (5), and given simply the location of these subsections in subsection (2) by using three separate qualifications signalling such textual mappings. This spatial and syntactic breaking up of semantic content into various subprovisions and indexing of these subprovisions by backward and forward cross-referencing in order to provide textual links with the preceding and preceded legislation helps the draftsman to reduce information load at a particular point in the syntax of a legislative statement.

Some fifty years ago, these textual-mapping devices were almost non-existent but, in present-day British legislation, they are quite common. Bhatia (1987a) compares the use of textual-mapping devices in two British Housing Acts, the Housing Act 1957 and the Housing Act 1980. The frequencies of these text-cohering devices in the two Acts were as follows:

Name of the Act	No. of pages	No. of sections	Frequency of textual-mapping devices	% per section
Housing Act 1957	120	193	020	0.10
Housing Act 1980	109	155	200	1.29

It is true that the situation may not be the same in the whole of the British statute book. There may still be many cases with high density of information at various points within the syntax of the legislative statement, sometimes because of the nature of the subject-matter of legislation, at other times because of some other considerations. On the whole, the present-day legislative writing is generally quite rich in the use of textual-mapping devices. However, in other Commonwealth countries the use of such text-cohering devices is still very rare and as a result legislative acts seem to carry a relatively higher load of information at various points. In many of these countries, legislative genres even now display more orthodoxy in the use of some linguistic resources than they do innovation and creativity.

5.5 Concluding remarks

In this chapter we have looked at two closely related written genres from legal settings. The two genres are related in terms of the settings in which they are used, the participants taking part in these professional communicative activities, in the way both are validly used as legal authority in the negotiation of justice and more importantly, the way they encode and represent legal processes. As stated earlier, no legislative provision is of universal application. It becomes operative only in a specific set of circumstances, which represents a selection of contexts from the model world of rights and obligations, permissions and prohibitions created by the legislative writer. This selection of facts from the model world is used as a basis to create definite legal relationship(s) between two parties. Legal cases represent the other side of the picture. They represent the legal process by which legislative rules are applied to the facts of the real world. In order to understand the true nature and function of legislative rules, it is important to understand not simply the way the facts of the model world are identified and used to create specific legal relationships but also to appreciate how such legislative rules are applied to a selection of relevant facts from the world of reality. We shall have a more detailed discussion of the relationship between the two genres and how such a relationship can be advantageously exploited for a variety of academic and professional purposes in the next part of the book.

PART 3: APPLICATIONS

The aim of this section is to discuss applications of genre analysis to two main areas of language use, language teaching in general and ESP in particular, and language reform in public documents. However, in order to take up applications in these areas, it is necessary to discuss the notion of simplification as used in language-teaching pedagogy and the way it affects authenticity of genres in professional and academic discourse.

Simplification v. easification – generic integrity in discourse

Simplification, as generally understood and frequently practised in language-teaching pedagogy, is a special form of intra-lingual translation, the purpose of which is to make a given text simpler in terms of its content and/or form. This is usually done by bringing its content or linguistic form within the area of experience of a particular group of readers. Simplification, therefore, involves a kind of tampering with the original linguistic input in order to produce either a *simplified version* or a *simple account* of the original text. Widdowson (1978:88) discusses the two terms in detail. Simplified versions, he points out, are passages derived from genuine instances of discourse by a process of lexical and syntactic substitution, and hence are regarded as alternative textualizations of a given authentic discourse. Simple accounts, on the other hand, are genuine instances of discourse designed to meet a communicative purpose, and do not represent alternative textualizations. They are genuine instances of discourse in their own right. However, in either case the authenticity of the original genre which the text represents is compromised. Whether it is a simplified version or a simple account, the resulting discourse is less likely to be a genuine instance of the genre which the original text represents. In the case of simplified versions, the content and/or lexico-grammatical resources are tampered with in order to bring the text within the linguistic competence of a specific readership. This certainly changes the authentic nature of the genre. In the case of simple accounts, it is even more likely that the original text will lose its essential communicative purpose. It will certainly, as Widdowson (1979) claims, be a genuine instance of discourse but will not necessarily represent the same genre as the original. A typical instance of this phenomenon is found in simple accounts of scientific research reports, which are called popular accounts of scientific discoveries and are simplified for non-specialist science enthusiasts in magazines like the *Popular Science* or the *Scientific American*. They may be called simple accounts and considered genuine instances of discourse, which, of course, they are, but they are different from original authentic scientific research reports because they represent two different genres, in that they serve two very different communicative purposes. The moment one simplifies an original to produce an alternative or a different version of the original, the generic integrity of the original text is likely to be completely lost or at least neutralized to a certain extent.

Loss in generic integrity, resulting from the simplification of an original text, may have negative repercussions for a number of applied linguistic situations (see Bhatia, 1983a), particularly for the teaching, learning and testing of languages in specific contexts as well as in language reform. If that is the case, is there an alternative which can make a particular text more accessible to a non-specialist readership and yet maintain the generic integrity of the original? Bhatia (1983a) introduces the notion of *easification* as an alternative to simplification. Easification, as he points out, attempts to make the text more accessible to the learner by using a variety of what he calls *easification devices*, the purpose of which is to guide the reader through the text without making any drastic changes to the content or linguistic form of the text, thus maintaining its generic integrity. He suggests a wide range of easification devices to make an authentic text more easily accessible to the reader depending upon the nature of the genre which the text represents, and the purpose of reading. Easification is not only a technique for text presentation, he points out, but also a learning strategy which helps the learner to simplify the text for himself, depending upon his background knowledge of the subject matter and of the language. These concepts of easification and generic integrity have useful applications in the teaching and testing of ESP and in language reform, particularly in the designing of public documents.

6 From description to explanation in language teaching

In this chapter, I would like to look at some of the important language-teaching contexts, particularly ESP, where findings of genre analysis can be used to understand and appreciate some of the general issues in present-day language teaching, especially in countries where English is a second language. Section 6.1 will take up the teaching of grammar and within that a special case of the use of nominal expressions in professional and academic discourse, and illustrate why grammatical explanation is necessary in language teaching, particularly in ESP. Section 6.2 will consider syllabus design with special reference to the use of input to teaching materials in language teaching. Here, another specific case, the use of English in newspapers illustrates how genre analysis can help ESL/EFL course designers to make theoretically well-motivated decisions in the choice of appropriate genre-based tasks. Section 6.3 is concerned with the concept of appropriate text-task relationship for further comment, and illustrates it by referring to an ESP situation. It discusses one of the most difficult questions in English for Academic or Occupational Purpose Legal (EA/OLP) contexts, i.e., genre-specificity and the notion of inter-textuality in legal contexts and suggests how to exploit it for EA/OLP courses. Section 6.4 discusses a case study of actual genre-based English for Business and Technology (EBT) teaching materials written for use on a self-access basis, and demonstrates how pre-knowledge of formal and content schemata can facilitate not only the learning of generic conventions and rhetorical action but also the linguistic resources to realize them. Section 6.5 considers some of the relevant questions frequently raised in the context of evaluation of purpose in ESP. The final section briefly discusses the application of genre analysis for the development of sensitivity in ESP learners and teachers towards creativity and orthodoxy in the use of generic conventions in cross-cultural ESP settings.

English language teaching, whether as a second or foreign language, has for a long time been prescriptive. Prescriptions, which either came from the teacher's authority or the grammar book, determined language-teaching syllabuses, teaching materials, classroom practices and even evaluation procedures. This was a favourite pattern till about the early seventies and still persists in many English language teaching contexts. In the late sixties and early seventies, the introduction of linguistics and discourse analysis started having some influence on a wide range of language teaching courses, especially in the case of English courses for a variety of specific or specifiable purposes. In the last twenty-five years, models of discourse analysis have changed considerably; however, language description continues to be the main source of strength for ESP theory and practice.

6.1 Genre-based grammatical explanation in ESP – the case of nominal expressions

Complex nominal expressions of various kinds are typically associated with academic and professional genres and have gained a certain degree of notoriety in recent years. To the specialist community they are a useful linguistic device to bring in text cohesion, facilitating reference to (associated) technical concepts already mentioned; however, to the non-specialist outsider this is nothing but jargon. I would like to consider three areas of academic and professional writing and look at the use of various types of nominal expressions in them in order to find out why academic and professional writers use nominal expressions the way they do. The areas of professional activities we shall concentrate on are advertisements, scientific, more generally, scientific academic and research writing, and legislative provisions.

Let me first take up three major types of nominal expressions. The first type is the **complex nominal phrases** (Quirk et al., 1982), which is significantly used in advertisements of a particular kind. The second type is known either as **nominal compounds** (Williams, 1984) or **compound nominal phrases** (Salager, 1984), and these are typically associated with scientific writing. The third type is conventionally called **nominalization**, and is overwhelmingly used in legislative provisions (Bhatia, 1983b). Although all three types of nominals are generally grouped together under the broad category of complex noun phrases (see Quirk et al., 1982), it is more appropriate to consider them as distinct for two reasons. First, although they perform a more or less similar grammatical function in the language, they have different grammatical realizations, and secondly, they seem to textualize different aspects of the three genres with which they have traditionally been associated. In other words, they have different grammatical realizations and carry different discoursal values in the three genres. Let me give examples from the three genres, first from advertising.

[1]   **The world's first packless, cordless, lightweight, compact, integrated video light.**

This illustrates precisely the true character of the noun phrase in advertising.

The most striking characteristic of this type of complex nominal phrase is the degree and to a lesser extent the complexity of modification of the noun head. A series of adjectives, linearly arranged in the pre-modifying position in such complex nominal phrases is rarely matched elsewhere in English. The typical syntactic structure of such a complex nominal phrase is **(Modifier) Head (Qualifier)** where (M) is realized primarily in terms of a series of linearly arranged attributes as follows: (Det) (adj) (adj) (adj) (adj) . . . H (Q).

Although scientific English displays a wide range of nominals, we shall take up only one of them here. Williams (1984) calls them **nominal compounds**; we shall call them **compound nominal phrases** and some typical examples are:

pulmonary artery mean pressure electrocardiogram V1 lead,
airport building roof truss failures,
nozzle gas ejection space ship attitude control, etc.

The common structure underlying these compound nominal phrases is the following: **(M) (M) (M) (M) (M)** . . . **H (Q)** where (M) is realized in terms of a series of linearly arranged nouns, occasionally incorporating adjectives as well. The final example comes from legislative provisions, which are notorious for being nominal in character, and display an above-average use of nominalization:

[2] The power to make regulations under this section shall be exercisable by statutory instrument which shall be subject to annulment in pursuance of a resolution of either House of Parliament.
(Ch.25/78: Nuclear Safeguards and Electricity (Finance Act) 1978, UK)

In any other genre, as Swales and Bhatia (1983) point out, this sentence would probably be in its more typical verbal version:

[3] A statutory instrument can be used to make regulations under this section and such a statutory instrument can be annulled if either House of Parliament passes a resolution to that effect.

This type of nominalization is also used in all kinds of academic, particularly scientific research writing, but we shall look at that later on. For the time being, let us consider these three types of nominals and study why they are typically associated with the three genres referred to above. The questions we would like to ask ourselves would be of the following kind:

- Why do the specialist writers of these genres use nominal compounds the way they do?
- To what extent do these nominals serve genre-specific functions?
- What aspects of specialist communication do they textualize in individual genres?

In order to answer some or all of these questions, we need to look at these texts, taking a genre perspective as defined in the introductory section.

First, the case of advertising. The main communicative purpose of advertising is to promote a particular product or service to a specific group of potential customers. In one of the major types of advertisement, this is done by an adequately attractive description of the product or service, which is positive and convincing (see Bhatia and Tay, 1987). Some form of product-detailing is necessary if the consumer is to be persuaded to buy the product or use the service. The following are a few typical examples of such a product description:

[4] All these Sensor technologies combine to give your individual face a personalized shave – the closest, smoothest, safest, and most comfortable.

[5] Most important, you can have this scientific advance without compromising looks or luxury features. This unique power plant delivers its high performance wrapped in a sculptured body that turns science into art.

[6] If this sounds like a smart system, consider the brains behind it. Or more accurately, the lateral and longitudinal G-force sensors along with vehicle height sensors. These devices measure the typical float, roll, dive and squat characteristics a road puts a car through and then instantaneously tells hydraulic actuators to counter these forces.

These are some of the typical examples of product-detailing in advertising. In fact, the most striking linguistic feature of the text is its use of complex nominal phrases. The examples display an overwhelming use of long and complex nominal compounds full of adjectival attributes positively evaluating the detailed descriptive account of the product being promoted. Obviously, the use of complex nominal compounds makes available to the copywriter a number of syntactic slots in which to insert suitable modifiers to accomplish the right kind of product-detailing.

Let me now turn to academic scientific genres. As I mentioned earlier, scientific writing displays a range of nominal expressions used for a variety of purposes. In fact, the nominal phrase is the main carrier of information in academic scientific writing. Compound nominal phrases, nominalization and, to a far lesser extent, complex nominal phrases, all are used in academic scientific writing. Let me take the following two examples.

[7] The discrete donor-acceptor pair (DAP) emission bands in ZnSe, which are recognized as the P, Q and R series, have been extensively investigated by means of time-resolved photoluminescence (PL) and selective PL excitation measurements.
    (Y. Yamada, I. Kidoguchi, T. Taguchi and A. Hiraki, 1989, L837)

One of the major concerns of scientific research writing, as we all know, is to communicate very specialized and precise knowledge to an audience, who would seem to share with the writer the required level of knowledge of the subject-discipline. In order to communicate their specialist knowledge, scientists constantly need to refer to technical concepts like:

The discrete donor-acceptor pair (DAP) emission bands in ZnSe, which are recognized as the P, Q and R series
and
time-resolved photoluminescence (PL) and selective PL excitation measurements

But they also create new terms for new concepts, as in the following extracts of a research article:

[8]

LASER GLAZING OF SPRAYED METAL COATINGS

I. Introduction

The high power density of lasers permits the surface melting of many materials in a time during which negligible heat conduction occurs to the substrate. The resulting sharp temperature gradients cause rapid quench

LASER GLAZING OF SPRAYED METAL COATINGS *continued*

rates which have been utilized for the production of novel and useful metallurgical microstructures.

We have employed for another purpose the ability of *laser melting* to maintain *low substrate temperatures* while fusing a thin surface layer. It is often desirable to impart certain physical or chemical properties of one relatively expensive material to a less expensive substrate by applying a thin coating of the former to the latter. In particular, we wished to apply a thin layer of titanium to a graphite substrate. . .

Scanning the surface with a laser effectively cauterized the microporosity in the upper half of the titanium coating without causing titanium carbide formation at the titanium/graphite interface. . .

II. Surface

The preglazed surface consisted of a graphite substrate onto which had been plasma sprayed a titanium coating 50 um thick. . .

III. Laser treatment

The microporosity apparent in Fig.1 renders the titanium coating permeable. If the material is to exhibit the corrosion resistant properties of solid titanium the film must be made impervious by sealing the micro-porosity endemic to plasma-deposited coatings. . .

Determination of the optimum conditions for sealing the microporosity involved varying the energy per unit area, as well as the power per unit area, delivered by the laster . . .

IV. Analysis of treated surface

The effect of laser treating the plasma sprayed surface is graphically depicted in Fig. 2, a cross-sectional photomicrograph of the titanium layer. Figure 3 is an enlargement of a laser treated surface. Comparison with Fig. 1 shows that laser treatment produces a fused skin on the plasma-deposited titanium layer which is smooth and sound. The absence of cracking during the severe thermal cycling caused by the rapid quench rates characteristic of laser melting indicates that the titanium is ductile . . .

V. Conclusions

The rapid quench rates characteristic of laser melting have been successfully exploited to seal the porosity of titanium coatings, plasma sprayed atop graphite substrates, without the formation of titanium carbide . . .

(Pangborn, R.J. and Beaman, D.R., 1980)

This extract illustrates how a scientific writer uses nominal expressions to refer to specialized technical terms, and it also demonstrates how new knowledge is converted into known technical concepts for further reference. In the introductory paragraph of the article the writers refer to the use of lasers for the surface melting of materials and this very knowledge is referred to again in the second paragraph as a new compound nominal phrase *laser melting*. Similarly, the knowledge that there is negligible heat conduction occurring to the substrate is again converted into another compound nominal phrase *low substrate temperatures*. This process of creating new compound nominal phrases to refer to new concepts continues, as and when the authors need to refer to the knowledge of the subject-discipline they have already mentioned. The new compound and complex nominal phrases in this article are the following:

- titanium carbide formation at the titanium/graphite interface. . .
- the titanium coating
- the corrosion resistant properties of solid titanium
- the microporosity endemic to plasma-deposited coatings
- the effect of laser treating the plasma sprayed surface
- a cross-sectional photomicrograph of the titanium layer
- enlargement of a laser treated surface
- the plasma-deposited titanium layer which is smooth and sound
- the rapid quench rates characteristic of laser melting

In the concluding section of the article, the process is taken to its logical extreme when the authors summarize almost the entire article in terms of a few very complex as well as compound nominal phrases.

The rapid quench rates characteristic of laser melting have been successfully exploited to seal the porosity of titanium coatings, plasma sprayed atop graphite substrates, without the formation of titanium carbide. . .

In academic scientific writing, therefore, the need for compound nominal phrases arises from the fact that the scientific writer must then refer repeatedly to very precise and complex concepts. In order to facilitate concise reference, s/he invariably creates compound nominal phrases, which not only promote discourse coherence but also spare him tedious repetitions of long descriptions.

Of course, good scientific writers are well aware of the difficulties that such compound nominal phrases might pose to their readership, particularly if they do not share the same background knowledge of the subject-discipline at a particular point. Candlin and Loftipour-Saedi (1983) point out

> the production and presentation of W-discourse (writer's discourse) is conditioned by the linear on-going *accumulation principle*. According to this principle each discourse element and its textual presentation at any stage in the on-going process of discourse is premised upon the collection of all the foregoing elements and builds upon it, and each element is produced with full awareness of the foregoing elements. It is as if each element is (in its deep structure) repeating all the previous elements while adding something new to them.
>
> (Candlin and Loftipour-Saedi, 1983)

Dubois (1981) points in the same direction when she argues that a simpler phrase, as in example [9] is more likely to appear at the beginning of the article than the phrase in [8], which is a more difficult compound nominal phrase, and is more suitable for the later parts of the article, where, it is assumed that the reader has acquired the relevant knowledge.

> [9] Studies of the oxidative NADP in enzymes in *Drosophilla melanogaster* have concentrated on the relationship of gene dosage to the in vitro tissue enzyme level and on allelozyme variation.

> [10] *Drosophilla melanogaster oxidative NADP-enzymes studies* have concentrated on the gene dosage
> to *in vitro tissue enzyme level relationship.*

Finally, let me turn to legislative writing, which is notoriously rich in the use of nominals of a third kind, which we have earlier on referred to as **nominalizations**. As already discussed in the previous chapter, legislative writing must be both precise and all-inclusive. Reconciling the two requirements is not always an easy task. One of the many linguistic devices which make this possible is the use of nominalizations, others include the use of qualificational insertions, complex-prepositions, syntactic discontinuities, binomial and multi-nomial expressions (for more details see Bhatia, 1982, 1983b, 1984, 1987 and Swales and Bhatia, 1983).

To illustrate how nominalization is used in legislative provisions, let us look at an example from Singapore's Wills Act (1970).

> [11] No obliteration, interlineation or other alteration made in any will after the execution thereof shall be valid or have effect except so far as the words or effect of the will before such alteration shall not be apparent, unless such alteration shall be executed in like manner as hereinbefore is required for the execution of the will; but the will, with such alteration as part thereof,

shall be deemed to be duly executed if the signature of the testator and the subscription of the witnesses be made in the margin or on some other part of the will opposite or near to such alteration or at the foot or end of or opposite to a memorandum referring to such alteration and written at the end or some other part of the will.
(Section 16 of the Wills Act, 1970, Republic of Singapore)

In this 132-word sentence, there are eleven instances of nominal expressions with five different verbs being nominalized. Of these eleven, there are only two which have been repeatedly used, *execution* twice, and *alteration*, which is the topic of the section, six times. This means that the legislative draftsman uses nominalization for two reasons. First, of course, to refer to the same concept or idea repeatedly and, as in academic and scientific discourse, this promotes coherence and saves the writer from repeating lengthy descriptions. Second, and perhaps more typically, it is a convenient device to refer to as many aspects of human behaviour as required and, at the same time, to be able to incorporate as many qualificational insertions as necessary at various syntactic points in the legislative sentence. The use of nominal rather than verbal elements is likely to provide 'more mileage' for the legislative writer, when one of his main concerns is to be able to cram detail after detail and qualification after qualification in his sentence. It is entirely a different matter that such a highly nominal style is bound to create difficulties for the uninitiated readership in what Halliday calls the 'unpacking' of such expressions. Sometimes, even a seemingly simple and innocent-looking provision like

[12] No will shall be revoked by any presumption of an intention on the ground of an alteration in circumstances.
(Section 14 of the Wills Act, Republic of Singapore)

can make one wonder whether it is the best and the only way of putting it, when one finds that, of the three nominals, at least two, *presumption* and *alteration*, are rarely, if ever, used in everyday discourse.

Although nominals have traditionally been treated as a single entity, particularly for various applied linguistic purposes, and there are good reasons for treating them so for some language-teaching purposes, especially at lower levels, there are equally compelling reasons for treating them as distinct linguistic devices, particularly for more advanced and specialized language-teaching purposes. First, they display not only distinct linguistic forms but also seem to have a very different distribution in academic and professional genres. Second, and more important, they realize somewhat different aspects of the genres in which they are used. The writers of these genres are often led to the use of one or the other of these nominal forms for very different genre-specific considerations. In order to appreciate the full potential of these linguistic forms, one essentially needs to adopt a generic perspective.

In advertising, one often finds an above-average use of complex nominals because the copywriter's main concern is to find as many syntactic slots as possible for adjectival insertions. This facilitates suitably precise, desirably positive and effective description of the product or service being advertised. Scientific research writing predominantly uses compound nominal phrases to refer to concepts that are either created as the discourse proceeds or to refer to further-refined and often-repeated scientific concepts, in which case the use of compound nominal phrases is a convenient linguistic device to create and refer to technical terms. In legislative rules and regulations, one finds an overwhelming use of nominalizations simply because the parliamentary draftsman needs to condense his longish provisions into somewhat more precise, unambiguous and all-inclusive statements by incorporating all types of possible conditions and contingencies that may arise during the course of the interpretation of a particular legislative provision. Nominalization is a very ancient and trusted linguistic device used by the legal expert to achieve condensation and all-inclusiveness in his writing.

The analysis of nominal use, presented here, has strong implications for many applied linguistic purposes, particularly for ESL, ESP and the teaching of professional and academic writing. Grammar has long been an integral part of our language-teaching programmes. In earlier days our approach was invariably prescriptive. With the availability of various linguistic descriptions of language, we introduced an important element of description. Since the advent of discourse and genre analysis in recent years, language-teaching programmes have needed to become more explanatory, so that the learner understands why s/he should write an essay or academic or professional text in a particular way. This will also make for better awareness of the rationale of the text-genre that s/he is required to read or write. After all, the most important function of learning is not simply to be able to read and produce a piece of text as a computer does, but to become sensitive to the conventions, in order to ensure the pragmatic success of the text in the academic or the professional context in which it is likely to be used. The explanation for the use of nominal expressions of various kinds (and perhaps also for a number of other areas of grammar) comes not so much from the general grammar of English as from the grammar of the genre in which they regularly occur. In other words, these features of grammar carry genre-specific restricted values rather than general grammatical values. The teaching of general grammar, therefore, has very little role to play in ESP. In fact, it is not only counter-productive to teach grammar, as such, but inaccurate too. The explanation for the use of any aspect of syntax in ESP comes from the analysis and understanding of the genre in which it is conventionally used.

6.2 Genre-based language curriculum – the case of English in newspapers

The teaching and learning of English in many parts of the world, especially where it is taught as a second language, continues to be teacher-based. The curriculum is determined and designed by language planners and teachers as part of a formal system. Although learning a language goes well beyond the limits of any academic curriculum and becomes a lifelong process which extends further than institutionalized goals or objectives, learners are rarely called upon to play any significant role in it. A genre-based flexible language curriculum can facilitate language learning within, across and beyond the confines of a curriculum, which will allow more freedom to the participants in the teaching and learning process. This can be effectively realized by using a daily newspaper, which is easily available and also contains a wide variety of genres and sub-genres that can enrich the linguistic repertoire of any language learner.

The language of newspapers is a rich source of linguistic data which can be exploited for ESP/ESL courses. However, there are some serious constraints which must be looked into before making any curriculum decisions. One of the things that make newspapers attractive for language-teaching purposes is the wide variety of genres that one finds in them. These include headlines, news reports, sports reports, editorials, feature articles, comments, letters to the editor, classified advertisements, reviews, book reviews, weather and ordinary reports, and fashion columns. The news reports cover a very wide range of topics, including accidents and disasters, crimes and the police beat, court cases, politics, matters related to consumers, financial and business matters, sports. There are also articles on every subject under the sun, including arts and leisure, personal investing, travel, real estate, coins, films, fashion, food, gardens, home design, music, stamps, television and radio programmes, theatre. A reasonable selection from such a wide variety of genres and topics can motivate a wide variety of language learners. But the greatest attraction in newspaper writing comes from its appeal to a general audience, unlike many other types of written discourse, which are generally aimed at relatively small, well-defined, homogeneous groups of like-minded people. Most other forms of discourse require specific expertise and are relatively difficult to understand because they are written for a selective and specialist audience.

Newspaper writing generally combines the virtues of standard language use, which is internationally recognized, and of a typical national variety. It represents an internationally recognized and understood variety of language and yet maintains local flavour, both of which ought to be valued very highly in most language-development programmes. The use of newspaper language as input to language-teaching materials is less likely to create problems of cultural bias which otherwise crop up so often in most second-language learning situations.

Newspapers also present the use of language which is fresh, topical and current. Every day we get fresh linguistic data on different topics. Once the principles are understood and agreed upon, language developers and teachers can afford to be more innovative, and use fresh and varied linguistic data while still remaining within the bounds of a specific curriculum. This can also help the teacher to preserve human interest and motivation in his or her teaching programme because s/he will not have to use the same linguistic input year after year in English lessons. Newspapers have not been fully exploited for this purpose, although there have been quite a few articles on using newspapers in language teaching. It is possible to use this source for EGP (English for General Purposes), EAP (English for Academic Purposes) and ESP (English for Specific Purposes); it is equally good for use across, as well as beyond, the curriculum.

Let me now refer to some of the problems. The wide variety of genres in newspapers can also be a disadvantage in that each genre serves a distinct communicative purpose, and thus represents a particular type of English. If these generic distinctions are not handled properly, the learner may get a misleading picture of the use of language for different communicative purposes. Genre distinctions in newspapers are so very significantly used that sometimes they can be very prominently and significantly practised even at the level of a sub-genre. Let me take a very simple example from newspaper writing. We all know that sports activities are not reported the same way as news reports on other pages of the newspaper. Lexis and certain syntactic devices are used differently, although the two share to a large extent the regularities of discourse organization. Although the general purpose of communication is not very different in the two types of report, some aspects of linguistic resources used are significantly different. Let me take up the following two instances, one is the front page news report and the other (p. 160) a sports page report of the same sporting event.

[13]

Holmes loses his title and calls it quits

ONE piece of history was made, and another denied, when 29-year-old Michael Spinks became the new world heavyweight boxing champion in Las Vegas yesterday.

Spinks is the first light-heavyweight champion to win the heavyweight title. He ended the seven-year-reign of Lary Holmes on a unanimous 15 rounds points decision.

In his 49th fight, the 35-year-old Holmes had been attempting to equal the unbeaten record of Rocky Marciano, but he has now decided to retire.

"I am going to quit. I don't need no more boxing," he said. "It would probably have been my last fight even if I had won because the symptoms were starting to show."

Spinks, who was a 5–1 underdog according to the Las Vegas bookmakers,

succeeded where nine other light-heavyweight challengers had failed. Despite conceding 9.7 kg he carried the fight to the tiring champion and won a close but narrow decision.

He now joins his elder brother Leon as the only two brothers to hold the world heavyweight title. Leon, like Michael, a former Olympic champion, defeated Muhammad Ali in a similar upset in 1978, also in Las Vegas.

"I knew I could do it," said an exuberant Spinks. "If you don't try you don't succeed in life."

Holmes earned US$3 million (S$6.6 million) for the fight and Spinks US$1.5 million. It was telecast live around the world, and Singapore viewers saiw it on RTM 1.

• Full report and Alan Hubbard's view: Page 25

(From the *Straits Times*, 23 September, 1985)

These reports of the same event, one on the front page and the other on the sports page, seem to represent the two very closely related sub-genres of news reporting. Although both of them use roughly the same discourse structure to organize the message, they differ significantly in terms of vocabulary, and also in the way popular explanation has been brought in to add 'colour' to the second one. The headlines in the

[14]

Spinks sinks the Holmes dream

MICHAEL SPINKS denied Larry Holmes a share of boxing immortality when he scored a stunning, unanimous 15-round decision to become the first light-heavyweight to win a heavyweight world title.

In his 28th consecutive victory, Spinks thwarted the 35-year-old Inter-national Boxing Federation title-holder's bid on the late Rocky Marciano's record of 49 fights straight without loss.

A 5-1 underdog, the unorthodox Spinks achieved his unprecedented feat by landing the more effective blows and waging a more aggressive fight before a capacity crowd of more than 11,000 at the Riveria Hotel.

LAS VEGAS, Sun.

Spinks, 29, succeeded where nine other light-heavyweights have failed over the past 78 years, surpassing the feat of his heavyweight brother Leon in upsetting Muhammad Ali seven years ago.

Holmes, who out-weighed his opponent by 10 kilograms, stalked Spinks throughout the bout, vainly seeking an opening for a knockout.

Asked if he would continue to fight, Holmes said: "No. I've got nothing to prove. I'll go home and take care of business."

But he wasn't hiding his disappointment. "You think about it and it takes something out of you . You fought hard for 18 years and still you don't get the respect , the reputation you deserve."

The last round proved decisive, Spinks winning it on the cards of two of the three judges even though he spent most of the round retreating.

Two judges gave Spinks a 143–142 scoring edge in the bout, and the third judge had Spinks ahead 145–142.

Holmes earned US$3.5 million ($7.7 million) and Spinks, who will have to relinquish his undisputed light heavyweight crown, received US$1.1 million.

In aother fight here, Bernard Benton, of the United States, became the World Boxing Council cruiserweight champion by beating fellow-American Alfonzo Ratliff over 12 rounds.

In the curtain raiser to the main event, Julio Cesar Chavez, of Mexico, retained his WBC junior-lightweight title when he outpointed Dwight Pratchett, of the United States, over 12 rounds. – Reuter, AFP.

Computer backs judges

LAS VEGAS, Sun. – **A computer agreed with the judges' view that Michael Spinks beat Larry Holmes fairly and squarely.**

The computer, set up by an American cable television network, counted punches that connected and attempted blows that missed.

It recorded that Spinks made 697 attempts to hit his opponent, of which 318 hit Holmes on the head or body.

Holmes unleashed only 567 would-be punches, of which 248 struck Spinks and 319 ended in thin air, according to the computer. – AFP.

(From the *Straits Times*, 23 September, 1985)

two reports present an interesting contrast; in the news report Holmes simply 'loses his title', whereas on the sports page it becomes more spectacular when 'Spinks sinks the Holmes dream'. Further, in the news report, 'Spinks, who was a 5–1 underdog according to the Las Vegas bookmakers, succeeded . . .', whereas in the spectacular and certainly more colourful sports reporting, the reporter adds, 'A 5–1 underdog, the unorthodox Spinks achieved his unprecedented feat by landing the more effective blows and waging a more aggressive fight. . . .'. Genre specificity, thus, within the pages of newspapers is so significant that any attempt to use newspaper language without being aware of it can become misleading. In other words, if the learner is not made sensitive to genre distinctions, then the very strength of newspaper language can become its weakness. Let us now take two more instances (pp. 162–4) of newspaper English, this time representing two different genres, news reporting and a lead article.

In the first excerpt, the purpose of the reporter is to bring the news to readers as accurately and dispassionately as possible. Newspaper reports generally are short, fresh and direct. They have something specific and precise to tell. The reporter takes the reader directly to the heart of the event, and the linguistic resources generally serve that purpose. Notice how the reporter in example [15] has used what is known as the verbal style:

Tass . . . accused the White House . . .

The Agency . . . claimed the move had been forced on him . . .

Tass said President Reagan had accused the Kremlin . . .

This kind of objective reporting with explicit source specifications is an excellent instance of what might be referred to as 'the language of doing'. On the other hand, the first sentence of the next excerpt begins with a rather longish nominalization,

> The President's announcement last Tuesday that he will no longer be bound by the second strategic arms limitation treaty and would violate one of its central provisions later this year if the Soviet Union does not make "radical changes" in its behaviour

and is equated with another noun phrase in the sentence *his most serious mistake* by the verb phrase *may be judged as*. This process of condensing ideas (particularly those assumed by the writer to be

[15]

Moscow says US lied on Salt 2

From Christopher Walker
Moscow

Tass, the official Soviet news agency, yesterday accused the White House of resorting to "a pile of lies" in an attempt to justify breaking the unratified Salt 2 nuclear arms limitation treaty.

The agency, giving the first official reaction to President Reagan's decision to dismantle two Poseidon submarines and stay for the moment within Salt 2 limits, claimed the move had been forced on him by public opinion.

"The White House's decision is a forced step," Tass said. "It has been taken under the powerful pressure of the US and international community demanding that the Soviet–US accords in the field of control over armaments be observed and the sliding of the world to a nuclear disaster be stopped."

Tass said President Reagan had accused the Kremlin of violating existing arms control agreements. "It goes without saying that these accusations were not backed up by a single fact," the agency said.

Senior Western observers described the criticism as perfunctory and mild and noted that it had taken a long time to appear, indicating that Moscow may be hoping that the second part of Washington's threat to breach the treaty in December may be averted by the second Reagan–Gorbachov summit, which is expected to take place around then.

Tass recalled that the US had declared in May 1982 that it would not take any action to break the treaty, which was originally signed by former President Jimmy Carter, and the late Mr Leonid Brezhnev. It alleged that the purpose of the new moves was to evade the strict limitations on strategic missiles imposed by the treaty and leave the US freedom of manoeuvre to gain military superiority.

"The latest decision of the White House regarding the Salt 2 treaty can be assessed as a demand by Washington for the unilateral right, unprecedented in international practice, to throw out some provisions of a treaty and temporarily retain others," wrote Mr Vladimir Bogachov, a leading military analyst.

● WARSAW: Poland and Czechoslovakia yesterday accused the US of seeking military superiority over the Soviet Union since their encouraging summit meeting in Geneva last November. President Husak of Czechoslovakia and General Jaruzelski, the Polish leader, condemned US air attacks on Libya last month and accused Washington of aggravating tension and conflict in various parts of the world.

The breakdown, page 6
Leading article, page 11

(From *The Times*, London, 29 May, 1986)

[16]

Why Mr. Reagan Blundered on SALT

By Albert Gore Jr.

GENEVA – The President's announcement last Tuesday that we will no longer be bound by the second strategic arms limitation treaty _ and would violate one of its central provisions later this year if the Soviet Union does not make "radical changes" in its behavior _ may be judged by history as his most serious mistake. Both in its substance and in the manner in which it was made, this decision illustrates the Reagan Administration's ambivalence about arms control and its deep confusion about our nation's strategic goals. The President is justified in condemning Moscow's violations of existing arms control agreements. But his proposed remedy would hurt us far more than it would hurt the Russians and would greatly increase the danger to both nations.

To begin with, the Soviet Union now has four "hot" production lines for making intercontinental ballistic missiles and can quickly expand the number of warheads on its already deployed SS-18 heavy missiles. By contrast, we have one "lukewarm" production line and no real ability to quickly increase the number of warheads we have deployed.

Second, if both countries continue to respect the treaty, the Russians will have to dismantle and destroy far more launchers than we will in the next several years. Indeed, Moscow has already destroyed more than 1,000 missiles in order to comply with SALT restrictions, while we have had to destroy fewer than 100.

Third, the Soviet leadership does not need a political consensus to assign top budget priority to its military or to produce and deploy new weapons. As a self-governing people, we do require such a consensus. This decision will itself make that already difficult process even more difficult. The new fiscal constraints of the Gramm-Rudman-Hollings balanced-budget law will further complicate

our ability to engage in an accelerated arms race with the Soviet Union.

Fourth, we are part of a strategic alliance with truly independent partners, while Moscow's Warsaw Pact allies are really subservient puppets. The abandonment of SALT II has already meant new strains for the North Atlantic Treaty Organization.

Fifth, the decision is based on what may be a tragic miscalculation of the Soviet Union's most likely response. Instead of making the "radical changes" that President Reagan has demanded of them, the Russians may well see the lifting of the SALT II limitations, coupled with an aggressive American effort to build missile defense systems, as a simple one-word message: "Build!" _ build offensive missiles and build them fast.

But what about Soviet noncompliance? Don't we have an obligation to hold the Russians accountable? They have deliberately impeded our efforts to verify their compliance with SALT II by heavily encrypting, or encoding, information from their missile tests. They have developed two new types of missiles instead of the one permitted by the treaty. And they have brazenly violated the Anti-Ballistic Missile Treaty's restrictions by building a new defensive radar at Krasnoyarsk, in central Siberia.

These three violations clearly call for a response in actions as well as words. Luckily, there are alternatives to the abandonment of SALT II. We can, for example, go forward with our plans to deploy our own new single-warhead mobile missile as a "proportionate response" to its Soviet counterpart, the SS-25. We can increase the number of "penetration aids" carried by missiles targeted in the vicinity of the Krasnoyarsk radar in order to eliminate whatever military advantage comes from its inland location.

His proposed remedy would hurt us more than the Russians – and endanger both nations

Albert Gore Jr., Democrat of Tennessee, is a member of the Senate Arms Control Observer Group.

(From the *New York Times*, 1 June, 1986)

Continued overleaf

[16] *continued*

There are alternatives to scrapping it

Solutions for the data-encrypting problem are more difficult to find. Nevertheless, the changes required of the Russians in this area may not turn out to be "radical," and a meaningful change could produce a very significant result. Some people close to President Reagan are convinced that an end to encrypting of missile tests would greatly improve his basic view of Soviet motives.

For our own part, we should consider what changes in our behavior might contribute to the kind of strategic outcome the Administration says it wants. After all, we have failed to ratify the last three treaties we signed with the Russians. And President Reagan has called into question the ABM treaty with what many believe is a preposterous reinterpretation of one of its important provisions governing new and exotic defensive systems.

The President has wisely abandoned the reckless rhetoric of his first two years in office, but serious doubts remain about his basic goal in our relationship with the Soviet Union. What he must clarify most of all - in his own mind and in his policies - is whether or not we really want to establish a working relationship with the Russians that relieves the enormous pressure we are now placing on them and they on us. Do we or do we not really want stability in our nuclear relationship with Moscow?

Some of the President's key advisers seem genuinely to believe that the basic character and motivation of the Soviet regime make it impossible to work out a useful modus vivendi - that all such efforts, of which arms control is the most important, merely serve to constrain us, while the Russians press on toward global domination. In this view, we can emerge free and secure from our competition with the Russians only if their system is somehow transformed by external and internal stresses. From this perspective, arms control - with its promise of diminished competition and risk - only eases pressures on the Soviet Union and is therefore inherently undesirable.

According to this view, our tack, though unstated goal must be to re-establish some form of strategic superiority. It happens to be politically unfeasible to accomplish this by beating the Russians in an offensive arms race. So hardliners now seek to achieve it through another means - a version of the Strategic Defense Initiative quite different from what the President originally proposed.

The President still speaks of the S.D.I. as a comprehensive defense that will replace our dependence on classical deterrence - the threat of retaliation against a Soviet attack. But many in his Administration define S.D.I. as a limited defense of our retaliatory missiles that will enhance rather than replace deterrence. While the President still envisions a "cost-effective and invulnerable" defensive system to be jointly deployed by us and the Soviet Union - cooperation orchestrated through arms control - his Secretary of Defense is designing a quick and dirty system to be deployed as rapidly as possible without regard to cost effectiveness or Soviet cooperation.

We must clear up this confusion in our strategic goals and our methods of pursuing them. The next few months will be an especially critical period - particularly dangerous but also an opportunity for a breakthrough. The possible convergence in early December of a second summit meeting and the scheduled reconsideration of SALT II makes it imperative for both superpowers to reassess their goals and practices.

A plausible agreement would include an American decision not to undercut SALT II; a decision by Moscow to reduce its encrypting; an agreement on a genuine and fair 50 percent reduction in strategic offensive forces; a moratorium, of a decade or more, on actual deployment of strategic defenses; and an agreement to redefine key imprecise terms in the ABM Treaty.

Such an agreement may be accessible and acceptable to both countries if the proper decisions are made between now and early December.

shared knowledge) in the form of complex nominals or nominalizations is very characteristic of advanced academic writing. Halliday (1986) refers to this phenomenon as grammatical metaphor, and associates it with the language of thinking. The use of this linguistic phenomenon is quite common and appropriate in a genre in which the writer argues persuasively to offer views and opinions that he holds or believes in. He takes a specific position with regard to events around him or issues that may be political, economic, socio-cultural or any other, and tries to justify his point of view. This phenomenon is found in certain types of persuasive academic writing too. Even the discourse strategies and the finally emerging discourse regularities in such lead articles and editorials have a lot in common with what we are very likely to find in many academic essays. They typically seem to have the following four-part cognitive structure.

1. PRESENTING THE CASE, which concerns actual events, i.e., what is or what was in the world of everyday events. It may be seen as framing issues, clarifying choices or defining areas of concern.

2. OFFERING THE ARGUMENT, where the editor discusses the possible alternative worlds, i.e., what was not or what might have been and can be seen in terms of Kinneavy's (1971) confutation and confirmation.

3. REACHING THE VERDICT, which concerns the world of desired events, i.e., what should be or what should have been and is generally seen as the writer's conclusion.

4. RECOMMENDING ACTION, where the writer is seen as suggesting how the desired world of events can be realized.

The discourse structure of a typical news report, on the other hand, is very characteristic of news reports only. It is very much like an inverted pyramid where the movement from top to bottom represents *general* → *specific*; or, *summary* → *expansion*; or, *preview* → *detail* (see Hoey, 1983). This downward movement also represents the expected decrease in the number of readers. In fact, it can be counter-productive to introduce the ESL learner to news report discourse without making him aware of the pitfalls that lie ahead because it is one of those genres which systematically break the rules of chronological sequencing in narrative, which is valued so very highly in many other genres with which language learners are mostly concerned. So once again, we are likely to run into problems if genre specificity is overlooked. It is true that some genres can give us directly utilizable insights for various types of academic discourse whereas others are likely to be counter-productive in the sense that they may mislead the language learner into believing that technical and business reports are written the same way as the journalist writes his news reports. Or it will be even more misleading if the learner starts making indiscriminate use of news-reporting language with its typical and exclusive lexis (*bid* for *attempt, probe* for *investigation, rap* for *reprimand, row* for *dispute,* or *pact* for *agreement* etc.), outlandish construction of adjectives (*seven-to-ten hour delay, sex-in-air hostess, out-of-court settlement,* etc.), predominant use of verbal style where nominal style is more appropriate, or exclusive *solution → situation → problem → evaluation* information structure, where the unmarked *situation → problem → solution → evaluation* is required. Let me illustrate this by taking the following two examples, one from a news report and the other from a technical report (p. 167):

[17]

Test for bone marrow graft rejection found

SOLUTION / PROBLEM → ←SITUATION→ / PROBLEM→

BOSTON, Fri. – A team of American doctors reported on Wednesday the discovery of a test to determine if a bone marrow transplant will be rejected – a discovery that could dramatically reduce the danger of a powerful yet risky cancer treatment.

Transplanted marrow is used to treat several forms of leukaemia and other diseases in which the marrow is defective.

Although doctors try to check compatibility of donors and recipients, immune cells in the transplanted bone marrow some

←PROBLEM / ←EVALUATION

times launch a deadly attack on all the other cells.

The condition, called graft-versus-host disease, is exactly the opposite of the problem that plagues conventional transplant patients.

The new test, developed by researchers at Baltimore's Johns Hopkins University and reported in the latest New England Journal of Medicine, was evaluated on 32 patients scheduled to receive bone marrow transplants. – Reuter.

(From the *Straits Times*)

[18]

When small printed circuits boards or microcircuits etc. are exposed, in service, to vibration and "rough handling" etc., they are prone to many failings. These include the actual components becoming separated from the boards themselves, or even the cracking of the boards. The most common situation where this occurs is the case of a missile. The "rough handling" in this case is the acceleration as the missile is launched. Obviously it would be useless if such an important component was lost from the firing circuit of the missile and all the money involved in the manufacturing and launching would have been spent without obtaining results.	**Situation**

The question is, of course, how can this situation be avoided? Not only do we have the possibility of circuits failing when components actually fall off. There is also the case of components moving and "shorting" against one another. Printed circuit boards are a convenient method of manufacturing in large numbers, they are also very compact, but the situation has to be avoided somehow in order to continue in their use. **Problem**

An answer is found in encapsulation, or potting of the circuit. Here, a mould is required of a convenient shape. The complete circuit board is then mounted inside the mould and the latter fitted with a material such as an epoxy resin. This fills the spaces between the components, the linking wires, and when the resin has "gone off", the circuit is like one solid brick. Obviously wires may be left protruding as required for connection purposes. **Solution**

The resulting block may be mounted using GNOME fixing methods and the problem of boards cracking and components moving no longer arises. Epoxy resins are comparatively light and therefore do not affect the height of the complete system to any great extent. There are new costs involved to the manufacturer, i.e., mould tools etc., but these may be justified as the desired result is obtained. The shape of the mould may be varied to not only encapsulate the material but also to incorporate mounting facilities. This encapsulation also has the advantage that dirt and dust is excluded from the circuit. **Evaluation**

A student example reported in Winter (1976)

Winter (1976) has referred to several alternatives to this standard *situation → problem → solution → evaluation* pattern and some of these are *situation → problem → evaluation*; *situation → evaluation*; but *solution → situation → problem → evaluation* is exclusive only to news reports because it is only in them that the journalist starts with the freshest information at the top. It is necessary to make the learner aware of generic distinctions in the language of newspapers so that s/he can not only distinguish discourse organization of news reports from that of editorials but account for such distinctions, too.

Coming to the exploitation of English in newspapers, there seem to be three main areas of pedagogical application. In the case of English-language awareness courses, where the primary concern is to make the learner familiar with a range of genres of English and not to prepare him to make use of this language to pursue his academic courses, such an awareness of language use will certainly extend beyond the university curriculum. This situation is not radically different from English for General Purposes (EGP). The second major area of application is English for Academic Purposes (EAP) where the learner needs to be proficient in the range of academic English either for receptive or productive use, or both, and in this case the learning of language is more specifically controlled by an existing curriculum. The third might be an ESP (English for Specific Purposes, Academic or Occupational) situation, where the aim definitely is to prepare learners for specific tasks associated with the teaching/learning of journalism.

In EGP courses teaching/learning is neither strictly controlled by any subject curriculum nor by any specific purpose. In such programmes, it is advantageous for the learner to be made aware of a large variety of functional genres, particularly those s/he is likely to continue to read after his or her formal education. In fact, it will develop awareness and interest in reading English through newspapers, which will certainly help his or her English education beyond the curriculum stage.

In the second case, where teaching and learning of English serves an academic purpose, sensitivity to genre specificity is likely to be more crucial because newspaper English will have to be used as a tool to master other academic varieties of the language. To what extent this will be possible depends largely on the selection of genres used as input to language-development courses, and, more importantly, on what tasks are set on such a selection. In principle, it is possible to use even news reports for teaching academic writing, provided the tasks are relevant to the academic purpose in question. It is relatively less important to select the right genre but more important to set the right tasks on what one may have selected. Let me illustrate this with the help of the following example of the news report.

[19]

Washington set to 'go bust' on Oct 15

Unless debt ceiling is raised to $4,000 b, warns Treasury

WASHINGTON, Wed. – The Treasury Department has said the government will run out of money next month unless Congress raises the ceiling on the federal debt to a new high of more than US$2,000 billion (S$4,000 billion).

Without a US$255 billion increase to a record US$2,078 billion, the government's bank account will run into the red on Oct 15, acting Assistant Treasury Secretary John Niehenke told a Senate finance subcommittee hearing yesterday.

"The word for that would be bankrupt," Senator Daniel Moynihan said.

He noted that the national debt has doubled in slightly less than five years.

"It took 189 years to reach a trillion (a thousand billion)," subcommittee chairman John Chafee said.

The Treasury Department also asked to be allowed to sell another US$50 billion in long-term bonds without regard to a legal interest payment limit of 4 per cent. It would prefer that this interest limit be abolished.

The increase in long-term bonds to US$250 billion and the debt limit increase should carry government financing needs through the year starting Oct 1, Mr Niehenke said.

Senator Steven Symms, a long-time opponent of the routine debt ceiling increases, said he will seek an amendment to prevent the government from spending more money than it takes in tax revenue.

"We're in a (spending) crisis," Mr Symms said. He explained that the current debt is costing each American US$650 annually, a figure that will rise to US$1,000 by 1990 at current rates.

Congressional sources said this amendment has little chance of passage.

The committee is to vote next week and Senate action is expected late this month.

Senate leaders have said Senate approval of the Bill will come after a long debate. – Reuter, UPI.

(From the *Straits Times*)

Here we have a news report on the problem of overdraft by the US government, which can be of interest to those studying economics, law or even political science. One of the things that makes this particular text suitable for a newspaper is the presence of what Kinneavy (1971) calls the 'surprise value'. And this, to a large extent, governs the typical discourse organization of this news report. The item that carries the highest surprise value has been chosen as the headline, and is further elaborated in what in the newspaper world is known as the 'lead' or 'intro'. Any explanatory, background, or secondary materials, follow in that order. This principle of organization gives news reports the structure of an inverted pyramid in which the most important points of the story are given first, and the remainder of the story gives the items in decreasing order of importance and increasing order of finer detail. The lexico-grammatical system uses typical lexis, that is generally associated with newspaper language, particularly the use of 'go bust', 'debt ceiling', 'a US $255 billion increase to a record US $2.087 billion'. This is done to further reinforce the element of surprise value, adding at the same time factuality and some degree of comprehensiveness to the news story. The use of specialist lexis, i.e., economic vocabulary – in this case, 'debt ceiling', 'long-term bond', 'a legal interest payment', 'the routine debt ceiling increases' – is a good instance of role borrowing where lexis from business and economics has been used to add factuality to the news report. Similarly, the use of numbers and quotes from acknowledged sources is not simply to present evidence for what the reporter is claiming but for objectivity, and to signal the writer's withdrawal.

In order to use such a news report for an EAP purpose, i.e., to enable the learner to write a short academic assignment on the status of US overdraft position, we might set a task which teaches the learner to play down the role of surprise value and to play up the role of factuality and comprehensiveness. The lexico-grammatical and discourse features that are selected for more elaborate treatment (particularly the use of technical lexis, nominal against the verbal style, different discourse organization, etc.) should also make this distinction clear. This kind of transformation exercise will not only make the learner more sensitive to the newspaper genre but also help him or her to differentiate it from other academic genres.

Let me now take one final example (p. 171), this time from an editorial, to suggest how we can exploit it for EAP courses.

The editorial page of a newspaper is radically different from the rest of the paper; whereas the other pages are dedicated to reporting news as accurately and dispassionately as possible, the editorial page offers views and opinions of the newspaper. The editorial is generally regarded as the newspaper's analysis, discussion, opinion or verdict on the issues of the day. Unlike news reports, editorials are written to provoke some reaction by expressing a strong opinion. The most significant aspect of this genre is the way the editorial writer makes use of linguistic resources to create favourable or unfavourable bias in his

[20]

The Straits Times says

Unwarranted and inequitable

AN attempt by the US Congress to rein in the United Nations by the purse-string has, quite unnecessarily, added another contentious issue to the many divisive ones on the agenda as the General Assembly convenes its 40th sessions this week. A bill passed by Congress last month threatens to cut the US contribution to the UN from the current 25 per cent to 20 per cent, unless voting in the assembly on budgetary matters is weighted according to member states' contributions, thus effectively giving the US a veto over the UN budget.

Congress's action is obviously prompted more by disenchantment due to a loss of US influence at the UN in recent years than by concern over alleged fiscal profligacy by the world organisation. Although the US pays the biggest single proportion of the budget as determined according to a formula that takes into account a state's gross national product and population size, the absolute amount is estimated to be less than what its citizens spend on pet food every year. The 5 per cent certainly would not enable the Reagan administration to balance the US budget.

The UN, on the other hand, has not been deaf to warnings since the 1973 oil crisis to curb its spending. Few new posts have been created, and recruitment has largely been limited to filling vacancies arising from resignation, retirement or death. It has been difficult, however, to trim the budget, as the membership has more than trebled since the founding of the UN in 1945, and there are increasing requirements for conference, printing, translation and other facilities and ser-

vices. Because almost all the newer member states are from the relatively less developed South, there is also a need to spend more on administering social and economic programmes, of which the UN can justifiably be proud, even if it cannot claim credit for defusing tensions that relate more directly to immediate political and security problems.

If the US feels that, given the increase in membership, there should be a more even sharing of the budget, it should make its case on the basis of accepted criteria such as national income and population. The previous reduction of the US contribution rate, after all, was made largely on that basis. The present threat therefore appears to be unsubstantiated and has obviously been made to bolster the demand for what amounts to a veto over the budget. The move begs the question whether Congress now feels that the political returns to the US contribution to the UN have diminished and have to be restored by budgetary manipulation.

Even more objectionable is the violence the US threat of weighted voting, if not resisted, would do to the one-state one-vote principle on which the General Assembly is founded. That principle was allowed by the framers of the UN Charter, the majority of whom were the victorious Western states of World War II, in return for which the five big powers were given the veto as permanent members of the Security Council. Congress only betrays the democratic ideal on which it is itself founded if it tries to set such an unwarranted and inequitable precedent in the General Assembly. President Reagan should veto Congress's attempt to veto the world.

(From the *Straits Times*)

arguments. In editorial [20] we find a typical four-move discourse structure: **case, argument, verdict, action**. It is interesting to note how each move is signalled in each paragraph, particularly **offering the argument**, against the Congress's action and for the UN, which has been signalled as the topic in the opening sentences. Also interesting is the way a shift in tense pattern in **reaching the verdict** and in **recommending the action** has been used as a signal to refer to the world of desirable events. All this signalling is closely related to the communicative purpose of the genre which this particular text illustrates. Since the editorial expresses a strong opinion against the action of the US Congress, it is interesting to see how the writer selects linguistic resources to realize favourable or unfavourable bias. Opinion has been expressed in no uncertain terms in the headline **Unwarranted and inequitable**. In the editorial, this bias against the attempt on the part of US Congress to block US contribution to UN budget has been realized and reinforced by a careful selection of lexis. Lexical selection can work in a number of ways. In example [14], discussed earlier, lexical selection was very cleverly used to add colour to reports on sports, turning them from matter-of-fact reports into popular explanation. In the present editorial there is a very subtle use of lexical selection which helps the writer to achieve favourable or unfavourable bias, favourable to the UN and unfavourable to the US Congress. The following expressions make the point clear:

Unfavourable bias towards the US Congress:

- An attempt by the US Congress to rein in the United Nations by purse-string
- A bill passed by Congress ... threatens to cut the US contribution
- Even more objectionable is the violence the US threat of weighted voting, if not resisted, would do to the one-state one-vote principle on which the General Assembly is founded
- Congress betrays the democratic ideal

Favourable bias towards the UN:

- The UN, on the other hand, has not been deaf to warnings
- It has been difficult, however, to trim the budget

- There is also a need to spend more on administering social and economic programmes, of which the UN can justifiably be proud

The other important aspect of this editorial is the use of nominal expressions, which refer to the concepts that are either taken as part of shared knowledge or assumed to be given in the prior discourse, i.e., news reports on which the editorial is based or certain parts of this same editorial. Genre analysis allows one to rationalize what aspects of a particular genre are textualized by some of these grammatical resources. Some of these linguistic devices are used in other genres too, especially where the communicative purposes overlap, and it is these areas of overlap which should motivate language teachers to exploit a variety of genres for a better understanding of language. However, inadequate sensitivity to genre specificity can reduce the effectiveness of the learning experience.

As for ESP, the importance of newspaper English can hardly be overstated. If the learner has to acquire the ability to operate successfully in journalism, either in an academic or professional setting, s/he must be sensitized to most of the genres that s/he will eventually be operating in (see Bhatia, 1983b and 1986 for a detailed discussion of this issue). Any indirect means of achieving this will only make the process more difficult.

To sum up, newspaper English has great potential as input to materials design programmes. It is attractive because of its variety and accessibility, international acceptability and local flavour. However, its full potential for various language-teaching purposes can be best realized only by looking at this vast resource of linguistic data from the point of view of genre analysis. Failure to sensitize language users to the various genre distinctions might result in ineffective teaching and learning. A genre-based language curriculum facilitates the use of new and varied linguistic input in the language classroom. But for a successful application, there must be a principled generic basis for the curriculum and an understanding of the importance of text-task relationship in order to ensure discourse competence in the language learner. A genre-based language syllabus need not contain a set of preselected texts in the form of a reading anthology. Instead, it may list a set of genres and task-types that can be designed for specific text-genres. Selection of texts for use in the classroom can then be left to the teacher and the learner, depending upon their interest, motivation and purpose. This kind of flexible curriculum will give greater freedom to the learner and the teacher to participate actively in their learning and teaching activities. It will also make the learner more sensitive to the use of language in newspapers for various communicative purposes.

6.3 Text-task relationship in English for legal purposes

The teaching of English for Legal Purposes, whether academic or occupational, has always been guided by pedagogical convenience rather than effectiveness. Since the ESP teacher finds it difficult to deal with complicated authentic legal texts, s/he tends to use either simplified texts or texts of general interest. Crocker (1982:6) confirms this when he admits,

> Although students valued "relevance" in the language course, the prospect of requiring instructors, whose control of English covered the domains of general educated social use, to handle samples of use well outside their normal domains (texts on international law, company contracts, etc.) was sufficient to preclude (matters of principles outside) initiating any task with inspection of a sample of legal text.

Therefore, many of these practising teachers either select general reading material and focus on grammatical form (Crocker, 1982) or select cases from legal casebooks because they 'exhibit discourse which is often simple and the opposite of obscure; and which is therefore accessible to the language student of lower intermediate to higher intermediate level' (Calderbank, 1982:3) and focus on general comprehension exercises. Both strategies turn out to be equally ineffective for legal English courses. A few teachers use legal cases because they find them convenient; however, they rarely use legislative writing as input to their courses simply because they find it extremely complex, and what White (1982) calls 'invisible'. Referring to legislative discourse, White (1982) claims that

> the most serious obstacles to comprehensibility are not the vocabulary and sentence structure employed in the law, but the unstated conventions by which the language operates.

He points out that there are expectations about the way in which language is used in legal settings but such expectations do not find explicit expression anywhere but in the legal culture that the surface language simply assumes. As a consequence of these difficulties, there is a heavy emphasis on the use of cases in legal English courses at the expense of legislative texts. This results in two undesirable consequences. First, legal cases tend to be treated in English courses as narratives, and learners are never given any opportunity to get engaged in the procedural activities or tasks which are relevant to the study of the law. This invariably leads to a lack of appropriate text-task relationship. Second, learners are never given an opportunity to appreciate the essential intertextual relationship between the various genres and the purpose they serve in a variety of legal settings. Legal cases and legislative provisions are complementary to each other. If cases, on the one hand, attempt to interpret legal provisions in terms of the facts of the world, legislative provisions, on the other hand, are attempts to account for the unlimited facts of the world in terms of legal relations. This complementarity of the two genres is evidenced in what de Beaugrande and Dressler (1981) call the **intertextuality** in legal cases, particularly in the richness of elaborate legal argumentation in legal judgments.

This kind of failure to take into account the appropriate text-task relationship in ESP courses can lead to two kinds of problems. First, there is always a danger that an uninitiated teacher of EALP or EOLP is likely to treat these cases as narrative because, in one sense, they do appear to be a narration of events, particularly in the description of the facts of the case. As a legal genre, however, cases are entirely different from traditional narratives. As already discussed in Chapter 5, they have a typical four-move cognitive structure, consisting of **identification of the case**, **description of the facts of the case**, **arguments of the judge** and the **pronouncement of judgment**. The cases differ from ordinary narratives not simply in the way they are structured but also, and perhaps more significantly, in the tasks that law students are required to engage in while handling cases appropriately and adequately. Students are required to study cases because legal decisions are based on the doctrine of precedent, which means that courts follow previous decisions within more or less well-defined limits. The part of the case that is said to possess authority is known as the *ratio decidendi*, which Glanville Williams, a distinguished legal writer, defines as 'the material facts of the case plus the decision thereon' (Williams, 1982:67). On the importance of *ratio decidendi*, he asserts:

Finding the *ratio decidendi* of a case is an important part of the training of a lawyer. It is not a mechanical process but is an art that one gradually acquires through practice and study ... The ascertainment of the *ratio decidendi* of a case depends upon a process of abstraction from a totality of facts that occurred in it. The higher the abstraction, the wider the *ratio decidendi*.

Therefore, a major concern of law students when reading legal cases is not simply to understand them as stories and then to answer comprehension questions on them, but to appreciate which facts of the case are legally material and to distinguish them from those that are legally immaterial, whether an earlier decision or a rule of law is relevant, whether a particular case is distinguishable from another, and to deduce the *ratio decidendi* of the case. The task of the ESP teacher, therefore, is to ensure such an appreciation. Failure to perceive these specialized tasks might lead to confusion on the part of the student and will make his job more difficult. Let me take an example to illustrate this:

[21]

Letang v. *Cooper*

[Court of Appeal (1965) 1 Q.B. 232; (1964) 3 W.L.R. 573; 108 S.J. 519; (1964) 2 Lloyd's Rep. 339; (1964) 2 All E.R. 929

The defendant appealed from a judgment for the plaintiff by Elwes J., who held that the plaintiff's claim was not time-barred [1964] 2 Q.B. 53. The appeal was allowed.

Lord Denning M. R.: On July 10, 1957, the plaintiff was on holiday in Cornwall. She was staying at an hotel and thought she would sunbathe on a piece of grass where cars were parked. While she was lying there the defendant came into the car park driving his Jaguar motor-car. He did not see her. The car went over her legs and she was injured.

On February 2, 1961, more than three years after the accident, the plaintiff brought this action against the defendant for damages for loss and injury caused by (1) negligence of the defendant in driving a motor-car and (2) the commission by the defendant of a trespass to the person.

The sole question is whether the action is statute-barred. The plaintiff admits that the action for negligence is barred after three years, but she claims that the action for trespass to the person is not barred until six years have elapsed. The judge has so held and awarded her $575 damages for trespass to the person.

Under the limitation Act 1939 the period of limitation was six years in

---

Letang v. *Cooper continued*

all actions founded "on tort"; but, in 1954, Parliament reduced it to three years in action for damages for personal injuries, provided that the actions come within these words of section 2(1) of the Land Reform (Limitation of Actions, etc.) Act 1954, "actions for damages for negligence, nuisance or breach of duty (whether the duty exists by virtue of a contract or of a provision made by or under a statute or independently of any contract or any such provision) where the damages claimed by the plaintiff for the negligence, nuisance or breach of duty consist of or include damages in respect of personal injuries to any person".

The plaintiff says that these words do not cover an action for trespass to the person and that therefore the time bar is not the new period of three years, but the old period of six years. ... I must say that if we are, at this distance of time, to revive this distinction between trespass and case, we should get into the most utter confusion.

I must decline, therefore, to go back to old forms of action in order to construe this statute. ... The truth is that the distinction between trespass and case is obsolete. We have a different sub-division altogether. Instead of dividing actions for personal injuries into trespass (direct damage) or case (consequential damage), we divide the causes of action now according as the defendant did the injury intentionally or unintentionally. If one man intentionally applies force directly to another, the plaintiff has a cause of action in assault and battery, or, if you so please to describe it, in trespass to the person. ... If he does not inflict injury intentionally, but only unintentionally, the plaintiff has no cause of action today in trespass. His only cause of action is in negligence, and then only on proof of want of reasonable care. If the plaintiff cannot prove want of reasonable care, he may have no cause of action at all. Thus it is not enough nowadays for the plaintiff to plead that "the defendant shot the plaintiff." He must also allege that he did it intentionally or negligently. If intentional, it is the tort of assault and battery. If negligent and causing damage, it is tort of negligence.

In my judgment, therefore, the only cause of action in the present case, where the injury was unintentional, is negligence and is barred by reason of the express provision of the statute.

This is an interesting case, based on the interpretation of section 2(1) of the Land Reform (Limitation of Actions, etc.) Act 1954, which Lord Denning construes in the light of modern-day interpretation of trespass and negligence. In this case, if one were to bring back old precedents, the judge says, one should produce the most absurd anomalies. In a case like this the reader is not simply trying to understand narrative in the form of case description but also interpreting legislative provisions in order to formulate the *ratio decidendi* of the case, which will be more or less in the following form:

> Any person, who intentionally causes injury to another person, is liable to that other person in trespass

or

> If a person causes injury only unintentionally, then he is not liable in trespass. The person injured has action only in negligence, and it is for that person to prove want of reasonable care.

In following these steps, the EA/OLP learner is required to interpret the world of facts in terms of legal relations, thereby creating a unique world of rights and obligations that we, as members of civilized society, live in. In fact, this process of relating the outside world to the typical world of rules and regulations is the essence of all legal education. These steps may appear to be a simple process of abstracting from the totality of facts to generalize in the form of legal rules, but the way past authorities and established rules of law are interpreted and made relevant by the presiding judge in his judgment makes these cases one of the richest genres in **intertextuality** of the text.

What kinds of tasks are relevant for the learner of ESP on such texts? The cases provide the learner with an opportunity to appreciate how legally-material facts are woven into a rational and reasonable argument, and how they are used to extract a *ratio decidendi*. In doing so, they must be able to distinguish one set of legally material facts from another with obvious surface similarities but some very crucial differences. This also gives an opportunity to the learner to appreciate and interpret legislation in its simplest form in small quantities, as it were. Moreover, the learner will also learn to appreciate and understand the nature of legal reasoning, particularly the way legal authorities, in the form of precedents in earlier cases or legislative provisions, are made relevant and used as evidence for or against a particular point of view. All these skills are vital to the training of apprentice legal professionals. Williams (1982:142) has these very things in mind when talking to law students about examination questions:

> It need hardly be added that the examiner *always* wants reasoning and authorities for the answer, even though he does not expressly ask for them.

At another point, in the same book, on the use of statutory provisions and earlier cases, he points out:

> One of the most important of a lawyer's accomplishments is the ability to resolve facts into their legal categories. The student should therefore take pains to argue in terms of legal rules and concepts. . . When citing cases, the mere giving of the name is of little use. What is wanted is not only the name but a statement of the legal points involved in the decision, and perhaps also a consideration of its standing.
>
> (Williams, 1982:118–119)

Learners need to appreciate the way social justice is negotiated in legal settings. Cases demonstrate the process of legal reasoning and decision-making in law. When using cases as input to ESP courses, it is necessary for an ESP teacher to engage the learner in tasks that ensure an appreciation and understanding of decision-making. However, it is often not realistic to attempt to teach these skills and abilities without the genres through which they are realized. In fact, it is not simply a question of handling one genre but several at the same time because of the essential intertextuality of the legal documents, whether one considers legal cases, legislative provisions or textbooks. None of these genres can be handled adequately in isolation. It is certainly true that legislative provisions are the most complex of all the legal genres, characteristically displaying a kind of cognitive structuring that requires very specific reading and interpreting strategies on the part of the apprentice readers (see Bhatia, 1982). Some of these strategies the learners will have learnt to use while working through legal cases, which make accessible to them the role of preparatory qualifications, especially the way they describe circumstances to which a particular provision becomes applicable (see Bhatia, 1982, and also Chapter 5 of this book). Let us take section 2 (1) of Limitations Act, 1939 as amended by the Law Reform (Limitation of Actions &c.) Act 1954, s. 2(1), a part of which has been used by the judge in the case mentioned above, and see what part the facts of the real world play in the world of legal relations.

[22]   **Limitation of actions of contract and tort,**
and certain other actions

(1) The following actions shall not be brought after the expiration of six years from the date on which the cause of action accrued, that is to say: –

(a) actions founded on simple contract or on tort;
(b) actions to enforce recognisance;

(c) actions to enforce an award, where the submission is not by an instrument under seal;
(d) actions to recover any sum recoverable by virtue of any enactment, other than a penalty or forfeiture or sum by way of penalty or forfeiture.

Provided that, in the case of actions for damages for negligence, nuisance or breach of duty (whether the duty exists by virtue of a contract or of provision made by or under a statute or independently of any contract or any such provision) where the damages claimed by the plaintiff for the negligence, nuisance or breach of duty consist of or include damages in respect of personal injury to any person, this section will have effect as if for the reference of six years there were substituted a reference to three years.

(Limitations Act, 1939)

The case of *Letang* v. *Cooper* rests on the interpretation of section 2 (1) of the Limitations Act, 1939 as amended in 1954, particularly on the last proviso-clause, which disallows action for negligence after a lapse of three years. The plaintiff takes the position that her action comes under trespass, which includes damages for personal injury, and hence should not be considered as time-barred after three years. Any reasonable decision on the issue requires analysis of the facts of the case to match the legal relationship favoured in the statutory provision referred to above. Lord Denning takes the position that the facts of the case indicate that it can only be interpreted as action for negligence and not for trespass, and, as such, it must be time-barred after the lapse of three years. The main point of the case, therefore, can never be adequately understood and appreciated unless one moves systematically from the real world of facts to the world of legal relations envisaged in the form of legislative provisions. On the other hand, legislative provisions, as we discussed in the chapter on legal discourse, are rarely, if ever, of universal application. They become operative only in a specific set of circumstances, a selection of which is used as a basis to create legal relationship(s) represented in a rule of law. In order to understand the nature and function of legislation, the learner must develop a capacity not only to appreciate how specific facts of the world are used to create legal relations but also to apply specific legal provisions to relevant facts of the world. Therefore, specialist learners must be trained to handle both – legislative provisions so that they can apply such legal relations to the facts of the world outside, and legal cases so that they can perceive legal relations from the facts of the world. So, in exploiting the two types of authentic legal texts, the ESP teacher has to be able to create an awareness of various genres used in different legal settings and also to bring them together in a meaningful relationship. Training of this kind can be given effectively and economically only if the ESP course designer engages the learner in appropriate tasks, with input from authentic legal genres.

6.4 Genre-based ESP materials – the case of UNDP-Government of Singapore self-access project

Genre-based approach to ESP materials development for ESP is relatively new. There is very little available in the form of any complete set of teaching materials, except the two, one for business and the other for technology, produced by the UNDP-Government of Singapore Project in the Teaching of English in Meeting the Needs of Business and Technology. This project was undertaken to develop EBT (English for Business and Technology) materials to be used on a self-access basis to supplement the existing mainline programmes at the two existing polytechnics in Singapore. The two volumes of materials, which were the outcome, were produced by the joint effort of a team of EBT specialists and practising teachers representing the three participating institutions, namely, the National University of Singapore, Ngee Ann Polytechnic and Singapore Polytechnic. Volume 1 contains materials to be used in English for Business, and Volume 2 in English for Technology.

In order to ensure that the materials were realistic and relevant to the needs of the students in the two institutions, a detailed needs analysis was carried out to obtain information on, and descriptions of, subject activity, and to understand the expectations that subject teachers had of their students. The project team sought co-operation not only from the subject departments but also from the world of business and technology beyond the two polytechnics in an attempt to collect authentic linguistic data, to get descriptions of circumstances in which the students would be operating, and to understand those circumstances, in general terms. To ensure such relevance, a large database of authentic resource materials from local sources was created and analysed using principles of genre analysis. The analysis was carried out at various linguistic levels (lexico-grammatical as well as discoursal) in the context of sociolinguistic and cognitive constraints that seemed to operate on these genres. The aim was to arrive at as 'thick' a description of these genres as possible, in order to give psychological reality to the analysis and the materials. The project team also obtained specialist reactions not only on the analyses of various genres but also on the final versions of teaching materials from the subject specialists at the two polytechnics. In order to serve specific departmental requirements more adequately, teaching materials for technology were written on a departmental basis, in spite of a great degree of overlap in the way genre distinctions were realized in these disciplines.

The materials are primarily based on the description of authentic linguistic data, where the focus was not just on the language (lexico-grammar and cognitive structure) but also on the conventions and procedures that shape the genres in question. The materials, therefore, do not simply promote the awareness of the linguistic system underlying a particular genre but also offer genre-specific explanation as to why certain features of language realize specific values in individual genres. The underlying principle, therefore, is to take the learner from pure descriptive linguistic tasks towards genre-specific explanation of why such linguistic features are used and to what effect. This, it is hoped, will help the learner to use language more effectively in academic and professional settings, and to bring much needed psychological reality and relevance to the learning task. The approach to genre analysis and materials design is not prescriptive but clarificatory. The idea is that once the conventions and procedures are learnt and adequately understood, the learner can then be encouraged to exploit them creatively to achieve private ends within the socially recognized communicative purposes.

Volume 1 on Business consists of eight units, six of which are devoted to letters of various types, one to memos and one to job application letters. Volume 2 on Technology consists of five units, two on Lab Reports and the remaining three on Project Reports for various departments of the two polytechnics. In Technology the main emphasis is on writing Introductions and Discussion and Conclusion sections of the reports. Each unit is devoted to a specific (sub)genre, and consists of a head text followed in most cases by a set of three head worksheets. The head text represents a standard or model example of that particular (sub)genre and sets out the main rhetorical moves or steps needed for its adequate realization by colour-coding each move. Each head text is followed by a set of three head worksheets.

Head worksheet 1, in each unit, is meant to help the learner internalize the interpretative generic structure of the genre in question. This highlights the main discoursal strategies that are conventionally exploited to achieve communicative ends in specific academic and professional settings. This gives the learner what Carrell (1983) refers to as 'formal schemata' in the form of discoursal conventions that are typically associated with the genre. Head worksheet 1 in the Business volume, for example, begins with a head text, which is taken as a standard or model example of a sales promotion letter (see Bhatia and Tay, 1987:1).

After reading the head text the learner is given in simple terms a detailed explanation of the communicative purpose of the (sub)genre and the various moves the writer makes use of to achieve that purpose. The moves are also colour-coded in the head text in order to make them obvious to the learner. The explanation does not contain any technical or other difficult vocabulary, except the names of the moves, which are also kept in communicative terms. The purpose of such an explanation is to make available to the learner what Carrell (1983) refers to as 'content schemata' against which the learner tries to understand the strategies that an expert genre writer employs to achieve his communicative purpose(s). The explanation can be given on the audio or video tape or in written form. Having made sure that the learner has understood and internalized both a typical communicative structure (formal schema) and the conventionalized patterns of knowledge, beliefs and experience of the specialist community associated with the genre in question, the head worksheet gives further practice to the learner in the following three aspects of genre construction and comprehension:

1.   Identifying and assigning discoursal values to various parts of the text
2.   Internalizing the discourse structure of the genre
3.   Introducing the learner gradually to the variation in the use of strategies to realize specific moves

Each exercise is, therefore, preceded by significant explanation of the strategy used by the author to achieve his or her intention. Exercise 2, for example, is not simply a mechanical exercise in the identification of various moves in the genre, but it also introduces the learner to different ways of **establishing credentials,** (as in part A below), including a case where the author needs to skip such a conventional realization of the first move, as in B below (slightly modified versions from Bhatia and Tay, 1987:5).

[23]

STANDARD BANK

268 Orchard Road, Yen Sun Building, Singapore 0923

4 December 1987

Mr Albert Chan
1 Sophia Road, 05–06
Peace Centre
Singapore 0922

Dear Sir

We are expertly aware that international financial managers need to be able to ask the right questions and work in the market place with confidence.	**Establishing credentials**
Corporate Treasury Services, Standard Bank, now provides a week-long Treasury Training programme designed to develop awareness and confidence in managers.	**Introducing the offer** *Offering product / service*
We explain the mechanics of foreign exchange and money markets. We discuss risk from an overall standpoint and practical hedging techniques to manage foreign exchange risks. We also discuss treasury management information systems, taxation and the latest treasury techniques.	*Essential detailing of the offer*
We will be holding our next Treasury Training Programme from 24–28 February 1987, inclusive. The fee for the Training Programme will be US$1,500 per person to include all luncheons and a dinner as indicated in the schedule as well as all course material.	
The programme is both rigorous and flexible. It can be tailored to fit the needs of a whole corporation or just a few levels within the company.	*Indicating value of the offer*
We are pleased to inform you that if your company sponsors 6 or more staff for the course, we will offer you a discount of US$100 per person.	**Offering incentives**
For your convenience, I enclose a reservation form which should be completed and returned directly to me.	**Enclosing documents**
If you have any questions or would like to discuss the programme in more detail, please do not hesitate to contact me (Telephone No. 532 6488 / telex No. 29052).	**Soliciting response**
As the number of participants at each training programme is limited, we would urge you to finalize as soon as possible your plans to participate.	**Using pressure tactics**
Thank you very much for your kind consideration.	**Ending politely**

Yours faithfully

Mr G. Huff

[24]

Exercise 2

(A)

Explanation

The writer of a promotional letter can use the move **establishing credentials** not only by **referring to the needs of the business world in general or the needs of a customer in particular** as in Mr Huff's letter given as the head text, but by **referring to his own company's achievements/speciality** as well. For instance in the following example,

> C & E Holidays, the name synonymous with the very best in travel trade with 20 years of professional expertise, will present you with a variety of programmes.

the writer **establishes credentials** by stating his company's past experiences and field of specialization. He may choose to use either of these two or, sometimes, both the strategies together to realize this move.

Instructions

Label the following text to indicate how many different strategies the author uses in **establishing credentials** of his company.

> The next 12 months are going to be difficult ones for Singapore industries as a whole. We, at Marco Polo are fully aware of the current market situation and are continuously upgrading our facilities and amenities to meet new competition.
>
> (Check with answer sheet)

(B)

Explanation

In certain cases when the company for which the writer is writing, has had past business dealings with the customer, he does not need to **establish credentials**. Instead, he would like to begin his letter by **thanking the customer for his continued support**. Look at the following example of this kind.

> You have now been a member of International Airline Passenger Association for about three months. Your continuing support keeps our worldwide organization strong and we want you to know that we appreciate your confidence in our services.

Continued overleaf

Instructions

Label the strategies that the author is using in the following text examples to establish credentials.

(1) With the current economic downturn we would like to take this opportunity to express our sincere appreciation for your support during the past months.
(2) Have you ever wished there was one study providing you with a step-by-step guide to establish a joint venture in the People's Republic of China?

Head worksheet 2 focuses mainly on the linguistic realizations of various rhetorical moves and the genre as a whole. Although the worksheet is meant to provide practice in the use of appropriate language, the grammatical explanation offered at each stage is invariably genre-specific, and therefore, more relevant to the task in hand. Look at the examples on pp. 187–92 from Head worksheet 2 (Bhatia and Tay, 1987:9–11).

Head worksheet 3 gives more advanced practice in free-genre writing concentrating often on refinement and creative variation in style, grammatical appropriateness, and other aspects of genre construction, like editing and revision, often using easification devices (see Bhatia, 1983). Another thing which is significant about these exercises is that all of them make use of more or less authentic, though grammatically imperfect and stylistically weak and inadequate examples from the real world. This is much more useful for learning purposes than especially written texts with inserted lexico-grammatical or stylistic errors, because the learner is more likely to face errors that are actually committed by a community of people, professional or academic, rather than the ones invented by the teacher. Exercises in this worksheet also take the learner systematically from relatively simple and controlled to more complex and advanced free genre writing, like Exercise 5 (Bhatia and Tay, 1987:26–27).

Although the materials in their present form contain only one set of worksheets, called the head worksheets, there is provision for several sets of additional worksheets to bring in more variety, focusing more and more on advanced creative aspects of genre writing.

Since the course has been designed to be used on a self-access basis to support the mainline programme, it offers several entry points for learners, depending upon the areas they need help in and how much they already know. It is possible for learners to work in their own time, at their own pace, in areas they find most useful. Some may be interested in grammar, others in organizing discourse, yet others in

[25]

Head worksheet 2

Exercise 1

(A)

Explanation

The writer of a promotional letter establishes the importance of his company either by referring to the business needs in general and the customer needs in particular or by referring to his company's achievements/speciality. There are certain typical language features which characterize the different ways of establishing credentials. For instance, notice the use of the pronouns you/we and the general/specific references in the examples that follow.

1 **Referring to the customer's needs:** Have you ever thought how much time your typist wastes in taking down your letters?

   Pronominal Reference: You

2 **Referring to the general business needs:** Every woman dreams of having at least one really beautiful coat and here is a splendid opportunity to make that dream come true.

   General Reference: Every woman

3 **Referring to the company's achievements/speciality:** We are fully aware of the current market situation and are continuously upgrading our facilities and amenities to meet new competition.

   Pronominal Reference: We

   C & E Holidays, the name synonymous with the very best in the travel trade, present you with a wide variety of tour programmes.

   Specific Reference: Name of the Company – 'C & E Holidays'

Instructions

Now, observe the use of references in the following sentences and tick them under the headings given to indicate the two ways (needs/achievements) of establishing credentials.

	Customer's needs	General business needs	Company's achievements/ speciality
1 Are you deafened by the ceaseless noise of typewriters and calculating machines?			
2 Why do thousands of people who normally suffer from the miseries of cold weather wear Thermotex?			
3 At the Ideal Home Exhibition, which opens at Earls Court on 21 June, we have attractive new designs in furniture, and many new ideas.			
4 How can project managers plan and effect strategies which facilitate the accomplishments of an I/S project?			
5 We at Wright Services are experienced Management Consultants with experience in industries as diverse as mining, banking and manufacturing.			

(Check with Answer Sheet)

Head worksheet 2 (continued)

(B)

Explanation

Now observe that in the following examples, the writer refers to his company's achievements/speciality in two ways:

1 **Factual evidence:** He not only states that a product/service is good but also presents some data in the form of facts and figures to illustrate its worth.

EXAMPLE:

C & E Holidays, the name synonymous with the very best in the travel trade, with 20 years of professional expertise, will present you with a wide variety of tour programmes.

Factual evidence: 20 years of professional expertise

2 **Unsupported generalizations and high pressure talk:** He states that a product/service is efficient without presenting specific reasons and explanations to prove its worth.

EXAMPLE:

We are fully aware of the current market situation and are continuously upgrading our facilities and amenities to meet new competition.

Unsupported generalizations: Continuously upgrading our facilities and amenities.

Instructions

Indicate in the boxes which of the sentences below uses factual evidence or unsupported generalizations in **referring to the company's achievements/speciality.**

	Factual evidence	Unsupported generalizations
1 We, the experienced carpet-makers, guarantee our carpets to last for 10 years. We use oriental wool exclusively - every fibre of wool is at least 12 inches long and our carpets have 400 knots to every square inch.		
2 We at Tech Craft make the best plastic pipes on the market today. They represent the very latest in chemical research.		
3 How would you like to have solar heating installed in your home at 50% actual cost?		
4 What would you say to a gift that gave you a warmer and more comfortable home, free from draughts and a saving of over 20% in fuel costs?		

(Check with Answer Sheet)

(C)

Improve the following sentences by providing factual evidence.

1 We have insulated a large number of houses and reports from all over confirm that there is a considerable reduction in the fuel bill after insulation.

2 In Singapore, Lep International Ltd has been operational for a long time and the services offered by our aircargo division include in and out-bound aircargo consolidation, import clearance, cargo delivery and collection and warehousing at the Changi Aircargo complex.

3 The Valuation Department of this firm has been in existence since the setting up of the firm's office and now comprises many qualified valuers.

[26]

Head worksheet 3

Exercise 2
(A) Read the following letter carefully. The errors have been italicised in order to enable you to identify them. Comments have been provided in the margin under the heading **Grammatical Points** to guide you to supply the correct and missing forms. Rewrite the letter keeping in mind the comments in the margin.

Grammatical points

ALLIED SERVICES PTE LTD
1 Maritime Square, # 11-22
World Trade Centre
Singapore 0409

3 December 1987

Capital Properties Ltd
100 Beach Road
01-07/08 Shaw Towers
Singapore 0718

Dear Sir

1. Incorrect subject-verb agreement (e.g. He go to work every morning.)
2. Incorrect noun phrase (e.g. one of the outstanding banks managers.)
3. Incorrect use of tense (e.g. The company car now belonged to John.)
4. Incorrect noun ending (e.g. We have many multinational company in this region.)
5. Unnecessary use of prepositions (e.g. The following articles are found in Yoahan, C K Tang and in Isetan.)
6. Incorrect use of tense (e.g. We have improved our services today.)
7. Use of passive voice (e.g. We are regularly reminded.)
8. Missing articles (e.g. It is one of best and most splendid buildings.)
9. Incorrect subject-verb agreement (e.g. Our banking system have many advantages.)

A cleaning system that saves money and yet do[1] a better job
We write to introduce ourselves as one of the leading *offices and building cleaners.*[2] Allied Services Pte Ltd which *belonged*[3] to the Initial Services Groups (UK) was incorporated in April 1979 with a paid-up capital of $1.2 million. With associate cleaning companies all over the world who are also *leader*[4] in their localities such as Initial Services Cleaners in United Kingdom, Australia, in[5] Holland and just across the causeway Dynaklan Services in Kuala Lumpur and Modern Hygienic Cleaning Services in Penang. The vast experience gained by all these companies had[6] added to our knowledge and skill in the field of Cleaning Maintenance. Being a member of the British Institute of Cleaning Services and American Institute of Maintenance, we *are constantly updated*[7] with the latest development and products in cleaning and maintenance via monthly journals.

We provide complete maintenance services using dependable and experienced cleaning staff, who are fully trained. A fully trained supervisor is assigned to every job and we use *latest cleaning techniques and most modern cleaning equipment.*[8] Our cleaning system have[9] the following advantages:

(a) lower cost
(b) higher productivity
(c) reasonably good standard
We provide the following services:
(a) General spring cleaning
(b) Polishing of all types of flooring
(c) Carpet shampooing, window cleaning
(d) Parquet sanding/varnishing
(e) Complete cleaning and maintenance programmes for hotels, factories, etc.
(f) Consultancy services on maintenance problems
(g) Tree/grass cutting and rubbish disposal
(h) Transportation services
(i) Planning and high pressure cleaning

Head worksheet 3 (continued)	
10. Missing articles (see 8.)	We understand your problems and can help to solve them by tailoring our services to *needs and budget for a specific building*.[10] We always provide only the highest quality work for our clients.
	We offer free consultation, cost estimates and we submit detailed bids and specifications on all jobs, be it daily, weekly, monthly, or for one-time clean-ups. We also provide free demonstration on request, without obligation.
11. Use of archaic or old-fashioned language (e.g. Please advise us.) 12. Incorrect verb forms (e.g. We look forward to meet you.)	*Please be at liberty*[11] to give us a call or write to us, at your convenience, and we shall send our representative to look at your needs, with no obligation on your part. We sincerely look forward to hear[12] from you.
	Yours faithfully
	JOSEPH LEONG for Managing Director

[27]

(B) Now that you have learnt to use appropriate grammatical forms, we would like you to rewrite the letter more effectively by considering the questions raised in the margin under the heading economy.

ALLIED SERVICES PTE LTD
1 Maritime Square, # 11-22
World Trade Centre
Singapore 0409

3 December 1987

Capital Properties Ltd
100 Beach Road
01-07/08 Shaw Towers
Singapore 0718

Dear Sir

A cleaning system that saves money and yet does a better job

We write to introduce ourselves as one of the leading offices and building cleaners. Allied Services Pte Ltd which belongs to the Initial Services Groups (UK) was incorporated in April 1979 with a paid-up capital of $1.2 million. With associate cleaning companies all over the world who are also leaders in their localities such as Initial Services Cleaners in United Kingdom, Australia, Holland and just across the causeway Dynaklan Services in Kuala Lumpur and Modern Hygienic Cleaning Services in Penang. The vast experience gained by all these companies has added to our knowledge and skill in the field of Cleaning Maintenance. Being a member of the British Institute of Cleaning Services and American Institute of Maintenance, we constantly update ourselves with the latest development and products in cleaning and maintenance via monthly journals.

Economy

Establishing credentials
– Is this move duplicated in the letter?
– Is this move too long?
– Is there a repetition of content, phrases and words in this move?
– Are the sentences in this move too involved and lengthy?
– Is there an excessive use of modifiers?

Head worksheet 3 (continued)

We provide complete maintenance services using dependable and experienced cleaning staff, who are fully trained. A fully trained supervisor is assigned to every job and we use latest cleaning techniques and the most modern cleaning equipment. Our cleaning system has the following advantages:

(a) lower cost
(b) higher productivity
(c) reasonably good standard

We provide the following services:

(a) General spring cleaning
(b) Polishing of all types of flooring
(c) Carpet shampooing, window cleaning
(d) Parquet sanding/varnishing
(e) Complete cleaning and maintenance programmes for hotels, factories, etc.
(f) Consultancy services on maintenance problems
(g) Tree/grass cutting and rubbish disposal
(h) Transportation services
(i) Planning and high pressure cleaning

We understand your problems and can help to solve them by tailoring our services to the needs and budget for a specific building. We always provide only the highest quality work for our clients.

We offer free consultation, cost estimates and we submit detailed bids and specifications on all jobs, be it daily, weekly, monthly, or for one-time clean-ups. We also provide free demonstration on request, without obligation.

Please feel free to give us a call or write to us, at your convenience, and we shall send our representative to look at your needs, with no obligation on your part.

We sincerely look forward to hearing from you.

Yours faithfully

JOSEPH LEONG
for Managing Director

Introducing the offer
– Is this move or part of this move duplicated?
– Is there a repetition of content, phrases and words?
– Is there an excessive use of modifiers?
– Should the details about the services offered be included in this letter? Is there an alternative method of dealing with the details of an offer?

Offering incentives
– Is there a repetition of content, phrases and words?
– Can you convey all this incentives information in a brief sentence?

Soliciting reponse
– Is the sentence too long and involved?

(Check with Answer Sheet)

[28]

editing or advanced free writing in any of the genres. The programme allows almost everyone to begin anywhere and proceed in any direction. However, the programme makes sure, at various points, that the learner has enough background to finish a particular worksheet by ensuring that s/he has done the previous worksheet(s), if considered necessary, before proceeding to the next one he is interested in.

The UNDP materials for EBT are based on the genre analysis of a corpus of authentic resource materials, but they are not meant to undermine linguistic analyses in the old tradition. The materials, in this respect, seem to take into consideration the best of earlier work and take it further – from pure description to explanation.

Since the project involved several practising EBT teachers from the two polytechnics, it was decided to develop a good working relationship with the technical departments that the self-access programme was meant to serve. The reason for this close collaboration was two-fold. First, it was considered crucial to use some of the subject-teachers as specialist informants for authenticating not only the technical texts that were used as input to EBT materials but also the finished materials to ensure that the materials made good sense to the specialist community, and secondly, it was felt that, in order to serve the parent departments, the project needed their support.

6.5 Genre analysis and assessment of attainment in ESP

The nature of ESP teaching, as Widdowson (1984) rightly points out, is parasitic in that it depends heavily on the requirements of other disciplines and areas of expertise. In many cases, there are institutional arrangements by which learners are sponsored for specific ESP courses. ESP teaching is specialized, and requires advanced preparation in the form of elaborate needs analysis indicating specific knowledge and understanding of skills and abilities that the learners need to acquire, the texts and tasks they need to handle, the target situations they are likely to participate in and the roles they are likely to assume after they complete the ESP course. One of the strong implications of dependence on this kind of sponsorship is that ESP practitioners are expected to be accountable to their sponsors (they may be industrial or business organizations, or university departments) for the achievement and success of their learners. However, it is a strange paradox that, in spite of such expectations of accountability, assessment remains the most neglected aspect of ESP theory and practice.

One of the reasons for this lack of research may be the feeling that the real evaluation of attainment for any ESP activity lies in the performance of real life tasks after the learner has completed the course and has been placed in situations for which s/he has been prepared during the course. Testing can rarely be a genuine communicative activity, but this is particularly true of ESP; it is, therefore, difficult and, even, unrealistic to predict what students will do in a real situation, on the basis of their performance in a simulated situation. Attainment in ESP does not relate to the knowledge of language usage, but to an ability to use language to communicate in a specific area. The real test of success of any ESP course should be based on the performance of learners in actual target-situations, academic or professional, for which they have been trained. If a learner is given training in negotiating in business situations, the real success of the course will depend on the extent to which the learner can successfully participate and win contracts in actual business settings. However, for the sponsors, an ESP course is an investment, and they like to have some indication of the appreciation of their investment. It is also important for the learners to have some idea of their progress at various stages and at the end of the course.

For academic contexts, Alderson (1988:88) points out,

> Tests, and particularly pass/fail examinations, are often crucially important within ESP. Indeed, the test is often the only reason why a student is taking an ESP course. When an ESP course is being offered as a service course to other areas of study, as frequently happens, for example, at the university level, often the only reason students have for taking the course is to pass the examination in the language required by the academic system, before they are allowed to graduate as engineers, doctors, lawyers or whatever. Here the examination is a hurdle to be overcome by hook or by crook. In this situation, the test serves as a strong motivating force and is quite likely to influence teaching.

Therefore, in ESP, whether in professional or academic contexts, some form of assessment is desirable.

Authenticity v. simplification

This brings us to the question of the **relevance** of assessment to the target situation, which brings in two types of requirements: **authenticity of communication** and **authenticity of purpose** associated with a communicative task. By authenticity of communication I do not mean a simple surface-level authenticity of communication for the sake of face validity alone, but more of an underlying rationality that makes people recognize the use of language as purposeful and truly communicative in real-life settings. Whether one considers teaching materials or testing procedures, it is by no means a great achievement to use subject-specific authentic texts as input if all it brings is the relevance of the content for the sake of the psychological reality. More important, is what the test designer wants the learner to do with it. Specialist texts are used in specific disciplines in a particular way, and are designed to fulfil a specific purpose. If the ESP curriculum is meant to serve the specialist discipline, the tasks that an ESP materials writer or test designer sets up for his learners must also serve the purpose that the specialist texts serve in the discipline in question. After all, the true purpose of evaluation of attainment in ESP is the evaluation of purpose which the ESP course is designed to fulfil. It will be unwise, for example, to use an authentic case from a law report and use it for general comprehension purposes by devising traditional exercises to assess overall comprehension as part of ESP evaluation, because the purpose of reading a legal case in the context of law is fairly well-defined and highly specific. On the other hand it will be equally unwise to predict, on the basis of an overall comprehension test based on a simple narrative, the extent to which a law student will be able to distinguish facts which are considered legally material from those that are considered legally immaterial in the context of the judge's argument, or to understand the way the judge argues the case and negotiates justice in a particular legal case. The role of genre in task-based ESP teaching, as Swales (1990:72) points out, is crucially important.

> The danger of ignoring genre is precisely the danger of ignoring communicative purpose. Indeed, as I have confessed elsewhere (Swales, 1985c), this is a lesson that I have learnt the hard way. I used to teach an EAP course for students entering the largely English-medium Faculty of Law at the University of Khartoum in Sudan. One of the main genres that I used were Sudanese case reports, and for this choice I could put forward an elaborate justification. The case reports were relatively short authentic documents; they had certain similarities to the narratives the students had read in their English lessons at school; they introduced in a relatively easy-paced way useful Criminal Law vocabulary; they were situated within Sudanese culture; they had a consistent rhetorical structure consisting of front matter, narrative and judgment; and they were relatively easy to exploit for methodological activities. They thus formed, or so I thought, an excellent basis for a first series of reading comprehension units. However, the comprehension tasks I invited the students to undertake were misconceived because they were designed to help the students to understand the stories. It was only when I attended classes given by a Criminal Law professor that I belatedly came to realize that the reading strategy required in legal education was not to understand – and retain the gist of – a narrative, but to spot the crucial facts on which the decision (rightly or wrongly) rested. The problem-solving law professor's questions were quite different to my own. Because I had failed to appreciate the role of the genre in its environment, the reading strategies I was teaching, however well-founded in terms of ESL methodology, were probably doing the students more harm than good.

The selection and interpretation of texts, whether for materials development or assessment purposes, therefore, need to have a sound generic basis, if one wishes to make teaching and testing of ESP relevant to the needs of the learner. Sometimes one is tempted to compromise generic integrity of a particular text in order to make it more readily accessible to the learner by applying a variety of simplification procedures to produce simplified texts or simple accounts (see Mountford, 1975; Widdowson, 1978, 1979; Davies and Greene, 1984); however, all these procedures can be counter-productive in typical ESP situations. As I have argued elsewhere (see Bhatia, 1983a), and also in this book, simplification involves expansion as a result of paraphrasing and detransformation, which invariably flattens out information distribution in simplified versions. This may run contrary to the generic character of specific text-types, particularly the legal genres, which are characterized by an exceptionally high density of information loading. Simplification, therefore, may obscure or even destroy the generic integrity of the text in question, thus resulting in somwhat confusing text-task relationship in ESP.

Subject-matter specificity and generic integrity in the selection of textual material for assessment purposes are also important from the point of view of the learner. Reading is a highly personalized activity and a reader often employs a variety of techniques and strategies to develop an authentic relationship with the text. These strategies may differ from individual to individual, depending upon the purpose for reading the text, the generic nature of the text, the nature and extent of what Labov (1970) calls 'shared knowledge', and a number of other factors. In simplifying a text, one is likely to communicate one's own interpretation, which may be very different from what the learner may understand when reading the original. Text, as Winograd (1974) points out,

> does not convey meaning the way a truck conveys cargo, complete and packaged. It is more like a blueprint that allows the hearer to reconstruct meaning from his own knowledge.

Winograd's 'cargo', as Candlin (1978:3) suggests, while discussing variability in discourse, is the sense or signification of sentences; his 'blueprint' implies the 'force' or 'value' that sentences take on in actual communication, and his notion of 'reconstruction' emphasizes the interpretative 'work' performed by the reader. By simplifying the text one invariably minimizes opportunities for the learner to do interpretative work on the original.

Another serious implication of the neutralization of generic integrity of professional texts through simplification is the loss of opportunities to learn and assess genre-specific text-processing strategies. As pointed out in Bhatia (1983a, 1984), there are specific cognitive strategies that are often required to cope with the flow of information in different genres (see the case of syntactic discontinuities in legislative rules in chapter 5). If, in the process of the selection and authentication of textual material, generic characteristics are either lost or neutralized, it will be difficult to assess whether the learner has learned to use such strategies to handle specific genres which s/he will be concerned with in the relevant professional settings.

The above discussion suggests at least two important conclusions:

1.   ESP, whatever its objectives may be, will require some form of assessment to give the learner feedback on his or her achievement and to show accountability to the sponsors.
2.   ESP assessment, in order to be effective, must be towards the specific end of the general-specific continuum.

This raises the question, How specific should the tests be? Alderson and Urquhart (1985), in their study on the effect of students' academic discipline on their performance on ESP reading tests wanted to find out whether students reading texts in a familiar content area, that is, related to their area of study, would perform better than students unfamiliar with that subject. The latter, they argued, might lack familiarity not only with the content of the subject area, but also with such aspects as genre effect, rhetorical organization, and linguistic and non-linguistic relations. The results of the experiments supported the hypothesis that

> students from a particular discipline would perform better on tests based on texts taken from their own subject discipline than would students from other disciplines.

This indicated that students appeared to benefit by taking a test on a text in a familiar content area. Similar findings indicating an advantageous relationship between subject-matter familiarity and the ability of the learner to perform comprehension tasks have been reported elsewhere (see Carrell, 1987; Hale, 1988; Read, 1990; Tedick, 1990). Two main sources of concern remain which need further investigation. One is the need to confirm the above findings with qualitative evidence of an advantageous correlation between content familiarity and the reading behaviour of specialists and non-specialists. Bhatia (1988) reports on an experiment in which he looked at the relationship between the reader's familiarity with the textual subject-matter and his ability to understand and negotiate meaning in order to interpret a technical text, by analysing the retrospective, and often, introspective loud-thinking accounts of his subjects. He compared the reading strategies of two native-speaker subjects reading two texts, one from a familiar subject discipline and the other from an unfamiliar content area. The findings indicated that both the specialist readers read texts from their familiar content areas smoothly, silently and faster, often concentrating on larger chunks of text, skipping familiar details, wherever necessary. The same subjects, when asked to read texts from unfamiliar areas, read slowly and in smaller chunks, hesitating a lot, and stumbling on unfamilar words repeatedly, often coming back to them, as if they were haunted by these unfamiliar words. This leads to the conclusion that lack of content familiarity does affect reading processes and strategies adversely, sometimes turning good readers into poor performers.

The second point that needs further investigation is the use of different types of tasks, set on familiar text-types to determine whether a familiarity with subject-specific tasks will also have an advantageous relationship with the learner's performance in comprehension tests. As Widdowson (1983) points out, there are procedural activities which characterize various subject-disciplines; therefore familiarity with subject-matter will also mean familiarity with specific tasks that are routinely engaged in by specialists in particular disciplines. It is very likely that in measuring learner performance on specific tasks one may actually be measuring very specific abilities, rather than a general ability to perform overall comprehension activities.

Text and task specificity

This brings us to the question of specificity of texts and tasks in the devising of assessment procedures for ESP courses. If one goes for accuracy and effectiveness, one comes up with an almost impossible situation where one may be required to design a separate test for each learner. On the other hand, if one goes for convenience, one may design a general test for everyone, in order to assess underlying competence, which might be a combination of grammatical, socio-linguistic and strategic aspects of communication. In either case, one finds problems; Alderson (1988:96) sums them up neatly in the following extract.

> The fact is that we simply have no means of deciding at present how specific a specific test must be. There is a range of competing arguments to be considered – on the one hand, the practicality, economy and convenience of having only one test for all target situations, and on the other hand, the danger of injustice to particular sub-groups of students who might be required to take an inappropriate test which gives misleading information about their abilities.

One of the ways of finding a suitable compromise which may combine soundness of theory with the convenience of practice will be to adopt a genre-based approach to assessment in ESP, which will cut across subject-matter differences so that it will no longer be necessary to devise textual material for each subject discipline. Instead, the focus will shift to specificity in communicative purpose. Recent research in genre analysis indicates that, within genres, subject-matter differences do not play a very significant role, in the sense that generic integrity is invariably maintained whether one writes a research article introduction in physical sciences or social sciences, or a report in technology or in business. Textbook genre, similarly, shows an exceptionally high degree of overlap in a wide variety of areas like sociology, psychology, geography, physics, physical chemistry, and linguistics. Subject-matter differences most notably appear either in the use of lexis or, sometimes, in the form of tasks or activities that are routinely associated with certain areas of inquiry. So by adopting a genre-perspective in the selection of texts and tasks in the assessment of ESP one may get a three-way advantage. One may settle the question of specificity in testing procedures to the advantage of both, the learner as well as the test designer. The learner will not feel disadvantaged because of unfamiliarity with the text-content. Some degree of unfamiliarity with lexis will be amply compensated by the familiarity with the other aspects of the genre, particularly with the communicative purpose of the genre, the cognitive structures in it and the use of grammatical resources. The basic differences in the subject-disciplines will be taken care of in the test tasks that will be set for the learners. For the test designer, it will be a nice combination of specificity of content and practical convenience of not having to design separate tests for learners in individual subject-disciplines. The relevance of the test task will also ensure more accurate assessment of the learner's ability to operate in a specialist environment, giving the test a better predictive validity about the behaviour of the learner in relevant target situations. Finally, by maintaining the generic integrity of the texts selected, one is likely to ensure that there is minimal gap between the content of the test and the task, on the one hand, and the real life target situation, on the other. The most crucial condition for the success of these assessment procedures, therefore, is the concept of generic integrity, which requires all the texts and the tasks that are selected to be genuine, authentic and relevant. Any attempt to use simplified texts, whether in content or form, or simple accounts, is likely to result in the loss of an essential link between theory and practice in language testing. In other words, loss of generic validity in text and task selection will definitely mean a loss in construct validity for the test in question.

6.6 Cross-cultural factors in the teaching of ESP

Kachru (1988) raises an interesting issue for the ESP profession when he argues for a culturally and linguistically appropriate ESP paradigm. Unfortunately the evidence he cites comes largely from the genres which are rarely the concern of many ESP practitioners, except the Japanese example of the innovative use of phrases in advertising from *Asiaweek*, part of which I reproduce here.

> To produce one such phrase requires the expensive services of an ad agency as sophisticated as anywhere. A creative director gathers the team and concepts are tossed about, a first-rate copywriter works on the theme, a lengthy rationalisation is prepared for the client, a decision eventually made to launch. Cost: maybe millions of yen. Everone understands that it is substandard English. Explains a copywriter at Dentsu: 'Yes, of course, we know it sounds corny to an American, even objectionable to some. But what the foreigner thinks of it is immaterial. The ad is purely domestic, a lot of market research has gone into it. It evokes the right images. It sells.'
>
> (*Asiaweek*, 5 October, 1984:49, quoted in Kachru, 1988:22)

There is a 'social meaning', Kachru claims, in such innovations.

> . . . the norms of 'English in advertising' are context bound and variety dependent. This fact about non-native uses of English has yet to be recognized by the specialists in ESP.
>
> (Kachru, 1988:23)

He argues that in order to ensure pragmatic success in communication, the ESP profession can ill afford to ignore cultural and interpretative contexts.

Unfortunately, however, research in such contrastive discourse analysis is scant and rather restricted because most of the frameworks currently used are essentially linguistic and few of them pay any attention to cross-cultural variation in the use of language in academic or professional contexts. We have gathered some evidence in the preceeding chapters indicating that there can be significant differences in the way English is used in various nativized contexts for a variety of professional and social purposes. In most academic genres, particularly in the sciences, the trend is still towards conformity because of a wide majority of academics looking for recognition through publications in the English-speaking world, where established conventions and standards are observed rather rigorously. However, in the case of many other professional genres, particularly in certain types of business letters (Teh, 1986; Bhatia and Tay, 1987), job applications (Bhatia, 1989) and some legal genres, local constraints do seem to play a relatively more significant role in their linguistic realizations, indicating some degree of variation across cultures. But, curiously enough, these very genres also demonstrate a certain degree of orthodoxy in the use of linguistic resources.

As a matter of fact, the bilingual's linguistic repertoire displays a strange complex of linguistic and discoursal resources resulting from a range of reactions and influences. It exhibits a highly nativized use of lexico-grammatical and discoursal resources, resulting from variations in socio-cultural norms, particularly in literary genres, which can be seen as a kind of reaction or response to native writing. But it also shows a somewhat extreme fascination for orthodoxy in linguistic behaviour, especially in non-literary writings, including some profes-sional as well as academic genres, which can be seen as the influence of some kind of standardized, or even outdated in some cases, use of the native linguistic conventions. The first aspect of the bilingual's use of linguistic resources has been referred to as the **bilingual's creativity** and has been well-documented in recent literature on nativized varieties of English (see Kachru, 1982, 1983, 1986; Parthasarathy, 1983; Sridhar, 1982). However, relatively little attention has been paid so far to the second one, which is equally fascinating, and I would like to call it the **bilingual's orthodoxy**.

Let me go back to the discussion of promotional letters in Chapter 2, and particularly to the opening move we have called **establishing credentials**. Teh (1986) discusses the linguistic realization of this move in her corpus, which consisted of letters from two sources, i.e., from multinational companies, most of which were written by native speakers of English and their nativized versions written by the local companies; she concludes as follows:

(i) It was more or less formulaic in its linguistic realization, having either the 'we' kind of orientation as in the following case:

[29] We are an established courier company incorporated locally since 1971

or

'you' kind of orientation as in this one:

[30] Do you wish that you could have word processor that can do the attached examples?

(ii) Move 1 was not an obligatory move in her data; it occurred in 95% of the multinational letters and only 68% of the local letters. (iii) Although she did not draw this conclusion, it is clear from her data that there was far greater variation in the linguistic realizations of this move in the multinational promotional letters than in the letters from local companies. Most of these letters in which significant linguistic variation was found were written by native speakers whereas the others written by the local companies indicated a greater use of the typical formulaic linguistic realizations; however, it must be pointed out that the strategies and discoursal conventions used in both sets of letters were more or less similar.

Let me take two instances of the opening move from the multinational sources.

[31] During the last three years our firm has performed over 1,500 information systems planning engagements. These experiences have confirmed. . .

[32] You have now been a member of the International Airline Passengers Association for about three months. Your continuing support keeps our worldwide organization strong. . .

The interesting point is that all the four statements [29–32] are part of the opening move in these promotional efforts and all of them carry more or less similar discoursal values in the respective letters, but the first two [29 and 30] are somewhat like the typical formulaic expressions frequently associated with the rhetoric of advertising, whereas the last two [31 and 32] represent a kind of linguistic variation which is less typically associated with the language of advertising. Once again, we notice a greater tendency in nativized promotional genres to use fixed, formulaic linguistic realizations, whereas, in similar situations, native writing is likely to display greater variation in the use of linguistic realizations, in that they are more personalized.

As in sales promotion letters, the first move in job applications often begins with **establishing credentials** (see Chapter 2). The only difference is that in sales promotion letters this move is more often realized by referring to the well-established nature of the company and less often by referring to the needs of the potential customer, although both of them are legitimate strategies to establish credentials. However, in job applications, it is very rare, though not impossible, to find a person well established in the profession and still looking for a job. So, generally one finds a predominant reference to the needs of the potential employer, in a reference to the job specification in the advertisement, which implies that the candidate can fulfil those needs.

[33] With reference to your advertisement in the *Straits Times* of 1 December, 1988 for the position of fashion copywriter, I would like to offer myself as a candidate for your consideration.

The first part of the sentence, *With reference to your advertisement in the* Straits Times *of 1 December, 1988 for the position of a fashion copywriter*, is an attempt to **establish credentials** by referring to the needs of the employer. The rest of the sentence, *I would like to offer myself as a candidate for your consideration*, offers the candidature for the position referred to in the earlier part of the sentence. The opening phrase, *With reference to your advertisement in ... for ...*, has become almost formulaic in nature, and is typically associated with this genre, used by native as well as non-native speakers of English. There seems to be a significant linguistic variation, however, in the realization of this opening move in the job applications written by the native speakers of English. Let me take a few examples from native sources:

[34] This is in response to your recent advertisement in the *West Bend Tribune* for a part-time insurance secretary. I would like to apply for this position with your agency. I feel that my experience and education have prepared me for this position.

This represents a somewhat modified version of the formulaic opening move in the job application. A more daring one comes from Lesikar (1984:287), where we find an almost winning combination of what the employers need and what the applicant thinks s/he can boast of.

[35] Sound background in advertising ... well-trained ... work well with others. . . . These key words in your July 7 advertisement in the *Times* describe the person you want, and I believe I am that person.

Occasionally, we come across a few instances of job application letters in which the opening move is preceded by **Adversary glorification** (see Section 3.3.2) where the writer tends to glorify the credentials of the organization or institution of the prospective employer. Huseman and others (1986:450) give a good example of this kind of approach:

[36] The reputation and growth of your company in the textile industry have led me to make this application for a position in your management trainee program. In reading about Brockland, I have been impressed with your trainee program and the opportunities you offer to qualified university graduates.

As against this, Bhatia (1989) reports an overwhelming use of the formulaic opening move, with very little variation in linguistic realization, in job applications from South Asia, of which the following is a typical example:

[37] With reference to your advertisement for the post of *Personnel and P R Executive* published in *The Times* of India dated 12th March 1988, I hereby submit my personal resume for your kind consideration and disposal.

Bilinguals, it would seem, take rather seriously conventionalized and standardized use of linguistic expressions to realize the opening move in job application letters.

The bilingual's use of linguistic resources in professional genres represents a number of diametrically opposite influences. On the one hand, we find a certain degree of creativity and originality in the use of linguistic strategies and discoursal procedures, whereas on the other hand, we discover a rather extreme orthodoxy in the use of linguistic realizations. I think there are two different kinds of processes at work here. In order to better appreciate what underlies these processes, we need to understand the nature of professional texts as genres, particularly where generic constraints are exploited by the expert members of the discourse community to achieve private intentions within the framework of socially recognized purpose(s). It is often found that members of the professional or academic community have greater knowledge of the conventional purpose(s), construction and use of specific genres than those who are non-specialists. That is why expert genre writers often appear to be more creative in the use of genres they are most familiar with than those who are outside the specialist community. Obviously, one needs to be familiar with the conventions of the genre before one can exploit them for special effects.

The foregoing discussion brings two very different aspects of genre construction into focus: variability and orthodoxy. Variability is the result of an individual genre writer's creative response to lexico-grammatical and discoursal choices because of specific cultural factors. Orthodoxy, on the other hand, is the result of highly conventionalized and more or less standardized aspects of genre construction. It may derive from the standardized use of lexico-grammatical resources, including formulaic, often outdated and sometimes, even, frozen expressions, indicating rather fixed discoursal values in specific genres; regularities of discourse organization, assigning more or less similar interpretative discourse structure to individual genres; or, tried and tested discourse strategies to achieve the fulfilment of certain types of communicative purpose(s). Even now, for example, it is not uncommon to find the following expressions in formal letters used in many countries in South Asia:

[38] I am a graduate in mining engineering having a shining academic record to my credit

[39] I am enclosing my brief 'Bio-data' for your kind consideration and confirmation. I request you kindly give me a chance to serve your esteemed organization. I assure you, Sir, I can prove worth [sic] of your selection by hard work and devotion to duties

[40] I may bring to your gracious knowledge that

[41] I would accordingly beseech your gracious, generous and benevolent honour to be kind enough to confer upon me a scholarship sufficient to cover my educational expenses

[42] For this noble act of kindness, I shall remain grateful deep down the depths of my heart

[43] Please refer to your letter No ... dated ...... and our reply to the same dated ... vide which we had referred 5 female candidates for you interview for the post of

As Kachru (personal communication) says, the following pronouncement is still common in testimonials written in India almost to the point of obsession:

[44] ... to the best of my knowledge and belief the candidate bears a good moral character.

The bilingual's repertoire of professional genres, therefore, represents a strange mixture of variability and orthodoxy in the use of linguistic resources. On the one hand, it displays a range of variation, particularly in non-literary genres, including the creative use of lexico-grammatical resources in literary expression and innovative use of discourse strategies for self-presentation in job applications (see Bhatia, 1989). At the same time, nativized genres also display somewhat extreme fascination for those conventional expressions which have been traditionally associated with some of these genres.

The present level of research in contrastive discourse analysis indicates that academic and professional genres appear not to vary systematically cross-culturally, and that more evidence is needed to establish such a variation in professional writing. The ESP profession will, therefore, do well to suspend judgement on the question of whether it is really necessary to shift the ESP paradigm considering the nativized use of English in some social, professional and academic contexts. However, in a number of ESP situations, it appears appropriate that learners and, more importantly, ESP researchers and expatriate teachers are made aware of the local constraints which may seem to determine the nature and linguistic realizations in these genres, if one needs to ensure pragmatic success in real-life professional settings in local environments.

7 Generic integrity and language reform

In this final chapter, I would like to discuss the relevance of genre analysis to one more area of linguistic concern: the process of language reform, particularly in the context of present-day concern with the simplification, reader accessibility and usability of legal and public documents. Linguistic activities in these contexts are concerned with simplification of language use for the purpose of reader accessibility. A very important implication of text simplification is that, in a number of cases, the resulting text tends either to obscure or even lose the generic integrity of the original, which, in some cases, can result in the total loss of generic identity of the text.

7.1 Language reform in legislative provisions

In Chapter 5, a brief indication was given of a divide between the reformists seeking far-reaching changes in the direction of the use of plain English in legislative and other public documents and the members of the professional community, claiming that the present degree of complexity is a necessary evil for the sake of clarity, precision, unambiguity and certainty of legal effect. In this section, arguments from both sides will be examined in order to discover if there is a way of arriving at a compromise to facilitate comprehension and usability without sacrificing certainty of legal effect.

The case for the use of plain English has been well stated in the 1986 discussion paper of the Law Reform Commission of Victoria as follows:

> The central platform of the plain language movement is the right of the audience – the right to understand any document that confers a benefit or imposes an obligation. Due consideration of audience should be a feature of all documents. Sadly, however, much official writing largely ignores the needs of the audience. Official writers can forget that it is their obligation to make their materials accessible to their readers. It is not the reader's responsibility to have to labour to discover the meaning. . . . The plain

language movement has insisted that documents should be comprehensible. This means that Acts as well as more general documents are to be accessible to those who are to be regulated by them.
(Law Reform Commission of Victoria, Discussion Paper No.1, *Legislation, Legal Rights and Plain English*, August 1986, pp.8–9)

Richard Thomas (1985), quoting Falsenfeld (1981–82), points out,

Lawyers have two common failings. One is that they do not write well and the other that they think they do.

He continues to echo the same sentiments.

... Lawyers have an almost universal reputation for mystifying their clients. ... Their prose baffles their clients and alienates the public. Lawyers go on using a particular phrase, sentence, paragraph or entire agreement because it is familiar. They try to cover every contingency, but in doing so can easily get lost in obscurity. The wordy, repetitive phrases of legal documents in 1985 still conjure up a musty Dickensian image and make them unintelligible to most non-lawyers – the very people who are often the ultimate users.

(Thomas, 1985: 144)

On the other hand, it has been emphasized again and again by the drafting community that the ultimate aim of legislation is to drive the judge to adopt the meaning which Parliament wants him to take. If, in doing so, it is possible to use plain language, so much the better, but a majority of parliamentary counsels admit that it is almost impossible to achieve this objective. The Renton Committee Report also underlines the primary objective of legislation to be the certainty of legal effect:

Ordinary language relies upon the good offices of the reader to fill in omissions and give the sense intended to words or expressions capable of more than one meaning. It can afford to do this. In legal writing, on the other hand, not least in statutory writing, a primary objective is certainty of legal effect, and the United Kingdom legislature tends to prize this objective exceptionally highly. Statutes confer rights and impose obligations on people. If any room is left for arguments as to the meaning of an enactment which affects the liberty, the purse, or the comfort of individuals, that argument will be pursued by all available means. In this situation Parliament seeks to leave as little as possible to inference, and to use words which are capable of one meaning only.

(Renton, 1975:36)

From the foregoing it is clear that the competing demands imposed by the two sides are almost irreconcilable. The demand for plain language is seen by the specialist community as unrealistic, whereas the continued trend, in legislative drafting, to maintain precision and certainty of legal effect is seen by the members of the reformist groups as unreasonable. The inevitable result has been a slow and rather painful pace of language reform in the past few decades. The fact is that radical reforms suggested by the plain-language campaign are seen as demands which amount to transgression of the generic integrity of the whole tradition in legislative writing. There seem to be two possibilities open to the concerned parties. One is to use what are discussed in section 7.2, **easification devices**, to make legislation more easily accessible to a larger specialist audience without, in any serious manner, neutralizing the generic integrity of legislative statements. The other possibility is to create popular versions of these documents in plain language for a lay audience, so that we may have two different versions for two very different sets of readership: an authentic and authoritative one which has been 'easified' in a number of ways, for specialist use; and another popular one for the lay audience, for information and education.

7.2 Easification of legislative documents for specialist use

Legal writing in general, and legislative documents in particular, present specific psycholinguistic problems in their processing and comprehension (see Bhatia, 1982). Unlike many other areas of specialist writing, it is neither possible nor appropriate to tamper with the original documents to make them easily accessible to a wide range of lay readership. However, it is possible to make such texts more reader friendly without simplifying their content or form. This can be done by using **easification devices** (see Bhatia, 1983a), which provide an access structure around the text to help the reader to process the text appropriately without sacrificing its originality, authenticity or generic integrity.

[a] Clarification of cognitive structuring

One major problem that legislative texts pose to a non-specialist reader is the depth and complexity of modification. Many of these modifications appear in those syntactic positions where they create discontinuities in the structure of the legislative statement (see Bhatia, 1982, 1983a). The syntactic structure of a typical legislative statement (see Section 5.2.4), must be understood in terms of a complex interplay of qualifications and the main provisionary clause. The most serious obstacle to a clear understanding of these legislative documents, therefore, is the complexity of syntactic structure, which can be overcome by clarifying the cognitive structuring underlying the provisions. Since I have already discussed, in Chapter 5, how this can be achieved effectively without sacrificing generic integrity of the text, I shall look again at one of the examples [16] I used earlier for the analysis of cognitive structuring, and present another way of achieving the same clarity of cognitive structuring:

> [1] Where the dwelling-house with respect to which the right to buy is exercised is a registered land, **the Chief Land Registrar shall,** if so requested by the Secretary of State, **supply him** (on payment of the appropriate fee) **with an office copy of any document required by the Secretary of State** for the purpose of executing a vesting order with respect to the dwelling-house **and shall** (notwithstanding section 112 of the Land Registration Act 1925) **allow any person authorized by the Secretary of State to inspect and make copies of and extracts from any register or document which is in the custody of the Chief Land Registrar and relates to the dwelling-house.**
>
> (Section 24(5) of the Housing Act, 1980, UK)

The emboldened sections represent the main provisionary clause and the remaining sections give the attendant qualifications, which make the provision operative.

[b] Reducing information load at a particular point

The second serious obstacle to the comprehension of legislative statements is the high density of information at a particular point in the syntactic structure of the legislative sentence (see Bhatia, 1987a). The tension between simplicity and clarity on the one hand, and certainty of legal effect on the other, is very common in all legal systems. However, in some of them, particularly in countries of the Commonwealth, it is further complicated by the requirements of the parliamentary process. The demand for all-inclusiveness resulting in excessive elaboration comes not only from the Government and the instructing department but also from Parliament itself, as was disclosed by the First Parliamentary Counsel to the Renton Committee:

For good reason, Parliament is rarely ready to accept a simplification if it means potential injustice in any class of case, however small. In particular, this is true of everything in a Bill which intervenes in private life, or in business. Powers of entry, and powers of obtaining information, will be looked at jealously. And much detail will often be needed before the Government is able to persuade Parliament that in this field no more than essential powers are being taken by the proposed legislation. . . . In many of the fields in which legislation is frequent, broad propositions may be, or may appear to be, oppressive. Parliament may insist that the rights of the citizen should be spelt out precisely and may well refuse to accept the argument that the way legislation is to be worked out can be left to the courts.

(Renton, 1975:57)

However, the present-day legislative writing shows the use of a new device to reduce information load at a particular point in the expression of legislative content. I have referred to this as a **textual-mapping** device, and it is being increasingly used in present-day legislation. This easification procedure was briefly discussed in Section 5.4. Let me give further substance to it by taking up an example from an earlier legislative writing to demonstrate how textual-mapping devices can make it more easily accessible. Following is the original version of Section 32 of the Housing Act, 1957:

[2] A local authority may pay to any person displaced from a house to which a demolition order made under this Part of this Act, or a closing order, applies, or which has been purchased by them under this Part of this Act, such reasonable allowance as they think fit towards his expenses in removing, and to any person carrying on any trade or business in any such house they may pay also such reasonable allowance as they think fit towards the loss which, in their opinion, he will sustain by reason of the disturbance of his trade or business consequent on his having to quit the house, and in estimating that loss they shall have regard to the period for which the premises occupied by him might reasonably have been expected to be available for the purposes of his trade or business and the availability of other premises suitable for that purpose.

(Section 32 of the Housing Act, 1957:797)

This is a relatively simple legislative provision although it is written in the traditional old style, entirely self-contained, packed into a single sentence. It looks very neat, precise, unambiguous and all-inclusive but is difficult to understand because of its syntactic complexity and sentence length. Like most legislative statements, this one calls for a cross-word mentality to ferret out its meaning. However, it is possible to break it into a number of subsections without sacrificing its legal content, precision and all-inclusive quality. This alternative version of section 32 uses a textual-mapping device to preserve its generic integrity:

1.   Where a house, to which a demolition order made under this Part of the Act, or a closing order, applies or which has been purchased by the local authority under this Part of the Act, the local authority may pay to any person specified in subsection (2) below such reasonable allowance as they think fit towards his expenses mentioned in subsection (3) below and the loss mentioned in subsection (4) below.

2.   The person mentioned in subsection (1) above is –
(i) anybody who is displaced from a house mentioned in subsection 1 above, or
(ii) anybody who is carrying on any trade or business in a house mentioned in subsection 1(i) above.

3.   Expenses mentioned in subsection (1) above are the expenses incurred by any such person mentioned in subsection 2(i) above in removing as a result of displacement.

4.   The loss mentioned in subsection (1) above is that which, in the opinion of the local authority, any person specified in subsection (2)(ii) above will sustain by reason of the disturbance of his trade or business consequent on his having to quit the trade.

5.   In estimating the loss mentioned in subsection (4) above, the local authority shall have regard to the period for which the premises occupied by him might reasonably have been expected to be available for the purpose of his trade or business and the availability of other premises suitable for that purpose.

Breaking a lengthy legislative statement into several subsections obviously makes the main provisionary statement more easily accessible to its readers by postponing the less important and more complicating legal details to subsequent subsection(s). It may add to the length of the provision but it will certainly make it easier to construe and hence more readily accessible to a wider range of audience.

[c] Indicating legislative intentions

The third easification device that can make legislative writing more easily accessible without endangering its generic integrity is the use of statements of purpose to explain and clarify the legislative intent at various levels, particularly in the case of complex contingencies. This will tell readers, specialist and non-specialists alike, what the Act or any section of it is about. Conard (1985) aptly illustrates this point by looking at the Trading with the Enemy Act, of the USA.

> *The first thing that any law-reader wants to know is what the law is about. Does it affect him or doesn't it? Most laws fail . . . to answer this question. . . A typical example is the Trading with the Enemy Act, which in time of war suddenly applies to tens of thousands of Americans. But if it came in the mail to an American who was about to send some money to a foreign creditor, he would have to parse two or three pages before he found out whether he was likely to be affected by it.*
>
> *The first thing that the citizen would notice is that the Act begins with Section 2 (may be S.1 got lost, he thinks). Section 2, which has no subtitle, contains a long list of definitions, starting with a half-page definition of "enemy."*
>
> *Somewhere in the middle of the second page begins Section 3, also with no subtitle. If the citizen is still looking, he will see:*

> That it shall be unlawful:
> (a) For any person in the United States, except with a license of the President, granted to such person, or to the enemy, or ally of enemy, as provided in this Act, to trade, either directly or indirectly, with, to, or from, or for, or on account of, or on behalf of, or for the benefit of any other person. . .

> *If he keeps on for a few lines more, and understands what he reads, he will at last find out what the law is about."*

> (Conard, 1985:62–83)

Conard suggests that a better way to start a statute could have been to begin: "This law applies to everyone in the United States who has any dealings with foreigners." It could then have explained what foreigners and what dealings were specifically affected.

The Renton Committee Report (1975:63) also seems to be clear about the importance of such statements of purpose, when they recommend that *statements of purpose should be used when they are the most convenient method of delimiting or otherwise clarifying the scope and effect of legislation.*

Elsewhere, Lord Renton (1990:14) gives an excellent example of both clarity and certainty of effect achieved in the Children Bill by clarifying the governing principle which the courts must apply when making decisions affecting children.

[3] When a court determines any question with respect to

(a) the upbringing of a child; or
(b) the administration of a child's property or the application of any income arising from it,

the child's welfare shall be the court's paramount consideration.

Sometimes statements of purpose or intention are also given in the form of sub-heading(s) and/or additional notes, as in the following example from The Personal Injuries (Compensation Insurance) Act 1963, Government of India:

[4] **Compensation payable under the Act, by whom and how payable** –

[D] (1) There shall, subject to such condition as may be specified in the Scheme, be payable by an employer in respect of personal injury sustained by a gainfully occupied person who is a workman to whom this Act applies, compensation, in addition to any relief provided under the Personal Injuries (Emergency Provisions) Act, 1962 (59 of 1962), of the amount and kind provided by section 7:

Provided that. . .

(2). . .

(3). . .
NOTES – This section imposes on the employers a liability to pay compensation for "personal injuries" to the workmen and also provides for the circumstances in which the employer will be discharged from this obligation and the Central Government would then be liable.

[d] Illustrating legislative issues

In the communication of legislative intentions there are always areas where a particular interpretation can be viewed as doubtful or difficult. Conard (1985) cites a good example of this from a bill in the recent Congress which provided:

[5] That hereafter, except as otherwise specially provided by the Act of Congress, no action of recovery of wages, penalties or other damages, actual or exemplary, pursuant to any other law of the United States shall be maintained in any court unless the same was commenced within one year after such cause of action accrued:. . .

He comments:
"The only way a lawyer can know whether the one-year limitation of this law applies is to search the United States Code from stem to stern. If he can't find a limitation anywhere else, then this is it.

A catch-all limitation may be a good thing, just to cover the unknown and forgotten cases. But this wasn't that kind of a law. The draftsman knew precisely what actions he wanted to limit, and he listed them, with citation, in the Committee report. If he had listed them in the statute, he would have saved hours of research for thousands of lawyers... If the draftsman had wanted to enlighten his reader, he would have written:"

The following actions must be brought within one year after the cause of action accrued:
(1) Suits for treble damages based on infringement of a registered trademark (17 U.S.C., s25);
(2) Suits based on infringement of copyrights (27 U.S.C., s25);" and so on down the list.

(Conard, 1985:77–78)

In cases like these, it is always helpful to add notes or additional illustrations as part of the access structure of the legislative statement. Illustrations of this kind definitely are in use but very sparingly. Let me take an example from The Indian Code of Criminal Procedure, 1973.

[6] 212.(1) The charge shall contain such particulars as to the time and place of the alleged offence, and the person (if any) against whom, or the thing (if any) in respect of which, it was committed, as are reasonably sufficient to give the accused notice of the matter with which he is charged.

(2) When the accused is charged with criminal breach of trust or dishonest misappropriation of money or other movable property, it shall be sufficient to specify the gross sum or, as the case may be, describe the movable property in respect of which the offence is alleged to have been committed, and the dates between which the offence is alleged to have been committed, without specifying particular items or exact dates, and the charge so framed shall be deemed to be a charge of one offence within the meaning of section 219.

Provided that the time included between the first and the last of such dates shall not exceed one year.

213. When the nature of the case is such that the particulars mentioned in sections 211 and 212 do not give the accused sufficient notice of the matter with which he is charged, the charge shall also contain such particulars of the manner in which the alleged offence was committed as will be sufficient for that purpose.

Illustrations

(a) A is accused of theft of a certain article at a certain time and place. The charge need not set out the manner in which the theft was effected.

(b) A is accused of cheating B at a given time and place. The charge must set out the manner in which A cheated B.

(c) A is accused of giving false evidence at a given time and place. The charge must set out that portion of evidence given by A which is alleged to be false.

(The Code of Criminal Procedure, 1973, Government of India)

Illustrations of this kind, whether real cases from past judgments or imaginary ones, do not interfere with or neutralize the generic integrity of the legislative statement, but they stand outside as additional aid to interpretation and thus help comprehension of complicating legal content.

A variety of other easification procedures can be additionally devised to facilitate comprehension and interpretation of complex contingencies depending upon the nature of the genre, the kinds of psycholinguistic difficulties it poses to a set of readers, and the purpose of the reading activity.

Gunnarsson (1984) gives a good illustration of this use of easification devices when she applies rule-component analysis to clarify syntactic organization of legislative statements. Section 11 of the Joint Regulation Act and its alternate version illustrate the point.

[7] s11 Before an employer decides on important alteration to his activity, he shall, on his own initiative, negotiate with an organization of employees in relation to which he is bound by collective agreement. The same shall be observed before an employer decides on important alteration of work or employment conditions for employees who belong to the organization.

If urgent reasons so necessitate, the employer may make and implement a decision before he has fulfilled his duty to negotiate under the first part of this section.

The alternative version would be as follows:

	The employer's duty to initiate negotiations before making a decision
s.11 Where an employer is bound by a collective agreement with an organization of employees and where employer plans	
– an important alteration to his operations or – an important alteration to the working conditions or conditions of employment of an employee who is a member of the organization:	
The employer shall himself initiate negotiations on the planned alteration with the organization of employees and conclude these negotiations before making a	

decision on the alteration.

If exceptional circumstances arise such that
the employer cannot postpone making and
implementing the decision:

The employer may make and implement
the decision before negotiating.

(Gunnarsson, 1984:87–88)

Although in this example there is quite a bit of rewriting of the original legislative statements and modification to the original language, the resulting version retains the essential legislative character of the genre. So long as any of these easification strategies do not interfere with the generic integrity of the text, they should be acceptable to the specialist community. In plain language literature, however, we often come across examples which transform legislative statements into plain language quite effectively for non-specialist readership, but for the drafting community these versions invariably neutralize the generic integrity of the legislation, thus giving the impression that the essential certainty of legal effect is either reduced or completely lost. Let me take a very simple example I was given by a senior Parliamentary Counsel in London a few years ago.

We were discussing the use of complex prepositions in legislative statements and I was arguing in favour of simple prepositions like 'for' in place of a more complex one like 'for the purpose of', 'about' in place of 'with respect to', 'under' in place of 'in accordance with' or 'in pursuance of' etc. His argument was that although in a number of cases it really does not matter much if one substitutes a simple preposition like 'about' in place of 'with respect to' as in the following example:

[8] An Act to clarify and amend law with respect to investment and borrowings by trustee savings banks.
(Trustees Savings Bank Act, 1978, UK, *underlining added*)

He explained that in cases like these, a complex preposition is used to achieve greater formality. It is quite likely, he emphasized, that Parliament, or some members of it, may not like to see lack of formality and somewhat less dignified use of a commonplace preposition like 'about' in legislative expressions. In other cases, however, a simple preposition may result in either loss of certainty in legal effect or ambiguity in its interpretation. He gave the following example, which illustrates the point very effectively:

[9] Child benefit shall not be payable in respect of a child over the age of 16 years for any week beginning after 31st August 1978 in which financial support for that child is being provided by way of payment under arrangements made by virtue of section 2 of the Employment and Training Act 1973 (a).
(The Child Benefit (General) Amendment Regulations 1978, UK, No.1275)

In this case it is likely that one may suggest the use of either 'to' or 'for' in place of the complex preposition 'in respect of'. However, if one were to use 'to', the section would become inaccurate because the child benefit is payable to parents or even to someone else in respect of a child and not necessarily to the child. On the other hand, the use of 'for' will make the section vague, because it could be interpreted that the money collected must be used for the child, which is not true. The intention is to compensate parents or whoever acts as a guardian for the expenses incurred on the child. Therefore, 'in respect of' seems to convey the intention of Parliament more appropriately than any of the alternatives in this case.

7.3 Popular accounts for public consumption

The main thrust of plain-language documents has been to press for language reform for the benefit of ordinary citizens. The citizens, who are supposed to abide by legislation, have a right to understand the laws which govern their daily activities. Unfortunately, however, laws are unintelligible to a large section of the people who are supposed to abide by them. As a matter of fact, we must realize that legislative documents are written for two very different audiences, and that they have different communicative purposes. The specialists, who include lawyers, judges, government executive officers, need to be able to understand and interpret laws in order to negotiate and implement justice. Ordinary citizens, on the other hand, need to be aware of laws in order to be able to avoid violating them. In the sciences, there is a fairly well-established tradition to produce two different versions of scientific reports, one for fellow scientists and the other for popular consumption by science enthusiasts. A somewhat similar tradition needs to be firmly established in the legislative setting as well. Simple accounts of the kind that Widdowson (1973) talks about in the context of language simplification can be one strong possibility and alternative non-linear accounts of public documents, including laws, social security, insurance, public health documents etc. the other. There has been some effort in this direction in the past few years, but much more needs to be done.

Plain English versions

Much of the plain English movement has been directed to redrafting general commercial and administrative documents, including insurance policies, residential leases, tax return forms, social benefit claim forms and other papers for better accessibility and usability by a larger section of society. Its achievements in the past few years have been tremendous. However, when it comes to legislative provisions, it has not been able to soften the attitude of the parliamentary draftsmen significantly in many of the Commonwealth countries, in spite of some of the impressive re-written versions of complex legislative matter. The Law Reform Commission of Victoria, in their Discussion Paper No.1, cite section 35 of the Fair Trading Act 1985 as an example of the plain English simplification.

[10] 35. (1) Where, on the application of the Minister or the Director, the Court is satisfied that a person has engaged in conduct constituting a contravention of a provision of Part II, the Court may make either or both of the following orders:

(a) An order requiring that person or a person involved in the contravention to disclose to the public, to a particular person or to persons included in a particular class of persons, in such manner as is specified in the order, such information or information of such a kind as is so specified, being information that is in possession of the person to whom the order is directed or to which that last-mentioned person has access;

(b) An order requiring that person or a person involved in the contravention to publish, at the expense of the person, in a manner and at times specified in the order, advertisements the terms of which are specified in, or are to be determined in accordance with, the order.

(2) Where, on an application made under sub-section (1), the Court is satisfied that a contravention of a provision of Part II has been committed, the Court shall not, in respect of that contravention, make an order or orders under sub-section (1) that the Court considers would, or would be likely to, require the expenditure by the person or persons to whom the order or orders is or are directed of an amount that exceeds, or of amounts that, in the aggregate, exceed, £50,000.

(3) Where, on an application made under sub-section (1), the Court is satisfied that a person has committed, or been involved in, two or more contraventions of the same provision of Part II, being contraventions that appear to the Court to have been of the same nature or a substantially

similar nature and to have occurred at or about the same time (whether or not the person has also committed, or been involved in, another contravention or other contraventions of that provision that was or were of a different nature or occurred at a different time), the Court shall not, in respect of the first-mentioned contraventions, make an order or orders under sub-section (1) that the Court considers would, or would be likely to, require the expenditure by the person or persons to whom the order or orders is or are directed of an amount that exceeds, or of amounts that, in the aggregate, exceed, £50,000.

(4) Where –

(a) on an application made under sub-section (1), the Court is satisfied that a person has committed, or been involved in, a contravention or contraventions of a provision of Part II; and

(b) an order has, or orders have, previously been made under sub-section (1) against the person who committed, or against a person who was involved in, that contravention or those contraventions in respect of another contravention or other contraventions of the same provision, being a contravention which, or contraventions each of which, appears to the Court to have been of the same nature as, or of a substantially similar nature to, and to have occurred at or about the same time as, the first-mentioned contravention or contraventions (whether or not an order has, or orders have, also previously been made under sub-section (1) against any of those persons in respect of another contravention or other contraventions of that provision that was or were of a different nature or occurred at a different time) –

the Court shall not, in respect of the contravention or contraventions mentioned in paragraph (a), make an order or orders under sub-section (1) that the Court considers would be likely to require the expenditure by the person or persons to whom the order or orders is or are directed of an amount that exceeds, or of amounts that, in the aggregate, exceed, the amount (if any) by which £50,000 is greater than the amount, or the sum of the amounts that has or have been or that the Court considers would be or be likely to be, expended in accordance with the previous order or previous orders first mentioned in paragraph (b).

(Section 35 of the Fair Trading Act, 1985)

Admittedly, this is an extremely complicated legislative statement consisting of a series of embedded clauses, one within the other. The commission then gives a drastically simplified version of this section in plain English:

[11] £50,000 is the most that a person or persons may be required to spend by an order or orders under sub-section (1) (whether made on one or more occasions) for all contraventions of any one provision of Part II which are of the same or a substantially similar nature and which occurred at or about the same time.

This simple version in plain English is very brief and accessible to ordinary readership and gives a gist of the whole original section in a few words.

The second most popular textual device which is being increasingly used in public documents, is of various kinds of caption technique. These are meant to give the reader a quick understanding of what the specific section has to offer. These are very common in public documents which are meant to inform and educate ordinary readership. A typical example of this is the following pamphelet from REGO.

REGO'S CHANGED.

From July 1st, 1991 you cannot register your vehicle without first getting a *Green Slip*. This is the Compulsory third Party Insurance you must have.

Inside, how to arrange it and the benefits for you.

COMPULSORY READING

Compulsory third Party Insurance (often called CPT) has always been paid as part of your rego. This is the insurance you pay to cover you if your vehicle injures another person. For the past two years your Compulsory Third Party Insurance has been allocated to one of 14 approved insurance companies.

From July 1st, 1991, that all changed. If your vehicle registration is due on, or after, July 1, 1991, you won't be able to register your vehicle without a Green Slip. Trailers do not need to be insured after this date.

You will then be free to choose your own insurer from any of the 14 approved insurance companies. Price control restrictions come to an end and the insurance companies are free to compete on price. Most people will find that they will pay less for Compulsory Third Party Insurance, particularly if they have a safe driving record. Note that it is only the premium payment that is affected.

By law, the cover offered by each insurance company is exactly the same. It's a very fair system. The insurance companies get to compete on price, you get to choose which insurance company will give you the best deal. The most important thing for you to remember is this:

Third Party Insurance is compulsory. After July, 1991, you cannot register your vehicle without the endorsed Green Slip you'll get when you pay your Third Party Insurance premium.

OK? Now here's how it works and how you go about getting your all-important endorsed *Green Slip*

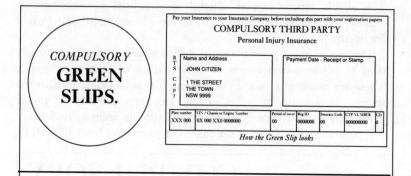

How the Green Slip looks

WHAT TO DO WHEN YOU GET YOUR MOTOR REGISTRATION RENEWAL NOTICE

PINK SLIP
(IF REQUIRED)
+
GREEN SLIP
=
REGO

PLEASE REMEMBER: NO ENDORSED *GREEN SLIP*, NO REGO. ALLOW YOURSELF PLENTY OF TIME TO OBTAIN YOUR *PINK* AND *GREEN SLIPS* BEFORE REGISTRATION. NEED ANY HELP? CALL THE *GREEN SLIPS* HELPLINE FREE ON 008 021031.

1.

If your renewal notice specifies an inspection required, you'll need to get a Pink Slip (Certificate of Roadworthiness) from an Authorised Inspection Station.

2.

To register your vehicle, you'll need to get an endorsed *Green Slip*. Your current insurer will send you, separately, a Compulsory Third Party renewal certificate (the *Green Slip*). You can simply pay the amount to the insurer nominated on that *Green Slip*. Or you can choose any of the licensed insurers from the list in this leaflet. When you pay your premium they will give you an endorsed *Green Slip*. It's an official receipt and proof that you have paid for your Compulsory Third Party.

3.

Take your endosed *Green Slip*, along with your Pink Slip (if you need one) and your vehicle Registration Certificate to your local Motor Registry to complete your vehicle registration. Or, if you prefer, you can mail the documents, together with your payment, to the Motor Registry.

Need Help? Call the Helpline 008 021031.

QUESTIONS AND ANSWERS.

Q: Can I register my vehicle without an endosed Green Slip?

A: *No.*

Q: What vehicles do I need a Green Slip for?

A: *All registered motor vehicles – cars, trucks, motor bikes, motor scooters, in fact any motorised vehicles using a public street. Trailers and caravans do not require Compulsory Third Party Insurance. However they must still be registered.*

Q: The change happens from July, 1991. Does that mean I have to do something immediately.

A: *No. Only if your registration falls due on or after July 1, 1991. Of course, if you buy a new vehicle after that time, you'll need an endorsed Green Slip before you can register it.*

Q: After 1st July, 1991, if I'm not happy with my current insurance company, can I change?

A: *Certainly, at your first registration renewal after that date.*

Q: You've said the premium rates will be competitive. What abour the cover?

A: *All the approved insurers will be offering exactly the same cover. It's only the dollar value of the premiums that may vary from insurer to insurer. There will be no "fine print".*

Q: What happens when I sell my vehicle?

A: *The Compulsory Third Party Personal Injury Insurance goes with the vehicle. So, if it still has, say, 6 months to run, the buyer gets the benefit. And of course, it works in your favour if you buy a second hand car.*

Q: What happens when I buy a new vehicle?

A: *You will need an endorsed Green Slip before you can register the vehicle. Speak to your dealer or insurer.*

Q: Am I still covered when I travel interstate and are motorists from other States covered in NSW?

A: *Yes. The amount of compensation payable will depend on where the accident happens. If you are injured in Victoria, then the law of Victoria applies. Similarly, if a Victorian is injured in New South Wales, the law of New South Wales applies.*

Q: If I'm in an accident which involves personal injury, can I find out who the Compulsory Third Party Insurer of the other vehicle is?

A: *Yes. If the owner of the other vehicle can't help, just contact the Motor Accidents Authority and they will advise you.*

Q: How do I lodge a claim if I am injured in a motor accident?

A: *Find out the name of the insurer of the vehicle you believe was responsible for the accident. Obtain a claim form from them. Send it to the insurer. Before doing so you may also wish to consult your solicitor.*

Q: If I'm a good driver will I pay less than someone with a bad accident history?

A: *After July, 1991, the 14 insurers will be competing with each other for your business. The answer is "most likely". Contact your Insurer.*

Q: Do pensioners get a reduced premium rate?

A: *Pensioner discounts will still apply. Contact your insurer.*

Q: What do I do if I have an accident?

A: *Any motor vehicle accident where someone is injured should be reported to the police as soon as possible, and in any event within 28 days. Any claim for compensation should be lodged within six months.*

As in public documents, the aim of simplification of legislation too is to increase the usability of the legislative document, as well as to achieve greater comprehensibility. We sometimes find the use of question captions in the plain English versions of legislation. Kelly (1988:64) reports the use of question captions by the Victoria Law Reform Commission in the rewriting of the Credit Act. The following is the original version of sections 105 and 106 of the Act.

[12] 105. The debter under a regulated contract may discharge his obligations under the contract by paying or tendering to the credit provider the net balance due to the credit provider at the time of payment or tender.

106. (1) Subject to this section, the mortgagor under a regulated mortgage, may, unless the mortgage is also security for a debt or obligation arising otherwise than in relation to a regulated contract, by notice in writing given to the mortgagee, require the mortgagee to sell goods that are subject to the mortgage.

(2) A notice given under sub-section (1) is of no force or effect unless –

(a) the goods to which the notice relates are, when the notice is given, in the possession of the mortgagee; or

(b) the mortgagor delivers the goods to the mortgagee in accordance with sub-section (3) not later than seven days after the giving of the notice or such longer time as is agreed between the mortgagee and the mortgagor or as the court permits on application by the mortgagee or the mortgagor.

(3) A mortgagor who gives a notice under sub-section (1) may, unless the goods to which the notice relates are in the possession of the mortgagee, deliver the goods to the mortgagee during ordinary business hours at a place at which the mortgagee ordinarily carries on business or at a time or place agreed upon by the mortgagee and the mortgagor or, if the mortgagee and the mortgagor fail to agree on a time and place, at a time or place determined by a court on application by the mortgagee or the mortgagor.

(4) Where –

(a) a notice has been given to the mortgagee under this section; and

(b) any goods to which the notice relates are in the possession of the mortgagee or have been delivered to him in accordance with sub-section (3)

the mortgagee shall, as soon as reasonable and practicable in the circumstances, sell the goods for the best price reasonably obtainable and shall account to the mortgagor as provided by section 114.

Penalty: 10 penalty units

The rewritten version of the above sections of the Act is much simpler and more readily accessible to a lay audience:

2. When is the debtor entitled to pay out the contract?
The debtor may pay out the contract any time. The contract is then discharged.

3. Is a mortgagor entitled to require the mortgagee to sell the goods?
The mortgagor may at any time require the mortgagee to sell the goods.

3.1 The mortgagor has to ask the mortgagee in writing.

3.2 If the goods are not in the mortgagee's possession, the mortgagor has to deliver them to the mortgagee at a place where the mortgagee carries on business during ordinary business hours – or as agreed by them, or ordered by a court on the application of either of them. The goods have to be delivered within 7 days of the notice given – or as agreed by the parties or ordered by the court.

3.3 The mortgagee must then sell the goods as soon as reasonably practicable for the best price reasonably obtainable.

Penalty: 10 penalty units

3.4 The mortgagor is not entitled to ask the mortgagee to sell the goods in this way if the mortgage is also a security for an unregulated obligation or contract.

Rewritten plain-English versions of public documents have become very popular in the past two decades. They reduce the length of the legislative sentence, clarify the complicating legal concepts, and spread the density of information by breaking a typically long legislative sentence into several shorter ones. However, as instruments of legislation, they leave the details to be worked out by the judiciary, which, in a way, may not be a totally undesirable situation. Whether it will be acceptable in many countries of the Commonwealth is certainly debatable. As the Hon. Mr Justice V.C.R.A.C. Crabbe (1989:84) declares,

> *Brevity may be the soul of wit. It is hardly the soul of a legislative sentence. Clarity is the soul of the legislative sentence. Precision does not necessarily mean brevity. Nor is brevity synonymous with simplicity. An economy of words is not necessarily beneficial in a legislative sentence.*

A little later he adds,

> there are calls for the legislative draftsman to use plain English in the drafting of legislation. But what is plain English? In an answer to a parliamentary question the Financial Secretary to the Treasury, asked if he will take steps to simplify the language of legislation, said that the primary objective in legislation must always be certainty. "The body of statutes which was deliberately designed in ordinary layman's language, namely, the Rent Acts, had probably as a result given rise to more litigation than any series of Statutes." Megarry also had this to say, "The Rent Acts ('a byword for confused draftsmanship') have evoked a rich volume of judicial vituperation. In this 'extraordinary and unique legislation', 'the Acts were passed in a hurry, the language used was often extremely vague', and the language 'resembles that of popular journalism rather than the terms of art of conveyancing'. 'It is patchwork legislation, has not been framed with any scientific accuracy of language, and presents great difficulties of interpretation to the Courts that had to give effect to it' ".

Similarly, Turnbull (1986:69) gives a good example of subsection (3) of section 8 of the Crimes (Hijacking of Aircraft) Act 1972, which created many problems for the Courts by its use of simple plain language. It provides,

> The punishment for an offence against this section is imprisonment for life.

This provision, in plain language, created for the Courts a difficult question as to whether the provision imposed a mandatory life imprisonment or whether the Courts had a discretion to impose penalty less than life imprisonment. The trial judge took the first interpretation whereas the appellate courts took the latter view. As a matter of fact, laws are consciously written for the judges, 'to box them in a corner', as it were. Even in the United States, where the plain-English movement forms a fairly well-established pressure group, legislative acts are rarely written in the same simple and plain language into which the original authentic legislative acts are translated for the benefit of Congressmen, so that they can vote understandingly on the bills. The simple reason is that the complex, detailed and, often considered, complete original version is meant for lawyers, public officials and judges, whose job is to discuss and negotiate justice; the plain version is meant for those who do not need to be thoroughly well-versed in the intricacies of legal content but who do need to be aware of specific laws in general terms. The two versions serve different communicative purpose(s) and they are meant for two different audiences, each of whom has a very different background knowledge and different motivations for reading and understanding the document. The two versions, therefore, represent two different genres. Popular versions or simple accounts can either be in simple prose as discussed above or in other non-linear forms, which have become popular in recent literature as alternatives to prose.

Alternatives to prose for popular consumption

Charrow (1988), Hartley (1978), Lewis, Horabin and Gane (1967), Redish (1979), Shuy and Larkin (1977), Wasan (1968), Wright (1978, 1979, 1980,), Wright and Reid (1973), and a number of other researchers have been working on alternatives to prose for expressing complex contingencies and have maintained that written information does not always have to be flowing prose. They have shown that abandoning the prose format for non-linear alternatives such as logical trees or flow charts, and tabulated presentations can often improve comprehension and, in particular, usability of public documents including some legislative rules. Lewis, Horabin and Gane (1967) illustrate how instructions from an income tax form for Capital Gains Tax could be presented alternatively either in the form of a list structure or a flow chart. The original version of the text runs as follows:

[13] If the asset consists of stocks or shares which have values quoted on a stock exchange (see also paragraph G below), or unit trust units whose values are regularly quoted, the amount of tax chargeable or allowable depends upon the relative sizes of the cost price of the asset, its market value on 6 April 1965, and the selling price of the asset.

If the selling price is greater than the market value, and the market value is greater than the cost price, tax is charged on the selling price less the market value (less allowable expenses.) If the selling price is greater than the market value, and the market value is less than the cost price, two possibilities arise. Either the selling price is greater than the cost price, in which case the tax is charged on the selling price less the cost price (less expenses.) Or the selling price is less than the cost price, in which case no tax is either charged or allowed.

If the selling price is less than the market value, and the market value is less than the cost price, tax is allowed on the market value less the selling price (plus allowable expenses.) If the selling price is less than the market value, and the market value is greater than the cost price, two possibilities arise. Either the selling price is less than the cost price, in which case tax is allowed on the cost price less the selling price (plus expenses) or the selling price is greater than the cost price, in which case no tax is either allowed or charged.

Lewis, Horabin and Gane (1967) then give an alternative version of the same text in the form of a list structure.

List structure

Instructions for determining chargeable gain or allowable loss

---

A Write down
(a) the cost price of your asset ....
(b) its market value at 6 April 1965 ....
(c) its selling price ....

B Answer the following questions:
1 Is the selling price greater than the market value?
If YES: Go to question 2.
If NO: Go to question 4.

---

2 Is the market value greater than the cost price?
If YES: Tax is charged on the selling price, less the market value, less expenses.
If NO: Go to question 3.

---

3 Is the selling price greater than the cost price?
If YES: Tax is charged on the selling price, less the cost price, less expenses.
If NO: No tax is either charged or allowed.

4 Is the market value greater than the cost price?
If YES: Go to question 5.
If NO: Tax is allowed on the market value, less the selling price, plus expenses.

5 Is the selling price greater than the cost price?
If YES: No tax is either allowed or charged.
If NO: Tax is allowed on the cost price, less the selling price, less expenses.

They also offer yet another simple account of the Capital Gains Tax in the form of a flow chart as follows.

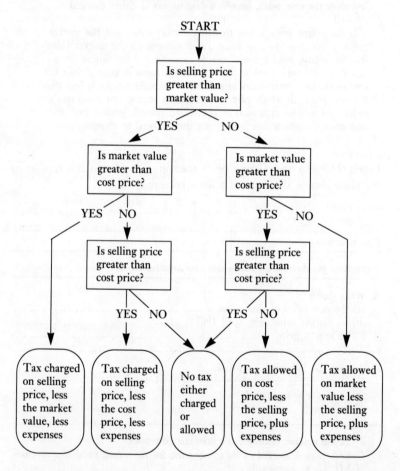

Note: 'Market Value' is based on the quoted value at April 1965.

This process of simplification, as Child (1988:224) points out, involves three stages:

1. The material is divided up into as many discrete propositions as possible.
2. Each proposition is divided into an assertion and its negation, in order to make the list exhaustive and the items on it mutually exclusive.
3. The propositions are put into a logical sequence moving them from general to specific, so that the first question produces an immediate result in as many cases as possible and each successive question moves to a lower common denominator, producing a result for fewer cases.

Wasan (1968:549) illustrates somewhat similar non-linear presentation strategies for the expression of complex contingencies. He uses the following original version of the rule to determine a seasonal worker's rate of unemployment benefit:

> **What is a seasonal worker's rate of unemployment benefit in his season?**
> [14] For the ordinary benefit claimant, full rate benefit requires 50 contributions to have been paid or credited in the preceding contribution year. Of these 39 must be in Class I. Benefit, even at a reduced rate, is not payable unless 26 Class I contributions have been paid or credited in the contribution year. But if a seasonable worker has not less than 13 Class I contributions paid or credited in a contribution year, he may count as Class I contributions any other contributions paid or credited in that year for the purpose of determining his rate of benefit if he is unemployed during his season. Thus if he should become unemployed in that part of the year when he is normally working for an employer, he should be entitled to full rate benefit so long as he has contributed according to his class of insurance throughout the preceding contribution year.

He then goes on to rewrite the same rule of law in the form of a logical tree. This non-linear format, he rightly points out, is not only economical in terms of effort and number of words used, but is also more effective in usability and decision-making.

Alternatives to prose in document designs have become a fairly well-established area of text construction in recent years. As Wright (1980) points out, these versions take into account reader characteristics, their familiarity with the subject matter and range of cognitive abilities including their background knowledge, and their purpose for reading the document: they also take account of the task constraints and generic characteristics of the text in question, and the usability is analysed in terms of perceptual, attentional, memory, response and decision

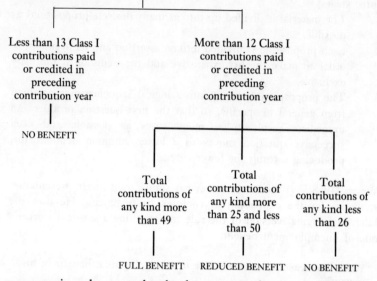

Seasonal Worker's rate of unemployment benefit in his season

Less than 13 Class I contributions paid or credited in preceding contribution year

More than 12 Class I contributions paid or credited in preceding contribution year

NO BENEFIT

Total contributions of any kind more than 49

Total contributions of any kind more than 25 and less than 50

Total contributions of any kind less than 26

FULL BENEFIT   REDUCED BENEFIT   NO BENEFIT

processes, in order to render the documents easier to use. The writer presents such non-linear versions for maximizing accessibility and usability of documents. These alternative forms are good for assessing the over-all cognitive structure of the legislative statement; they also tend to reveal any problematic gaps or ambiguities in the coverage of the legislative provision. The two institutions which have excelled in such efforts are the Medical Research Council, Applied Psychological Unit, Cambridge, England and the Document Design Center, Washington DC, both of which are helping organizations in the private and the public sector to design readable, comprehensible and usable public documents, including forms, leaflets, brochures and legal documents.

Although a non-linear form of communication like the one discussed above is an excellent method of presenting information, particularly for documents which need to be used to take decisions, it will have limitations, sometimes very serious ones, when used as an alternative to conventional forms of legislative statements, particularly the ones which are meant for specialist use. These alternative forms are being used for information and education purposes and are becoming increasingly popular in business, computers, public health, advertising and other areas where ordinary members of the public are meant to take decisions on the basis of technical information. All these alternative forms of popular versions, linear as well as non-linear, are effective and in some cases excellent examples of text presentation. However, none of these when used as an alternative to the legislative statement can be used to legislate, that is to negotiate justice in the court of law. In their non-linear alternative forms they will be difficult to quote in legal proceedings. As instruments of legislation, they have been and perhaps, for a long time to come, will continue to be rejected by the professional legal community as ineffective, inefficient, imprecise and devoid of legal content.

The main reason for this lack of interest in the so-called reformed writing is two-fold. First, the rewritten versions often obscure the generic integrity of the original legislative statement, and second, these can serve the communicative purpose of informing and educating the lay audience but are poor instruments for regulating human behaviour. The only way one can make them work is by changing the legal system. So long as the main function of legislation is to 'box the judge firmly in a corner', the legislative statements will continue to take the shape they conventionally do. However, the moment one transfers focus away from Parliament, and accepts the dominant role of the judiciary in the negotiation of social justice, the expression of legislative intentions will take the shape of general principles, thereby making plain language the obvious choice of legislative writers. As things are, the conventional legislative statement and its plain-English version serve two closely related yet slightly different communicative purposes and are hence seen by the specialist community and the legislators as somewhat different genres appropriate for two different settings.

Bibliography

Alderson, C. (1988). 'Testing and its administration in ESP' in Chamberlain, D. and Baumgardener, R. (eds.), *ESP in the classroom:Practice and Evaluation*, London, Modern English Publications and the British Council.

Alderson, J.C. and Urquhart, A.H. (1985). 'The effect of students' academic discipline on their performance on ESP reading tests', *Language Testing*, 2, 192–204.

Aman, R. (1982). 'Interlingual taboos in advertising: how not to name your product' in Di Pietro, R.J. (ed.), *Linguistics and the Professions*, Norwood, New Jersey, Ablex Publishing Corporation, 215–224.

ANSI (1979). *The American National Standard for Writing Abstracts*, ANSI Publication, New York.

Aristotle (Roberts, W. tr.) (1954). *Rhetoric*, Harvard University Press, Cambridge.

Barber, C.L. (1962). 'Some measurable characteristics of modern scientific prose' in *Contributions to English Syntax and Phonology*, Stockholm.

Bazerman, C. (1983). 'Scientific writing as a social act: a review of literature of the sociology of science' in Anderson, P.V., Brockmann, R.J. and Miller, C. (eds.), *New essays in technical writing and communication: Research, theory and practice*, Farmingdale, NY: Baywood.

de Beaugrande, R., and Dressler, W. (1981). *Introduction to text linguistics*, Longman, London.

Benson, (1984). 'Up a statute with a gun and camera: isolating linguistic and logical structures in the analysis of legislative language', *Seton Hall Legislative Journal*, 8, 279, 287–91, 296–300.

Bhatia, V.K. (1982). 'An investigation into formal and functional characteristics of qualifications in legislative writing and its application to English for Academic Legal Purposes'. A Ph.D thesis submitted to the University of Aston in Birmingham, UK.

Bhatia, V.K. (1983a). 'Simplification v. easification: the case of legal texts'. *Applied Linguistics*, 4(1), 42–54.

Bhatia, V.K. (1983b). *Applied Discourse Analysis of English Legislative Writing*. A Language Studies Unit Research Report, University of Aston in Birmingham, Birmingham.

Bhatia, V.K. (1984). 'Syntactic discontinuity in legislative writing and its implications for academic legal purposes' in Pugh, A.K. and Ulijn, J.M. (eds.), *Reading for Professional Purposes – Studies and Practices in Native and Foreign Languages*, Heinemann Educational Books, London, 90–96.

Bhatia, V.K. (1986). 'Specialist discipline and the ESP curriculum' in Tickoo, M.L. (ed.), *Language Across the Curriculum*, Singapore SEAMEO Regional Language Centre.

Bhatia, V.K. (1987a). 'Textual-mapping in British legislative writing', *World Englishes*, 6(1), 1–10.

Bhatia, V.K. (1987b). 'Language of the law', *Language Teaching*, October 1987, 227–234.

Bhatia, V.K. (1988). 'A genre-based approach to the analysis and teaching of business communication'. Paper presented at the XIV International Association of Language and Business, Reutlingen, West Germany, Nov. 1988.

Bhatia, V.K. (1989). 'Nativization of job application – a microethnographic study'. Paper presented at the International Conference on English in South Asia, Islamabad, Pakistan, 4–8 Jan., 1989.

Bhatia, V.K. (1991a). 'A genre-based approach to ESP materials development', *World Englishes*, 10(2), 1–14.

Bhatia, V.K. (1991b). 'Pragmatics of the use of nominals in academic and professional genres'. Paper presented at the Fifth Annual International Conference on Pragmatics and Language Learning, at the University of Illinois at Urbana-Champaign, Urbana, Apr. 1991.

Bhatia, V.K. and Tay, M. (eds.) (1987). *The Teaching of English in Meeting the Needs of Business and Technology*, Vol.1 and 2. The Report of the UNDP-Government of Singapore Project, Department of English Language and Literature, National University of Singapore.

Bley-Vroman, R. and Selinker, L. (1984). 'Research design in rhetorical/grammatical studies: a proposed optimal research strategy', *English for Specific Purposes*, 82–83, (1–4) and 84, (1–6).

Bradbury, P.L. (1984). *Cases and Statutes On Tort*, Sweet and Maxwell, London.

Calderbank, M. (1982). 'Case study in law', *English for Specific Purposes*, 68.

Candlin, C.N. (1978). 'Discoursal patterning and the equalising of interpretative opportunity'. Paper read at Culture Learning Institute, East-West Center, Hawaii, February 1978. Also published in Smith, L. (ed.), 1981. *English for Cross-cultural Communication*, Macmillan, London.

Candlin, C.N., Bruton, C.J. and Leather, J.H. (1974). *Doctor-patient Communication Skills: Working papers 1–4*, University of Lancaster, Department of Linguistics and Modern English Language, Lancaster.

Candlin, C.N., Leather, J.H. and Bruton, C.J. (1976). 'Doctors in casualty: applying communicative competence to components of specialist course design'. *IRAL*, 14, 3.

Candlin, C.N., Bruton, J. and Coleman, M. (1980). 'Dentist-patient communication'. Report to the General Dental Council, University of Lancaster, Lancaster.

Candlin, C.N. and Loftipour-Saedi, K. (1983). 'Processes of discourse', *Journal of Applied Language Study*, 1(2).

Carrell, P. (1983). 'Some issues in studying the role of schemata, or background knowledge', in *Readings in a Foreign Language*, 1, 81–92.

Carrell, P. (1987). 'Content and formal schemata in ESL reading', *TESOL Quarterly*, 21, 461–482.

Charrow, V. (1988). 'Readability vs. comprehensibility: a case study in improving a real document' in Davison, A. and Green, G. (eds.), *Linguistic Complexity and Text Comprehension: Readability Issues Reconsidered*, Lawrence Erlbaum Associates, Publishers, Hillsdale, New Jersey, London, 85–114.

Cheng, P.G. (1985). 'An analysis of contrastive rhetoric: English and Chinese expository prose, pedagogical implications, and strategies for the ESL teacher in a ninth-grade curriculum'. Unpublished doctoral dissertation, State College, Pennsylvania State University, Pennsylvania.

Child, B. (1988). *Drafting Legal Documents – Materials and Problems*, West Publishing Co., St Paul, Minnesota.

Clyne, M. (1981). 'Culture and discourse structure', *Journal of Pragmatics*, 5, 61–6.

Clyne, M. (1987). 'Cultural differences in the organization of academic discourse', *Journal of Pragmatics*, 11, 211–47.

Comeau, J. and Diehn, G. (1987). *Communication on the Job – A Practical Approach*, Prentice-Hall, Inc., New Jersey.

Conard, A.F. (1985). 'A legislative text – new ways to write laws', *Statute Law Review*, 62–83.

Connor, U. and McCagg, P. (1984). 'Cross-cultural differences and perceived quality in written paraphrases of English expository prose', *Applied Linguistics*, 4, 259–68.

Coode, G. (1848). On legislative expression or the language of written law. Introduction to a digest of the Poor Laws, appendixed to the 1843 Report of the Poor Law Commission. Repr. in Drieger, E.A. (1957), *The Composition of Legislation*.

Crabbe, V. C. R. A. C. (1989). 'The legislative sentence', *Statute Law Review*, 10(2), 79–94.

Crocker, A. (1982). 'LSP and methodology: some implications for course design and implementation in EALP', *English for Specific Purposes*, 67.

Crystal, D. and Davy, D. (1969). *Investigating English Style*, Longman, London.

Davies, F. and Greene, T. (1984). *Reading for Learning in the Sciences*, Oliver and Boyd, Edinburgh.

Dreidger, E.A. (1957). *The composition of Legislation*, Supply and Services Canada, (for) the Department of Justice, Ottawa.

Dubois, B.L. (1981). 'The construction of noun phrases in biomedical journal articles'. Paper presented at LSP Conference, Copenhagen, Aug. 1981.

Dudley-Evans, T. (1989). 'Genre analysis: an investigation of the introduction and discussion sections of MSc dissertations', in Coulthard, M. (ed.) *Talking about text*, English Language Research, University of Birmingham, Birmingham, UK.

Duke, S.O., Wauchope, R.D., Hoagland, R.E. and Wills, G.D. (1983). 'Influence of glyphosate on uptake and translocation of calcium ion in soyabean seedlings', *Weed Research*, 23/3, June 1983, Blackwell Scientific Publications, Oxford, 133–39.

Eagleson, R.D. (1988). 'Efficiency in legal drafting', in Kelly, D. (ed.), *Essays on Legislative Drafting: In Honour of J Q Ewens, CMG, CBE, QC,* The Adelaide Law Review Association, Law School, University of Adelaide, 13–27.

Ellis, J. and Ure, J.N. (1969). 'Language varieties: register', in Meeltham, A.R. (ed.), *Encyclopaedia of Linguistics, information and control,* Pergamon International Ed., London.

Fairclough, N. (1985). *Language and Power,* Longman, London.

Falsenfeld, C. (1981–82). 'The plain English movement in the United States', in *Canadian Business Law Journal,* 6, quoted in Thomas (1985).

French, A. (1989). 'The systematic acquisition of word forms by a child during the first fifty-word stage', *Journal of Child Language,* 16/1, Feb. 1989, 69–90.

Gan, K.A. (1989). 'Closings in business letters'. Unpublished academic exercise submitted to the Department of English Language and Literature, National University of Singapore, Singapore.

Garfinkel, H. (1967). *Studies in Ethnomethodology,* Prentice-Hall, Englewood Cliffs, NJ.

Garfinkel, H. (1972). 'Remarks on ethnomethodology', in Gumperz, J.J. and Hymes, D.H. (eds.), *Directions in Sociolinguistics: the ethnography of communication,* Holt, Rhinehart and Winston, New York.

Geertz, C. (1973). *The Interpretation of Cultures,* Basic Books, New York.

Genesee, F. (1989). 'Early bilingual development: one language or two?', *Journal of Child Language,* 16/1, Feb. 1989, 161–79.

Gimson, A.C. (1970). *An Introduction to the Pronunciation of English,* second edition, English Language Book Society and Edward Arnold (Publishers) Ltd., Hertford.

Gopnik, M. (1972). *Linguistic Structures in Scientific Texts,* Mouton, The Hague.

Government of India (1963). The Personal Injuries (Compensation Insurance) Act 1963.

Government of India (1947). The Prevention of Corruption Act 1947.

Government of India (1973). Indian Code of Criminal Procedure, 1973.

Greenfield, D.B. and Scott, M.S. (1986). 'Young children's preference for complementary pairs: evidence against a shift to a taxonomic preference', *Developmental Psychology,* 22(1), 19–21.

Gregory, M. (1967). 'Aspects of variety differentiation', *Journal of Linguistics,* 3/2, 177–98.

Gregory, M. and Carroll, S. (1978). *Language and Situation,* Kegan Paul, London.

Grice, H.P. (1975). 'Logic and conversation', in Cole, P. and Morgan, J.L. (eds), *Syntax and Semantics,* Volume 3, *Speech Acts,* Academic Press, New York.

Gunderson, L. (1991). *ESL literacy instruction – a guidebook to theory and practice,* Prentice-Hall Regents, Englewood Cliffs, New Jersey.

Gunnarsson, B.L. (1984). 'Functional comprehensibility of legislative texts: experiments with a Swedish Act of Parliament', *Text* 4(1–3), 71–105.

Gustafsson, M. (1975). *Some Syntactic Properties of English Law Language.* Department of English, University of Turku, Turku.

Gustafsson, M. (1984). 'The syntactic features of binomial expressions in legal English', *Text*, 4(1–3), 123–41.

Hale, G.A. (1988). 'Student major field and text content: interactive effects on reading comprehension in the tests of English as a Foreign Language', *Language Testing*, 5, 49–61.

Halliday, M.A.K. (1986). 'Language and learning: linguistic aspects of education and scientific knowledge'. Lecture series at National University of Singapore, Singapore, Singapore University Press.

Halliday, M.A.K. (1989). 'Some grammatical problems in scientific English'. Paper presented to the SPELT Symposium on Language in Education, Karachi, July 1989.

Halliday, M.A.K., McIntosh, A. and Strevens, P. (1964). *The Linguistic Sciences and Language Teaching*, The English Language Book Society and Longman Group Ltd., London.

Hart, R.P. (1986). 'Of Genre, computers and the Reagan inaugural', in H.W. Simons and A.A. Aghazarian (Ed.) *Form, genre and the study of political discourse*, University of South Carolina Press.

Hartley, J. (1978). 'Space and structure in instructional texts'. Paper presented at the NATO Coference on Visual Presentation of Information at Het Vennebos, Netherlands, Sept., 1978.

Hasan, R. (1973). 'Code, Register, and Social Dialect', in Bernstein, B. (ed.), *Class, Codes and Control: Applied Studies in the Sociology of Language*, Volume 2, Routledge and Kegan Paul, London.

Hawkins, S. (1983). 'How to understand your partner's cultural baggage', *International Management*, Sept. 1983, 48–51.

Hill, A.A. (1958). *Introduction to Linguistic Structures*, New York, Harcourt, Brace & Co.

Hill, S.S., Sophelsa, B.F. and West, G.K. (1982). 'Teaching ESL students to read and write experimental research papers'. *TESOL Quarterly*, 16(3), 333–47.

Hinds, J. (1983). 'Contrastive rhetoric: Japanese and English', *TEXT*, 3, 183–95.

Hinds, J. (1990). 'Inductive, deductive, quasi-inductive: expository writing in Japanese, Korean, Chinese, and Thai', in Connor, U. and Johns, A.M. (eds.), *Coherence in Writing – Research and Pedagogical Perspectives*, TESOL. 97–109, Washington, DC.

HMSO (1957). *The Housing Act, 1957*, HMSO, London.

HMSO (1978). *Trustees Savings Bank Act, 1978*, HMSO, London.

HMSO (1978). *Nuclear Safeguards and Electricity (Finance Act) 1978*, HMSO, London.

HMSO (1978). *The Child Benefit (General) Amendment Regulations 1978*, HMSO, London.

HMSO (1980). *The Housing Act, 1980*, HMSO, London.

HMSO (1981). *The British Nationality Act, 1981*, HMSO, London.

Hoey, M. (1979). *Signalling in Discourse*. Birmingham University ELR Monograph #6, Birmingham.

Hoey, M. (1983). *On the Surface of Discourse*, George Allen and Unwin, London.

Hofstede, G. (1983). 'The cultural relativity of organizational practices and theories', *Journal of International Business Studies*, Autumn 1983, 75–89.

Huckin T. and Olsen, L. (1983). *English for Science and Technology – A Handbook for Non-native Speakers*, McGraw-Hill Book Company, New York.

Huckin T. and Olsen, L. (1984). 'On the use of informants in LSP discourse analysis', in Pugh, A. and Ulijn, J. (eds), *Reading for professional purposes*, Heinemann, London, 120–29.

Huddleston, R. (1971). *The Sentence in Written English*, Cambridge University Press, Cambridge.

Huseman, R.C., Prescott, G.M., Lahiff, D., Penrose, J. and Hatfield, J. (1986). *Business Communication – Strategies and Skills*, Holt, Rinehart and Winston, Sydney.

Jordan, M.P. (1986). 'Co-associative lexical cohesion in promotional literature', *Journal of Technical Writing and Communication*, 6 (1/2), 33–53.

Kachru, B.B. (1982). *The Other Tongue: English Across Cultures*, University of Illinois Press, Urbana.

Kachru, B.B. (1983). 'The bilingual's creativity: discoursal and stylistic studies in contact literatures in English', *Studies in the Linguistic Sciences*, 13 (2), 37–55.

Kachru, B.B. (1986). *The Alchemy of English: the Spread, Functions and Models of Non-native Englishes*. Pergamon Press, Oxford.

Kachru, B.B. (1988). 'ESP and the non-native varieties of English: towards a shift in paradigm', in Chamberlain, D. and Baumgardener, R. (eds.), *ESP in the classroom: Practice and Evaluation*, Modern English Publications and the British Council, London.

Kaplan, R.B. (1983). 'Contrastive rhetorics: some implications for the writing process', in Freedman, A., Pringle, I. and Yalden, J. (eds.), *Learning to Write: First Language/Second Language*, Longman, New York, 139–61.

Kathpalia, S.S. (1992). 'A genre analysis of promotional texts'. PhD thesis submitted to the National University of Singapore, Singapore.

Kelly D.St.L. (ed.) (1988). *Essays on Legislative Drafting: In Honour of J.Q. Ewens, CMG, CBE, QC*, The Adelaide Law Review Association, Law School, University of Adelaide.

Kinneavy, J.L. (1971). *A Theory of Discourse*, W.W. Norton and Co., New York.

Kress, G. (1985). *Linguistic Processes in Sociocultural Practice*, Deakin Univeristy Press, Geelong.

Labov, W. (1970). 'The study of language in its social context', *Studium Generale*, 23, 30–87.

Law Reform Commission of Victoria (1986). 'Legislation, Legal Rights and Plain English'. Discussion Paper No.1, Aug. 1986.

Lesikar, R.V. (1984). *Business Communication: Theory and Application*, Richard D. Irwin, Inc., Homewood, Illinois.

Levinson, S.C. (1979). 'Activity-types and language', *Linguistics*, 17 (5–6), 365–99.

Lewis, B.N., Horabin, I.S. and Gane, C.P. (1967). 'Flow charts, logical trees and algorithms for rules and regulations', HMSO, London.

Limaye, M.R. (1984). 'The syntax of persuasion: two business letters of request', *Journal of Business Communication*, 20, 2, 17–30.

Love, C. and Tinervia, J. (1986). *Commercial Correspondence*, McGraw-Hill International Editions, London.

Miller, C.R. (1984). 'Genre as social action', *Quarterly Journal of Speech*, 70, 151–67.

Millett, T. (1986). 'A comparison of British and French legislative drafting (with particular reference to their respective Nationality Laws)', *Statute Law Review*, 7/3, 130–60.

Mountford, A. (1975). 'Discourse analysis and simplification of reading materials for English for Science and Technology'. Unpublished MLitt thesis, University of Edinburgh.

Munby, J. (1978). *Communicative Syllabus Design*, Cambridge University Press, Cambridge.

Nunan, D. (1989). *Understanding Language Classrooms – A Guide for Teacher-initiated Action*, Prentice Hall International English Language Teaching, London.

Oster, S. (1981). 'The use of tenses in reporting past literature', in Selinker, L., Tarone, E. and Hanzeli, V. (eds), *English for Academic and Technical Purposes*, Newbury House, Rowley, MA, 76–90.

Pangborn, R.J. and Beaman, D.R. (1980). 'Laser glazing of sprayed metal coatings', *Journal of Applied Physics*, 51(11), 5992–3.

Parthasarathy, R. (1983). 'South Asian literature in English: culture and discourse'. Paper given at the Conference on English as an International Language: Discourse Patterns Across Cultures, East-West Center, June, 1983.

Pettinari C. (1982). 'The function of a grammatical alternation in 14 surgical reports', *Applied Linguistics*, 4, 55–76.

Pikkarainen, L. (1982). 'Excess volumes of (N-methylmethanesulfonamide + an aliphatic alcohol)', *Journal of Chemical Thermodynamics*, 14, 503–07.

Pratt, D.V. (1989). *Legal Writing: A Systematic Approach*, West Publishing Co., St Paul, Minnesota.

Quirk, R., Greenbaum, S., Leech, G. and Svartvik, J. (1982). *A Grammar of Contemporary English*, Longman, London.

Ramachandra, S. (1988). 'The linguistic analysis of proviso clauses in Singapore legislation'. Unpublished Master's thesis submitted to the Department of English Language and Literature, National University of Singapore, Singapore.

Read, J. (1990). 'Providing relevant content in an EAP writing test', *English for Specific Purposes*, 9(2), 109–22.

Redish, J.C. (1979). 'How to draft more understandable legal documents', in MacDonald, D.A. (ed.), *Drafting Documents in Plain Language*, Practising Law Institute, New York.

Redish, J.C. (1981). 'Readability', in Felker, D.B. (ed.), *Document Design: A*

Review of Relevant Research, American Institute of Research, Washington DC.

Reid, T.B.S. (1956). 'Linguistics, structuralism and philology', *Archivum Linguisticum*, 8.

Renton, D. (1975). *The Preparation of Legislation*. Report of committee appointed by The Lord President of the Council, HMSO, London.

Renton, D. (1990). 'Current drafting practices and problems in the United Kingdom'. *Statute Law Review*, 11(1), 11–17.

Republic of Singapore (1970). Singapore's Wills Act, 1970, The Republic of Singapore.

Republic of Singapore (1980). Criminal Procedure Code, 1980, The Republic of Singapore.

Republic of Singapore (1980). The Income Tax Act, 1984, The Republic of Singapore.

Salager, F. (1984). 'Compound nominals phrases in scientific-technical literature: proportion and rationale', in Pugh, A.K. and Ulijn, J.M. (eds.), *Reading for Professional Purposes – Studies and Practices in Native and Foreign Languages*, Heinemann Educational Books, London, 136–45.

Saville-Troike, M. (1982). *The Ethnography of Communication*, Basil Blackwell, Oxford.

Schank, R. and Abelson, R. (1977). *Scripts, Plans, Goals, and Understanding*, Erlbaum, Hillsdale, N.J.

Scott, D.M.M. (1969). *Casebook on Torts*, Butterworths, London.

Selinker, L. (1979). 'On the use of informants in discourse analysis and "language for specialized purposes" ', *International Review of Applied Linguistics in Language Teaching*, 17(3), 189–215.

Selinker, L., Lackstrom, J. and Trimble, L. (1972). 'Grammar and technical English', *English Teaching Forum*, Sept.-Oct. 1972, 3–14.

Selinker, L., Lackstrom, J. and Trimble, L. (1973). 'Technical rhetorical principles and grammatical choice', *TESOL Quarterly* 7, 2.

Selinker, L., Trimble, L. and Bley-Vroman, R. (1974). 'Presupposition and technical rhetoric', *English Language Teaching Journal*, Oct. 1974.

Selinker, L., Trimble M. and Trimble, L. (1976). 'Presuppositional rhetorical information in EST discourse', *TESOL Quarterly*, 10, 3.

Selinker, L., Tarone E. and Hanzeli, V. (eds) (1981). *English for Academic and Technical Purposes*, Newbury House, Rowley, MA.

Shatz, M., Hoff-Ginsberg, E. and Maciver, D. (1989). 'Induction and the acquisition of English auxiliaries: the effects of differently enriched input', *Journal of Child Language*, 16(1), Feb. 1989, Cambridge University Press, Cambridge, UK, 121–40.

Shuy, R.W. and Larkin, D.K. (1977). 'Linguistic considerations in the simplification/clarification of insurance policy language', *Discourse Processes*, 1.

Sigband, N. (1984). *Business Communication*, Harcourt Brace Jovanovich Publishers, London.

Sinclair, J.M. and Coulthard, R.M. (1975). *Towards an Analysis of Discourse: The English Used by Teachers and Pupils*, Oxford University Press, London.

Smith, L. (ed.) (1981). *English for Cross-cultural Communication*, Macmillan, London.

Sridhar, S.N. (1982). 'Non-native English literatures: context and relevance', in Kachru, B.B. (ed.), *The Other Tongue: English Across Cultures*, University of Illinois Press, Urbana.

Stimpson, D.V., Robinson, P. and Gregory, J. (1987). 'Self-monitoring and competence as determinants of sex differences in social interaction', *Journal of Social Psychology*, 127(2), 159–62.

Swales, J.M. (1974). *Notes on the Function of Attributive en-Participles in Scientific Discourse*. Papers for Special University Purposes No. 1, ELSU, University of Khartoum.

Swales, J.M. (1981a). 'Definitions in science and law – evidence for subject-specific course component', *Fachsprache*, 3, 4.

Swales, J.M. (1981b). 'Aspects of Article Introductions'. Aston ESP Research Report No.1, Language Studies Unit, University of Aston in Birmingham, Birmingham, UK.

Swales, J.M. (1985). 'A genre-based approach to language across the curriculum'. Paper presented at the RELC Seminar on Language Across the Curriculum, at SEAMEO Regional Language Centre, Singapore, Apr. 1985. Published in Tickoo, M.L. (ed.) (1986), *Language Across the Curriculum*, Singapore, SEAMEO Regional Language Centre.

Swales, J.M. (1986). 'English for Specifiable Purposes', RELC Occasional Papers 42, SEAMEO RELC, Singapore.

Swales, J.M. (1990). *Genre Analysis – English in Academic and Research Settings*, Cambridge University Press, Cambridge.

Swales, J.M. and Bhatia, V.K. (1983). 'An approach to the linguistic study of legal documents', *Fachsprache*, 5(3), 98–108.

Tadros, A.A. (1981). 'Linguistic prediction in economics texts'. Unpublished PhD thesis, University of Birmingham.

Tarone, E., Dwyer, S., Gillette, S. and Icke, V. (1981). 'On the use of the passive in two astrophysics journal papers', *The ESP Journal*, 1(2), 123–40.

Tedick, D.J. (1990). 'ESL writing assessment: subject-matter knowledge and its impact on performance', *English for Specific Purposes*, 9(2), 123–44.

Teh, G.S. (1986). 'An applied discourse analysis of sales promotion letters'. MA thesis submitted to the National University of Singapore, Singapore.

Thomas, R. (1985). 'Plain English and the law', *Statute Law Review* 9(3), 144.

Trimble, L. (1985). *English for Science and Technology*, Cambridge University Press, Cambridge.

Turnbull, I.M.L. (1986). 'The problem of legislative drafting', *Statute Law Review*, 69. Quoted in Crabbe, V. C. R. A. C. (1989). The Legislative Sentence. *Statute Law Review*, 10(2), 92.

Wasan, P. (1968). 'The drafting of rules', *The New Law Journal*, 118, 548–49.

White, J.B. (1982). 'The invisible discourse of law: reflections on legal literacy and general education', *Michigan Quarterly Review*, 420–38.

Widdowson, H.G. (1973). 'An applied linguistics approach to discourse analysis'. Unpublished PhD thesis, University of Edinburgh.

Widdowson, H.G. (1978). *Teaching Language as Communication*, Oxford University Press, London.

Widdowson, H.G. (1979). *Explorations in Applied Linguistics*, Oxford University Press, Oxford.

Widdowson, H.G. (1983). *Learning Purpose and Language Use*, Oxford University Press, London.

Widdowson, H.G. (1984). *Explorations in Applied Linguistics 2*, Oxford University Press, Oxford.

Weir, T. (1983). *A Casebook on Tort*, Sweet and Maxwell, London.

Williams, G. (1982). *Learning the Law*, Eleventh edition. First published in 1945, Steven and Sons, London.

Williams, R. (1984). 'A cognitive approach to English nominal compounds', in Pugh, A.K. and Ulijn, J.M. (eds.), *Reading for Professional Purposes – Studies and Practices in Native and Foreign Languages*, Heinemann Educational Books, London, 146–53.

Winograd, T. (1974). 'Artificial intelligence: when will computers understand people?', *Psychology Today*, May 1974.

Winter, E.O. (1976). 'Fundamentals of information structure: pilot manual for further development according to student need'. Mimeo., Hatfield Polytechnic.

Winter, E. (1977). 'A clause relational approach to English texts: a study of some predictive lexical elements in written discourse', *Instructional Science*, 6/1, Elsevier Scientific Publishing Co., Amsterdam.

Wisdom, J. (1964). *Gods, Philosophy and Psycho-Analysis*, Basil Blackwell, Oxford.

Wright, P. (1978). 'Feeding the information eaters: suggestions for integrating pure and applied research on language comprehension', *Instructional Science*, 1978, 249–312.

Wright, P. (1979). 'Quality control aspects of document design', *Information Design Journal*, 1, 33–42.

Wright, P. (1980). 'Usability: the criterion for designing written information', in Kolers, P.A., Wrolstad, M.E. and Bouma, H. (eds.), *Processing Visible Language*, 2, Plenum Press, New York and London.

Wright, P. and Reid, F. (1973). 'Written information: some alternatives to prose for expressing the outcomes of complex contingencies', *Journal of Applied Psychology*, 57, 160–66.

Yamada, Y., Kidoguchi, I., Taguchi, T. and Hiraki, A. (1989). 'Bound-excitation and edge-emission spectra associated with Li and Na accepters in ZnSe', *Japanese Journal of Applied Physics*, 28, May 1989, L837.

Zappen, J.P. (1983). 'A rhetoric for research in sciences and technologies', in Anderson, P.V., Brockman, R.J. and Miller, C.R. (eds.), *New Essays in Technical and Scientific Communication*, Beywood, Farmingdale, New York, 123–38.

Subject Index

Author Index